The
Criminal
Mind

A Writer's Guide to Forensic Psychology

Katherine Ramsland, Ph.D.

WRITER'S DIGEST BOOKS
CINCINNATI, OHIO
www.writersdigestbooks.com

The Criminal Mind: A Writer's Guide to Forensic Psychology. © 2002 by Katherine Ramsland. Manufactured in the United States of America. All rights reserved. No part of this book may be reproduced in any form or by any electronic or mechanical means including information storage and retrieval systems without permission in writing from the publisher, except by a reviewer, who may quote brief passages in a review. Published by Writer's Digest Books, an imprint of F&W Publications, Inc., 4700 East Galbraith Road, Cincinnati, Ohio 45236. (800) 289-0963. First edition.

Visit our Web site at www.writersdigest.com for information on more resources for writers.

To receive a free weekly e-mail newsletter delivering tips and updates about writing and about Writer's Digest products, register directly at our Web site at newsletters.fwpublicatio ns.com.

06   05   04   03   02   5   4   3   2   1

Library of Congress Cataloging-in-Publication Data

Ramsland, Katherine M.
   The criminal mind: a writer's guide to forensic psychology / by Katherine Ramsland.
      p.   cm.
   Includes bibliographical references and index.
   ISBN 1-58297-079-3 (alk. paper)
      1. Psychology, Forensic. I. Title.

RA1148 .R35   2002
614'.1—dc21   2002016752
                                                      CIP

Edited by Jack Heffron, Anne Bowling, Donya Dickerson
Designed by Sandy Conopeotis Kent
Cover by Chris Gliebe, Tin Box Studio, Cincinnati, Ohio
Production coordinated by John Peavler

About the Author

Katherine Ramsland, Ph.D., has published seventeen books, among them biographies of Dean Koontz and Anne Rice, and *The Forensic Science of C.S.I.* She writes articles on crime for Courttv.com and teaches forensic psychology at DeSales University.

Photo by Caryn Cole Biehl © 1999

Also by Katherine Ramsland

The Forensic Science of C.S.I.

Ghost: Investigating the Other Side

Bliss: Writing to Find Your True Self

Cemetery Stories: Haunted Graveyards, Embalming Secrets, and the Life of a Corpse After Death

Piercing the Darkness: Undercover With Vampires in America Today

Dean Koontz: A Writer's Biography

Prism of the Night: A Biography of Anne Rice

The Vampire Companion: The Official Guide to Anne Rice's 'The Vampire Chronicles'

The Witches' Companion: The Official Guide to Anne Rice's 'Lives of the Mayfair Witches'

The Anne Rice Reader

The Roquelaure Reader: A Companion to Anne Rice's Erotica

The Art of Learning: A Self-Help Manual for Students

Engaging the Immediate: Employing Kierkegaard's Theory of Indirect Communication to the Practice of Psychotherapy

Table of Contents

Scale for Children–Revised (WISC-III); Rorschach; Thematic Apperception Test (TAT); California Psychological Inventory (CPI); Beck Depression Inventory; Neurological Tests; Forensic-Only Assessment Instruments (FAIs); Fictional Scenarios

Without a Conscience; Juvenile Assessment; Risk Assessment, Treatment, and Prevention; A Case for Fictional Development

11
The Psychologist as Consultant/Investigator... 193

Profiling; Examples of Accurate Profiles; Profiling and the Victim; Profiling and the Profiler; Assisting the Forensic Artist; Psychological Autopsy for Equivocal Death; Psychological Investigator/ Consultant; Stalker Evaluations; A Fictional Case

12
Other Applications... 213

A Quick Overview; Civil Proceedings; Screenings for Police Officers; Innocence Projects; Mental Health Court; Litigation Consulting/ Jury Analysis

13
Ethics... 231

Ethical Errors; Ethical Principles for Mental Health Professionals; The Relationship With Attorneys; Controversial Topics; Dangerousness Assessment Ethics; Duty to Warn/Protect; A Fictional Scenario Involving Ethics—How to Turn the Plot

Introduction

You've decided to write a novel that will involve a forensic psychologist. Let's decide that this psychologist will be male, so we'll call him Dr. Ted Webster. You think that it's now just a matter of reading some textbook on abnormal psychology to see how psychologists diagnose and treat the criminal mind. Then you'll have him do a little investigating, put him on the stand as an expert witness, and then get him involved in some action—perhaps action that endangers him. That doesn't seem very hard, right?

Maybe not, but it's an inaccurate idea of what psychologists do in the forensic arena. A little research will show you that your task of creating this character is much more complicated and that the methods and goals of a psychologist can often be at odds with those of the legal system. Before you even get Ted on the witness stand as an expert, you'll need to know the following specific details:

- where he went to school
- his field of expertise
- whether he's a psychiatrist, psychologist, or social worker
- whether he's board certified in forensics, and by which organization
- how and why he was contacted for his expertise
- which clinical assessment tools he uses
- his approach to working with a client
- how many connections he has in the court system
- whether he has experience with criminal interviewing
- whether the judge will allow his expertise
- which phase of the trial will give him a forum
- whether he's testifying for the prosecution or defense (or performing a

service for the court)
- whether he testifies frequently
- why he would be involved in any "action"

You will also need a more professional means of understanding forensic diagnosis and forensic reporting procedures than you might get from a textbook—particularly from a basic text in psychology. In fact, some forensic psychologists find that they have to devise entirely new motivational scenarios to be able to work within the court system.

Few published fiction writers really understand what a forensic mental health specialist does. They might think of Dr. Sam Waters on television's *Profiler*, as she uses her special gifts to "see" into the mind of a criminal. Or they might think being a profiler is like Clarice Starling's prison interview of the intimidating serial killer, Dr. Hannibal Lecter, in *The Silence of the Lambs*. Both of those techniques heighten drama, undoubtedly, but profiling is not about being a psychic, and getting a killer to talk can be far more difficult than author Thomas Harris lets on. Psychologists generally rely on the results of assessment tests rather than clairvoyance, and they see the defendant in an interview room, not a prison cell. Nor are they likely to be left without resources in a dangerous situation.

While it is true that if some defendant dislikes what the psychologist says and then manages to be acquitted or to escape, there may be danger to the expert and her family, but this is not generally the case. What psychologists do that could be dramatic is to study the criminal mind up close, get themselves into ethical dilemmas, trigger surprising confessions, help solve mysteries, and watch for patterns that might provide important information to the attornies who have hired them. They may also contribute to proactive methods of investigation and assist with advice in cornering or questioning suspects.

This book provides information about how a person like Ted would become a forensic psychologist, what he must do for either side in a criminal or civil dispute, how he deals with defendants, what he faces in a courtroom, his best courtroom strategy, and how he might serve as a consultant on such issues as juvenile treatment or risk management.

Basically, according to the American Academy of Psychiatry and the Law, a mental health practitioner will be called on for one or more of the following:

- criminal responsibility evaluation
- civil or criminal competency evaluation
- mental disability
- risk assessment
- juvenile assessment
- involuntary treatment or commitment
- child custody issues
- psychic injury cases
- malpractice cases
- corrections cases

While I will use examples from fiction, television, and film to show the different roles of a mental health professional, I will also point out where those examples diverge from reality for the sake of drama. In addition, I will make suggestions along the way for how fiction writers might work up a character or plot device that is consistent with what actually happens with psychologists in the legal arena.

The courtroom is adversarial, and any expert witness has to be aware that the other side will treat her as the enemy. In other words, someone to be discredited. Cross-examination can be intense, and issues of payment will always be raised as a way to nullify testimony. A "hired gun" is generally viewed as nonobjective, and the truth is, some psychologists will actually write unwarranted favorable reports just to keep getting work from a certain attorney. It's unfortunate, and such unethical professionals make the job more difficult for those who make honest evaluations (but they do make for good fictional characters). Yet honest or not, that person will come under close scrutiny in any courtroom. The mental health professional will need to keep calm, be well prepared, and avoid taking offense.

All types of mental health professionals may testify in court, from psychiatrists to psychologists to social workers. The generic "mental health professional" will hereafter be used whenever the specific role or situation mentioned can be filled by any type, and for readability mental health professional may be used interchangeably, where appropriate, with "researcher" or "clinician" or "expert."

The Court System

A quick overview of the judicial system will give you an idea of where the mental health professional fits in. Since most writers will be interested primarily in criminal trials, we'll focus on how those proceed, but it should be noted that civil trials can involve some very high stakes as well.

Once a suspect is arrested, he is booked and subjected to a criminal records check. He'll get fingerprinted and photographed and then put into a holding cell. At this time, the police may interrogate him, and it is his right to ask for a lawyer and to remain silent. The prosecutor looks at the evidence to decide whether to file an indictment that formally charges him with a crime. Depending on where the suspect was arrested, the next step is a grand jury hearing (a preliminary or probable cause hearing before a judge). In the first case, the prosecution presents its evidence in a closed session; in the second, the evidence is shared with the defense. Thus, defense attorneys can make plans for having certain pieces of evidence dismissed in other pretrial hearings. They may challenge the methods used in the police search or interrogation procedures at this point, or they may propose a change of venue, bail, or assessment of competency. The arraignment, in which the accused enters a plea of guilty or not guilty, may occur at this hearing or at a later time.

Once pretrial motions are heard and resolved, there may be an attempt at a plea bargain. If not, then the case moves toward court—coming before either a judge, a jury, or both. At court, each side gives an opening statement. Prosecutors outline the charges and how they intend to prove their case; the defense insists on a client's innocence or incapacity. Then the prosecutor presents all the evidence, including witnesses, documents, photographs, trace evidence, and fingerprints. She draws these together with logic and circumstantial evidence and then presents her list of witnesses for direct examination. The defense has an opportunity to cross-examine any witness. Once the prosecutor feels she has presented her entire case, she rests.

Next up is the defense, who follows roughly the same pattern as the prosecution did. This may or may not involve putting the defendant on the stand. When the defense rests, the prosecutor may call rebuttal witnesses or show evidence. The defense gets the same chance, but neither may offer new material during this phase. At any of these stages, a mental health professional may be called. She should come to court in preparation to be called, but it

Fingerprint Patterns Used in Criminal Investigations

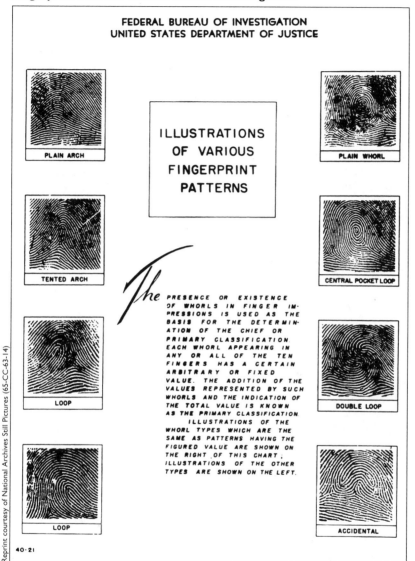

A record of a suspect's fingerprints are taken and saved. If fingerprints were left at the crime scene, forensic artists can use these patterns to help determine if any belong to the suspect.

is always possible that the judge will rule her testimony inadmissible. Throughout this book, you'll see how and why that happens.

When both sides are finished, each makes a closing argument, stressing their strong points and the other side's weaknesses. Then, the judge or jury comes back with a verdict of either guilty or not guilty. If warranted, the judge will pronounce a sentence.

Mental health professionals, then, may contribute to either side of a case as expert witnesses or may perform competency analyses. In juvenile hearings and situations such as civil commitment or child custody disputes, they may have a very active part in personality assessments, as well. When a case is decided, they may then get involved in correction decisions or parole hearings. In short, there are numerous areas in which they may be used as researchers, clinicians, or experts, and that means there are numerous potential opportunities for using them for plot and character development in fiction.

I

The Forensic Psychologist

What Is Forensic Psychology?

Most people don't really know what forensic psychology is. They can't quite figure out what psychologists do with corpses, but that's because they misunderstand the word *forensic*, which has more to do with the legal and judicial process than with the morgue. Because the popular television show *Quincy* focused on a medical examiner—a forensic pathologist—a lot of misconceptions about the term arose in popular culture.

Forensics is the analysis of information suitable for use in a court of law. Thus, the discipline of forensic psychology involves psychology in the law, by the law, and of the law. Wherever the legal system and psychology intersect, you have forensic psychology. Such professionals use their expertise with human behavior, motivation, and pathology to provide psychological services in the courts, play roles in criminal investigations, develop specialized knowledge of crimes and motives, assist with counseling, and conduct forensic research. Although there are civil applications, quite often mental health professionals are involved in the understanding of crime and criminal justice—especially in the case of mentally ill offenders.

Most forensic mental health professionals work either in a correctional setting or in a psychiatric hospital. Contrary to popular notions, they tend not to be active investigators, although in some places that's not altogether implausible (there is currently a program in England for this kind of training). They usually perform the more ordinary roles of assessment and treatment, or of therapeutic intervention. To do this kind of work, mental health professionals should have a good background in the following:

- abnormal psychology, especially criminal behavior patterns
- social psychology, with an emphasis on how the court system works and on social theories of crime and aggression
- psychological testing
- personality and developmental theory
- an area of specialization such as juvenile aggression or psychopathy

Psychological assessment in the forensic arena is relevant to a broad spectrum of cases, from juvenile delinquency to criminal competency to sexual allegations. With additional training in law and criminality, behavior specialists can assist in the fact-finding process that is involved in arriving at just court decisions. They may also assist in civil matters, such as child custody, disability, sexual harassment, or claims of emotional suffering.

Mental health professionals can do assessments for the court, the government, insurance companies, or any other decision-making fact finders involved in legal issues. They may also consult on investigative work. Yet for the most part—and of most interest to crime and mystery writers—mental health specialists with forensic background use their expertise within an adversarial arena. A forensic behavior specialist may serve as an expert witness for the defense or prosecution, or she may present findings as ordered by the court and be impartial to either side. When one side hires a mental health professional, the professional is generally viewed as part of the adversary's camp, and cross-examination aimed at diminishing witness credibility can be intense.

Mental health professionals are generally called on to present findings from test data and clinical interviews, specifically in terms of whether a defendant understands the charges and the legal process or what his mental state was at the time he allegedly committed a crime. One major difficulty for mental health professionals who are also clinicians is that they are trained to help, which can be a source of tension in the courtroom. That means they want their findings to make a positive difference. However, as with other types of forensic scientists, mental health professionals must remain neutral, present their findings to the best of their ability and within the limits of what the lawyers ask, and then let them decide how to use the information.

Try as they might to avoid it, they may be there strictly as a "hired gun." For example, a psychologist, who specialized in dissociation, was hired by the defense in an episode of *Law and Order*. Because he made a good living at being a court witness and had a heavy investment in defending his theory and expertise, he worked hard to help clear a woman charged with murder. When his own theory began to undermine his testimony, his conflicted response betrayed his personal agenda. He was clearly not an objective professional. Such experts are all too readily available, although their reputations among their peers usually suffer—and they become increasingly vulnerable to being discredited.

Varieties of Experts

Any of the types of professionals discussed in this section, with additional training in forensics procedures, may be utilized as expert witnesses in the courtroom. However, there are some differences in the way they approach criminality and the application of drugs and in the types of assessment tools and methods that they use. There are also differences in their education and training. Using a psychiatrist as a courtroom consultant or an investigative character would involve a different approach than using a psychologist or neuropsychologist.

Psychiatrists have medical degrees in addition to their clinical training in psychology, and they tend to make diagnoses based on the categories offered in the *Diagnostic and Statistical Manual of Mental Disorders: DSM-IV*, which describes various mental and behavioral disorders. Writers will need to understand how this manual is used and presented in court. Psychiatrists can also evaluate drug reactions and prescribe drugs, so writers developing such characters will need background in, and a good resource guide to, psychopharmacology. Forensic psychiatry is considered a "medical subspecialty," and some practitioners may specialize exclusively in legal issues. These days, psychiatry is divided on whether mental illness is primarily biological and thus treatable with pharmaceuticals, or is a product of psychosocial factors. If psychiatrists do therapy, they tend to assess causal factors of behavior from past influences—particularly the parents during early childhood. If they believe strictly in physiological manifestations of mental illness (which they are increasingly pressured to do within the managed care system), they tend merely to prescribe drugs and engage in little to no psychotherapy—but they may still consult on counseling strategies.

As for training, psychiatrists attend four years of medical school and serve a one-year medical internship. Then they spend around three years as residents specializing in psychiatry, in both hospital and outpatient settings. Forensic psychiatrists are often employed in psychiatric hospitals and prisons where they administer diagnostic assessment tests and evaluate the mental states of inmates. With the arrival of managed care, psychiatrists are more often used for psychological diagnoses, in part because of their access to hospitals.

Writers will need to know where their psychiatrist characters went to school, where they got their additional training, which model they prefer for making interpretations from assessments specific to psychiatry, and whether they are board-certified specifically in forensic psychiatry.

Likewise, forensic psychologists can do personality assessments for use in diagnosing a case, and their range of theoretical approaches is often greater than that of psychiatrists. They may emphasize cognitive, behavioral, or even existential criteria. They may have a preference for behavior modification procedures or for therapies that address deviant behavior via some broad-range context that includes family systems, environment, and sociological factors. In other words, they tend to deal with patients on a more individualized basis and to figure out treatments or therapeutic tools that seem relevant to the unique aspects of specific cases, rather than relying on a strict catalog of traits prematched to treatments. Psychologists cannot prescribe drugs, but they are familiar with psychopharmacology. They tend to work in a consulting partnership with psychiatrists or physicians so they can get drugs prescribed or can refer cases that may best be treated with drug therapy. (There is a movement afoot to allow them to prescribe drugs, so writers should stay updated.)

A neuropsychologist, on the other hand, tends to focus on the brain and the neurological system to make assessments of mental disorder. In recent years, with increasing evidence of mind/body interaction and the cellular imprinting of emotions, many clinicians have had to include some knowledge of neurology in their repertoire of clinical skills. For example, schizophrenia appears to have a greater physiological component than was previously believed, so neurological studies have become more relevant in its treatment. There is now less emphasis on blaming the mother or some disruptive element in the environment. Sociopathy is gaining the same status, particularly with new studies on the relationship between brain injuries and antisocial behavior. Neuropsychologists can administer the full battery of tests that psychologists ordinarily do, but they add such tests as vision, emotional processing, sleep disorders, and organic brain conditions. In other words, they tend to know more of the way the body and its disorders influence the mind than the average psychologist, which has greater scientific impact in a courtroom procedure. They cannot prescribe drugs, but they are expert in assessing drug-related manifestations in behavior. They may also utilize hypnosis more readily than psychiatrists, and they tend to have better training in it. Thus, neuropsychologists have as much expertise on the body as psychiatrists, but they have access to a greater range of approaches to interpretation, treatment, and diagnosis.

Licensed social workers, too, have their role in forensics, especially if they work within the corrections system. Their records from a hospital setting may become part of a court file, and they can also participate in assessment. In the McMartin case in California, where a family who ran a day care center was prosecuted after a social worker coached the children in the family's charge to tell horrendous stories of abuse, the social worker questioned and screened the children. Although she was unlicensed, she became the prosecution's star witness (and was discredited only after massive harm had been done to the family). However, unless the social worker has specific expertise on a subject or has a key association with someone involved in a trial, it is more likely that an expert witness in mental health will be one of the three mentioned previously.

The experts diverge on several key issues, so writers must keep their characters within the appropriate professional boundaries.

Prominent Psychologists in Books, Television, and Movies

One of the earliest fictional "psychologists" was Porfiry Petrovich, the shrewd police detective in Dostoevsky's *Crime and Punishment*. He's even been called the world's first profiler.

Porfiry must figure out the apparently motiveless and brutal double homicide of an elderly pawnbroker and her stepsister. As clues come together, he suspects a financially strapped student named Raskolnikov who wrote an article about how "extraordinary men" are above the law and can do as they please. Since nothing directly links Raskolnikov to the crime, Porfiry must think of a way to persuade the young man to confess.

At first, he merely plays cat and mouse with Raskolnikov, letting him know in roundabout ways that his actions have been noted. This makes Raskolnikov uncomfortable. He nearly spills the beans just to shed the pressure but holds back. Porfiry then says he knows about Raskolnikov's "extraordinary man" article and asks him to explain certain parts. This is a subtle way of letting Raskolnikov know he is under suspicion, but Porfiry proceeds to ask if Raskolnikov thinks of himself as the extraordinary man. When Raskolnikov refuses to go any further with this game, Porfiry switches tactics.

He says that some painters were at work in the apartment building where the murders occurred. Did Raskolnikov see them? When the suspect offers no real answer, Porfiry lets him know that the painters were there only on the day of the murder. Without saying so, he allows Raskolnikov to wonder if they were witnesses. Raskolnikov senses a trap. Porfiry apologizes, acting confused, and allows Raskolnikov to go. Nevertheless, the young student leaves believing he's in serious trouble, which was Porfiry's goal.

At this point, we've seen psychology at work: first, to figure out from the crime scene who the perpetrator might be, and second, to interrogate and pressure a suspect.

At their next meeting, Raskolnikov insists that Porfiry get right to the point, but the detective dances around, moving from one subject to another and occasionally stopping at the door to listen. Raskolnikov grows increasingly nervous until he loses his patience and tells Porfiry that he knows he is under suspicion for murder. He demands to be arrested or allowed to leave. Porfiry meets this confrontation with further gamesmanship, describing Raskolnikov's visit to the murder scene to see the blood.

Finally Porfiry claims that he already knows who murdered the old pawnbroker. He's aware that Raskolnikov has been ill, and he manipulates the young man's guilt into a burden too heavy to carry. Then he switches gears: He knows that Raskolnikov has a compassionate side that will not allow him to live easily with such a crime. Effectively, Porfiry plays one side of Raskolnikov against the other until Raskolnikov finally confesses. Although not a trained psychologist, Dostoevsky used the techniques of psychology in figuring out what might work—in the manner of a profiler initiating a proactive approach to flush out an offender.

In other nineteenth-century fiction, the characters Sherlock Holmes and C. Auguste Dupin also did some pretty slick profiling of a sort. Caleb Carr picked up on this technique in more recent times in *The Alienist*. His turn-of-the-century psychologist, Dr. Kreizler, creates a psychological portrait of "an imaginary man"—the sort of person who might commit the types of murders going on at the time in New York—and initially establishes that the serial killer of young male prostitutes is organized (makes a plan), does not like what he is doing (is conflicted), is triggered by something that the boys represent (is compulsive), and wants to be caught (is possibly dissociated). As the clues come in, Kreizler adds details to the portrait, and in the end, is proven correct in his extrapolation from the crimes to the criminal's personality and circumstances.

Forensic psychology is getting more popular as a subject for contemporary writers. It shows up in novels like James Patterson's *Kiss the Girls* and Thomas Harris's *The Silence of the Lambs*, as well as in television shows like *C.S.I.*, *Law and Order*, *Cracker*, and *Profiler*. In an episode of *Law and Order*, for example, a psychiatrist hired by the district attorney is asked to evaluate a young boy to see if he was capable of killing his infant brother. If so, then they will proceed against the boy, but if not, then their suspicions will go to the parents. In another episode, two mental health experts are in conflict during the evaluation of an eleven-year-old girl who had murdered a young boy. One declares her to be a budding psychopath who will continue to be dangerous, while the other sees her as a child who cannot understand the concept of murder and who, with help, can be guided away from such behavior.

Even movies get into the act, as shown in *Basic Instinct* with the conflict-of-interest prone police psychiatrist Beth Gardner. Authors who include forensic mental health professionals in their stories need to know both where the popular image has gone wrong and how to get it right.

Where Popular Media Get It Wrong

In an episode of *Profiler*, Rachel Burke, a member of the FBI's Violent Crime Task Force, must figure out the psychological contours of a sniper who has killed several people in a public park, and in the process, has trapped several more. She must sort through all the possible motives, from rage over a spouse's infidelity to an unprovoked attack like that of Texas sniper, Charles Whitman, who in 1966 shot from a tower on the University of Texas at Austin, killing thirteen and wounding thirty people. She expects that this aberrant behavior is about some emotional wound rather than a demand against a public utility. That leads her to believe the shooter was fired or replaced recently at work.

The victims themselves appear insignificant to him, and she suspects a history of mental illness or criminality. In fact, she ends up guessing wrong on several points, which correctly illustrates the "art" of profiling, but when she thinks she's got it right, she walks by herself toward the heavily armed killer, boldly assuming that he will not shoot her. That's quite a dramatic effect but would probably never happen.

First, the FBI would not send a woman alone to walk toward a man with an arsenal of weapons, trying to talk him down on a megaphone. Second, a behavioral science expert would probably stay behind the lines and advise other agents about what to do. Third, the expert knows how much of an art profiling is and would not entrust his life to guessing correctly.

Burke replaces FBI forensic psychologist Dr. Sam Waters. Waters had the unique gift of thinking in pictures so that she could visualize a crime from the perspectives of both the victim and the killer. On the show, we see her concentrating on some clue until she can envision exactly how that clue betrays the mind of the perpetrator. I'm sure most profilers wish they could do this, but in real life profiling "intuition" is based on observation, experience, and the constant exposure to a variety of cases.

It's likely that this idea of getting into the mind of the killer was derived from Thomas Harris's *Red Dragon*, his prequel to *The Silence of the Lambs*. Although his character, Will Graham, was an FBI instructor and detective, not a psychologist, he made famous the notion that investigators who immerse themselves in a series of crimes by the same person are able to think like killers.

It's almost as if the detectives allow themselves to be so similar to the killer that they could be pushed over the edge and become killers, too.

Many crime stories have picked up on this idea that a superior investigator has the ability—the gift, even—to think like the criminal. It's a form of intuition that links them together, threatening to infect the investigator and erode his or her stability. Each episode of *Profiler* that features Waters involves her in some inaccessible form of concentration that sets her apart from other behavioral science experts.

Many profilers object to the depiction that they are the other side of a very thin dime from the offender. Former FBI special agent Roy Hazelwood, who developed the technique of profiling serial rapists, claims that his knowledge derives from experience and hard work, not from having a deviant mentality. He takes offense at this depiction. Even putting aside its implications, the idea oversimplifies the way a profiler operates.

John Douglas, the FBI special agent who started the Behavioral Science Unit and the profiling instruction, insists that his expertise is not about walking the psychological edge—nor is it about getting a constipated look as you bring up images of what happened. His insights into the mind of a serial killer derive from a logic-based intuition that is built on extensive experience. He can quickly sift through all that he knows from prior cases to make specific deductions that might guide police in their search. He does *not*

- visit a crime scene during an investigation
- tell the forensic team that they must leave so he can concentrate
- visualize through a killer's eyes how the person did what he did
- try to put himself into the mind-set of a killer

What he does do is to think through a killer's logic, and from there, imagine the set of circumstances that brought victim and killer together. Yet that only provides an initial grounding for what comes next: an intense investigation to find out from other people who the victim was, where she was last seen, what the crime scene is like, and other such details. The fact is, most cases are cracked through detailed police work, not through a profiler's psychic intuition. Profiling is an aid—just one tool among many—not a flash of insight due to some brain mechanism that the profiler shares with the criminal.

Another example is psychologist Gerry Fitzgerald—"Fitz"—on the television series *Cracker*. Fitz supposedly has an uncanny ability to see evil in people, knows how to press the right buttons to get them to confess, and can walk away unscathed. He claims to understand the criminal mind because he's not that far removed from it. ("You gotta be one to think like one.") His mental feats affirm the popular notion that psychologists have some magical powers to figure people out and make them say things they don't want to say. If that were so, all criminal cases where an arrest is made would be solved. And psychologists would probably be at the heart of every criminal proceeding. Nothing could be further from the truth.

In *Basic Instinct*, a man is found murdered in his bed and Detective Nick Curran investigates. When Curran discovers that the murder appears to mimic the plot of a novel written by the man's girlfriend, police psychiatrist Beth Gardner is brought in on the case. Nice plot, but police psychiatrists are not there to take the place of detectives. They provide things like stress management (as seen in *Lethal Weapon*) and fitness assessments. One corrections officer told me that when staff psychologists attempt to join investigations, they are put firmly in their place. It's more likely that a psychiatrist might be asked informally by a friend in law enforcement to comment on an investigation than that one from the police station would be included as part of the investigative team. (On *C.S.I.*, for example, the investigators consult with a psychiatrist when they have a case with complex psychological dimensions, but aside from offering his expert opinion, the psychiatrist remains uninvolved.)

An example of getting the facts wrong in a novel is found in James Patterson's *Along Came a Spider*. The book initially caught my attention because it purported to supply an alternative explanation for who had kidnapped and killed the Lindbergh baby in 1932. I live near the body dump site, have been in the former Lindbergh home, and have seen the evidence in the police museum. I've also read nearly every scholarly book on the subject, along with FBI reports, so I was interested to see what Patterson offered.

Had I not had other reasons for reading this novel, I'd have put it back on the shelf. The explanation was so absurd—ignoring key facts and getting others wrong—that I wondered how much Patterson had researched the book. Did this early problem portend some jarring experience with his under-

Research and the Lindbergh Kidnapping Case

Research, such as this article on the Lindbergh kidnapping case, is available for many famous—and not-so-famous—cases. As a writer, researching the details of your subject matter is a crucial step in developing realistic characters and story lines.

standing of psychology? I knew that the narrator would be a forensic psychologist who would be looking at this case. However, he'd be basing his ideas on a false rendering of the facts as Patterson had them.

First, the three-part ladder used in the crime was too heavy for a twelve-year-old boy and was placed too far from the window for a boy to climb in or out of—particularly with a toddler in his arms. The FBI report said that this crime could not have been committed by a single man, let alone a boy with oversized shoes stuffed with newspapers (as Patterson wrote it).

Then there were the shoes: the boy's wearing size nine to make it look like a man. The prints found were larger than that. And what of the series of ransom notes that all shared a secret symbol that led to a man in Brooklyn? Not to mention that the ladder had broken and been carried away from the window. Again, did the boy do that with a child in his arms? Even worse, the boy claims that he had planned everything carefully, but in fact the Lindberghs had never stayed in that home over a Monday night. They had chosen to do so at the last minute because the child had a cold. So much for surveillance and planning.

It gets worse. Patterson writes that the boy ran across open fields for two miles (he later says four) and dumped the child in the woods, still alive. The autopsy report showed that the child had most likely died of a head injury, not from being buried alive. The truth is, the dump site was over four miles away. Between Lindbergh's house and that area was heavily wooded, rough terrain. The boy would have had to trudge with a toddler in his arms through dense woods (not fields), down a steep mountain, go through town (which by that time was already alerted), cross the main street, and walk up another difficult hill to where the dump site was.

I did not believe this account for a moment. Patterson did not check out this place, nor did he seem to have studied the facts of the crime. Upon further reading, it turns out that the entire description was a killer's fantasy, but he proclaimed himself a Lindbergh expert who had lived in the area, so it seemed unlikely he would have gotten so much wrong, even in his imagination. As for what the psychologist does on this case, we'll take that up later. My initial hunch about the book was correct, and I ended up distrusting the author.

Why Getting It Right Matters

As forensic psychology becomes increasingly popular and more schools offer courses and degrees in it, fiction that fails to build such characters accurately will be regarded as poorly researched. Other books by that same author will be suspect and may even be dismissed as not worth reading.

Let's say, for example, that a writer decides to have his forensic psychologist consult on a "cold case" (an unsolved case no longer under active investigation) in which a suspect has been identified. Then let's say that the psychologist feels the suspect is the wrong person. He believes he can identify the right person, so he goes off on his own to investigate it like a detective.

Sorry, that doesn't happen. What he or she may do is offer to the detectives some reason why they're going down the wrong road and why they should consider an alternative. He isn't going to just go off and do it on his own because (1) he may interfere with future investigations, and (2) he has been hired for a certain role and his options are either to agree to fill the role or to turn it down. He does not get the option to become a part of the investigation in some role that he develops on his own. Were this scenario to be developed in fiction, sophisticated audiences would disengage from the story. It might sell to mass market, and even be believed, but it would be regarded as pop entertainment that perpetuates a false image.

Potential readers are such practitioners themselves, and they will wince whenever they see something in error. For example, if you present the insanity defense as if it's a commonly used strategy, you've missed the boat. If you believe that most states are using the *Frye* standard to decide on the admissibility of novel evidence (or you fail to even address such restrictions), anyone in the field will know that you are relying on outdated material. If you say the "fact finder" in the courtroom is the lawyer, you'll lose anyone in your audience who knows court procedure.

For example, whenever I see the psychologist on *Cracker* listen to the facts of the case and then spin off a sophisticated character profile that wows everyone, I cringe. It's unlikely that any psychologist will spout an offhanded theory without studying all of the available facts of the case—autopsy reports, police reports, crime scene photos, witness interviews, etc. A psychologist needs to pore over papers, do assessments, and compare the facts to patterns before she will provide a report. Most psychologists resist the notion that they are mental magicians. They know they need to do careful research, and offering a two-minute diagnosis is just not good psychology. It may also be unethical if the psychologist urges cops or attorneys to follow her hasty lead.

To develop a credible character who will act as a professional on a court-room team—or even on an investigative team—you need to know what role the psychologist is likely to play. You also need to know the professional and ethical codes that proscribe his or her behavior. You want to achieve the kind of fiction that seems likely to be factual, such as in Scott Turow's legal dramas. If you make errors based on the popular notions of psychology, you will fail. Luckily, the information is available, and a good writer will do the research. It is also a good idea to watch a correct depiction, such as the way psychiatrist Emil Skoda operates on NBC's *Law and Order.*

With the numerous crime shows on television devoted to forensic science and a greater access to information on the Internet, readers are more aware of how crime investigation works. The writer who crafts a credible character is more likely to increase his or her readership—as well as readers' appreciation—than the writer who relies on superficial or erroneous notions. Any time a reader might say, "He wouldn't do that," you've broken the spell.

Understanding the Criminal Mind

Another aspect of getting the facts right means being accurate about the criminal element. While Thomas Harris worked hard to base his *The Silence of the Lambs* serial killer, "Buffalo Bill," on several real cases—Ed Gein, Ted Bundy, and Gary Heidnik—the emphasis in the film and fictional sequel was on the mythical Hannibal "The Cannibal" Lecter as the ultimate monster. He killed and ate his victims. Still, his presentation was rather simplistic. Lecter comes across as having a larger-than-life IQ and seems completely in control of compulsions that lead him to kill (and munch on) people. While his inflated narcissism is true to life, there is no sense that he's driven by fantasies (which is most likely) or that his behavior will escalate beyond his control—which happens in most cases. Until his aberrant behavior is explained in simplistic Freudian terms in the movie *Hannibal,* he comes across as evil incarnate. As true crime writer Ann Rule put it, "Dr. Lecter was all-knowing and so much smarter that he made the police look like dunces." In truth, killers typically pick on people much weaker than themselves whom they catch off-guard because the killers themselves otherwise feel powerless. They "prove" themselves with a victim, not because they're so clever and smart, but because they're empty and full of need.

Harris also fell short when he gave his notorious doctor real feelings for the FBI agent, Clarice Starling. Psychopaths, as demonstrated in numerous studies, don't bond with people. Their emotions are shallow, and they tend to go from one relationship to another in manipulative ways. They use people up. They're not likely to give up something unless they see that they'll get much more in return.

It's true that fiction relies on a certain suspension of belief, but that won't occur if the reader senses poor research and a false presentation.

The Informal Forensic Psychologist

Not all applications of forensic psychology in fiction will involve a psychologist. Instead of having a specific character do your criminal psychology, you might want to do it yourself. In that case, you still need grounding in some basic psychology and in courtroom procedure. Developing the offender's psyche involves understanding how a crime scene is the "artwork" of the "artist" and what occurs with that person during arrest and in court. Let's take a famous crime case that did get to court and see how one author tried to "get into the killer's head."

On August 4, 1892, the bodies of Andrew Borden, seventy, and Abby Borden, sixty-four, were discovered hacked to death in their Fall River home. Abby's body was on the floor of the upstairs guest bedroom, while Andrew's corpse lay on the living room couch. There were blood spots on the floor, the wall, and the picture hanging over the sofa, but Andrew's clothing was not disturbed, nor were there injuries other than to his face, which was pierced by eleven fierce blows. It appeared that, as he napped, he had been attacked from above and behind.

Mrs. Borden, lying face down, was slain in the guest room on the second floor with a sharp instrument that had inflicted upon the back of her head eighteen to twenty blows, thirteen of them crushing through the skull. Her blood was dark and congealed, and crimson spots spattered the pillow shams that she had gone into the room to change.

It soon became clear that Abby had been killed an hour and a half before Andrew. That meant that the murderer had been lurking in the house all that time.

Andrew's thirty-two-year-old daughter, Lizzie, was the first to come across his body, and she sent the maid, Bridget Sullivan, for Dr. Bowen. Then a neighbor, Mrs. Adelaide Churchill, came over and asked Lizzie where her mother was. Lizzie said that Abby had been visiting a sick friend, but she thought she had heard someone come in. "I don't know but that they killed her, too," she said—an odd remark, delivered without emotion. It wasn't long before Abby's corpse was discovered upstairs.

That someone could have just come in and killed these two elderly people in the middle of the day on a busy street is odd, since it was the family practice to keep all doors on the first floor locked. Yet on that day, Lizzie claimed to have been in the barn, leaving the back screen door unlocked. She was in the loft for twenty minutes, she said, although there was no evidence of a disturbance in the thick dust on the floor. It was oppressively hot where she claimed to have been, leading many to speculate that she could not have been up there that long.

No footprints were found on the grass and no workers in the yard next door had seen a stranger coming or going in the Borden yard, although someone spotted an agitated man out in the street.

Theories about who did the ghastly deed range from the following:
- Emma, Lizzie's older sister, who was in another town
- Bridget, told to wash windows when she was ill
- John Morse, brother to Andrew's first wife, who had unexpectedly arrived the night before
- Andrew's supposed illegitimate son, who wanted money
- a disgruntled customer of Andrew's
- a wandering maniac
- a potential boyfriend to Lizzie (never found)
- Lizzie herself

Lizzie was the one arrested, and her contradictory answers at an inquest, coupled with the grand jury testimony by a friend who said that Lizzie had burned a dress, resulted in a trial for murder. Nothing was ever proven and she was acquitted, but speculation still abounds and fiction allows for some interesting explorations.

One novel theorized that Lizzie had a secret lover, which was inconsistent with her personality and with the dynamics of small towns—not much remains secret when your family is prominent. This theory also did not explain the brutality of the killings. Likewise Evan Hunter's *Lizzie* made her a lesbian who was about to be outed by Abby. While Hunter does a good job with the facts of the trial, there is nothing to support Lizzie turning on Abby just to keep her secret intact. It also fails to account for why she would kill her father so brutally over an hour later—especially smashing his face. Hunter fails to grasp what a forensic psychologist knows about such frontal, personalized attacks.

Elizabeth Engstrom offers something more involved in her novel *Lizzie Borden*. She researched neurological and psychological disorders, since Lizzie suffered from "spells" similar to her mother's "black moods." Coupled with resentment of a controlling father, the potential for a prolonged explosive reaction is credible. Engstrom first immersed herself fully in medical and forensic material that she felt was relevant and then allowed a story to unfold.

"First I read everything," Engstrom said. "I read the newspaper accounts and the trial transcripts over and over, and then I went to the Knight Library at the University of Oregon and read everything on the criminally insane that pertained to Lizzie. Then I went to the law library on campus and read everything that pertained to Lizzie's case and its unusual finding. Then I read all the other novels about her, and all the other books about her with their own peculiar theories of what happened, and then I tried to put myself in her shoes, just turned the screws down on her, day after day, week after week, until something had to happen. Basically, I made it all up, but within historically accurate constraints."

No matter what theory about a real-life crime you want to spin, it needs to be grounded not just in the facts about the case but in a broader context of psychological research and the forensic arena. As authors like Engstrom and Hunter understood, the manner in which a police investigation and court system operate in a specific time and place will have ramifications on the kinds of theories one can spin. Had there been only one murder, Lizzie probably would not have been arrested. Had she been a man, it is likely that certain issues would have been more thoroughly investigated, such as the blood spot on her clothing. It's also likely that an all-male jury in 1892 who were disinclined to put a woman to death might have had a different verdict.

In addition, had she been poor, she could not have hired her "dream team" defense.

In short, to spin a good tale, writers need to know the facts of a criminal case, the psychological issues consistent with those facts, and how such personality manifestations would play out in the legal process, from arrest to jury trial and beyond.

2

Psychology and the Law

A Sample Case

To see what mental health professionals might be up against in court, let's look at a case in some detail—because mental health professionals certainly have to. As you read this, keep in mind that mental health professionals hired for a defense related to mental illness look for behaviors that support or fail to support the idea that the perpetrator acted in a way that could be construed as insane or compulsive.

On to the case: On Thanksgiving Day in 1996, Roderick Ferrell, 16, from Murray, Kentucky, led a pack of kids into a situation that resulted in the killing of an elderly couple in Eustis, Florida. Back in Kentucky, Ferrell had been involved with a fantasy role-playing game called "Vampire: The Masquerade." Too tame for him, he'd developed a game that was decidedly more dangerous and gathered kids around him who would obey his command. According to one gang member, Ferrell became obsessed with "opening the gates of Hell," which meant that he had to kill a large number of people to consume their souls.

At one point, Ferrell was arrested, but not held, for breaking into a local animal shelter, freeing all the dogs, and mutilating two puppies. Yet he didn't stop with that. Not long afterward, he beat to death Richard and Naoma Wendorf, the parents of a former girlfriend, Heather, who wanted to become a vampire and run away from home. Ferrell then used a cigarette to make burns in the shape of a V to signify his vampire clan.

He, Heather, and the three other kids drove the Wendorf's Ford Explorer to Louisiana, where they were arrested. In a grand jury hearing, Heather was cleared of all charges, although the other four were held for separate murder trials. Heather claimed that she'd had no idea what Ferrell was planning and was not even sure that he had actually done it until she saw him playing with her mother's pearl necklace.

Apparently Ferrell had decided to kill Heather's parents before arriving at their home. He and the others had visited another girl in Eustis and had revealed the plan. That meant that Ferrell would be charged with first-degree murder. Despite Ferrell's youth, prosecutors said they would seek the death penalty.

The severity of the charges meant that psychologists hired by the defense would have their hands full. This became a sensational media case, but Ferrell's family had no money, so everything went through the public defender's office. And Ferrell would not shut up. Initially, he told reporters from the *Orlando Sentinel* that a rival vampire clan had done the killings. Then he claimed to have been treated by psychiatrists for multiple personality disorder. He also said that his grandfather had abused him. Whatever mental health professional came in to work with him would have to evaluate all of those claims.

Then from Murray, Kentucky, came news of another bizarre arrest. Rod Ferrell's mother, Sondra Gibson, was indicted for allegedly writing sexually explicit letters to a fourteen-year-old boy. She pleaded guilty to a felony charge of unlawful transaction with a minor, and her attorney claimed that she was mentally ill, which gave Ferrell's defense psychologists something more to work with—the possibility of a genetic disorder.

As preparations began for the Ferrell trial, details emerged of exactly what had happened that day. Another boy, Scott Anderson, was in the house, but it was Ferrell who swung a crowbar at a sleeping Richard Wendorf. He then stabbed Naoma Wendorf in the head when she walked into the room. It was clearly cold-blooded and utterly unnecessary. Was this kid the monster he claimed to be?

The first role the mental health professionals played in this case was to assess Ferrell for competency to waive his rights. When first caught, he'd waived his right to silence before giving a videotaped confession. If proved incompetent, then the confession would be thrown out. Another issue was whether he was competent to understand the legal procedures and to participate in his own defense.

It seemed that he could. He was not psychotic, so he was deemed competent and the confession was in. He appeared to have simply killed two people for a thrill. He knew what it meant to be arrested and understood that what he had done was against the law.

Since there is no "diminished capacity" law in Florida—which mental health professionals and defense attorneys rely on in many other states—and since the plea of not guilty by reason of insanity has become less popular with juries, the defense stated in pretrial motions that the arguments to be advanced would include the following.

- the killings were committed while Ferrell was emotionally or mentally disturbed
- Ferrell was too disturbed to realize the seriousness of the crimes
- Ferrell was under the influence of drugs at the time of the murders
- Ferrell suffers from schizotypal personality disorder, which is a form of borderline psychosis
- Ferrell was raised by a divorced mother who failed to discipline him properly and who has her own mental problems, and he was neglected by his father
- Ferrell was sexually abused as a youth
- Ferrell was allowed to participate in violent and self-destructive role-playing fantasy games, which impaired his judgment about what was real or normal
- Ferrell feels persecuted by society
- Ferrell is developmentally disabled
- Ferrell suffers from his beliefs in vampirism

In other words, there was an underlying psychological reason for what Ferrell had done that an expert would have to evaluate. It's a rather complicated list, but defense lawyers reach for anything that may help a jury understand why a crime was committed and why there might be mitigating factors. Since there was no question that Ferrell did it, the issue now was whether he deserved to die. Defense lawyers wanted to find something—anything—that would beg for leniency.

Cold-blooded murders are distinguished in the courtroom from other types of violent crimes. They are not considered cold-blooded when

- the killing emerges from a situationally induced rage
- the killer fails to think through a plan of escape
- the killing exhibits compulsive sexual or sadistic practices
- mortal violence appears to be induced by a victim's resistance

The Eustis murders, then, were senseless and unrelated to any kind of threat, abuse, surprise attack, rage, or confrontation. Ferrell had a plan and he carried it out. On videotape he described without emotion how he bludgeoned a sleeping man and then struck a woman in a bathrobe who was demanding to know what he wanted. To a jury, this would be appalling.

Now if you were to write about this case in a fictional scenario, you'd have to be familiar with all of the factors described previously (and then some), and then create a character who responds to them.

Regardless of which side your character offers testimony for, his or her approach to the case will be influenced by the attitudes, background, and personality issues that you as the writer develop. For example, if your mental health professional is young, she might understand the teenage mind and the allure of fantasy games better than someone in his fifties. Yet perhaps she had a bad experience with a similar game. In that case, she could have a personal conflict with the job she must do that adds to the tension of interviewing a game-inspired murderer.

Even her attitudes about the testing procedure will have some effect. Perhaps she was trained to view psychological testing as an art, not a science, and she has difficulty feeling confident about test results. This might be a secret she keeps from colleagues but which affects her judgment when facing an accused criminal. Or perhaps she had a mother who was out of control, the way Ferrell's mother appeared to be, and she can relate to his situation.

She would also have to have some experience with, or opinion on, various issues like the death penalty, "designer defenses," trying juveniles as adults, and the vampire fad around the country. If she needs further information, she will consult certain sources or other experts. She will also have to know about any landmark legal decisions that may affect her approach to the case, such as what type of testimony is allowed.

At any rate, creating a character who is going to serve as a psychologist in a high profile criminal trial requires consideration of many factors, some of which will involve personality and character background, and others that will involve the intersection of psychology and the law. The first decision to be made will be the type of forensic behavioral expert the writer wishes to develop.

The next question is how a psychologist joins the legal team and what steps he or she will take. Before developing the character, the writer needs to know how a mental health professional can become a forensic expert.

Forensic Assessment Education

There are only a few schools around the country that offer a Ph.D. in forensic psychology, although many other schools provide exposure and even some internship experience. There are also schools that link the law and psychology programs, such as at the University of Arizona, or the psychology degree with the criminal justice program. The John Jay College of Criminal Justice in Manhattan offers a master's degree in forensic psychology with an internship that places the student directly in the hospital or court system. That program may develop into a Ph.D., but in general, those practitioners who end up in the courtroom are there because they

- can do competency and assessment tests
- can make competent observations from a firm background in mental health
- have experience in syndrome issues that generally come into court
- have experience with criminal responsibility evaluations or malingering

Such experience means that they may have a degree in a more general area of psychology but have done impressive research or taken a job (and thus have gained experience) in an area that gets the attention of the court or an attorney. In addition, they may have served the appropriate length of internship in a clinical setting and taken a stiff examination for clinical licensure. (Not all psychologists or social workers are licensed, just as not all clinicians are licensed.)

Although there are common courtroom procedures for mental health professionals, it is also true that unique situations arise that require the opinion of an expert. On an episode of *Law and Order*, the psychiatrist is asked about "computer addiction." He applies what he knows about substance abuse to this relatively new arena to give the prosecutor some idea of what he might be up against with this sort of defense. Yet it's qualified by the fact that no one really knows what this new "addiction" is.

Becoming Certified as a Forensic Behavior Specialist

Beyond getting a degree and license as a mental health practitioner, there are courses and certification programs for specializing in forensic work. A comprehensive training program would emphasize the following:

- definition of an expert
- nature of forensic evaluations
- competency evaluation procedures and forms
- ethical issues in the evaluation process
- mental state at the time of the offense evaluations
- sentencing issues
- juvenile and adult court procedures
- civil trials
- uses of clinical evidence in the court proceedings
- report writing and expert testimony

In some states, passing a course in these topics is sufficient for forensic certification. Other states require a course, an exam, experience in evaluations, a period of supervision, and visits to forensic institutions. Certification can make the difference between whether or not an expert is allowed to testify.

There are separate boards for forensic certification in each specialization.

Specialized Knowledge

Anyone hired as an expert will understand something about the layout of legal cases and how the various levels of the court system work. Writers need to familiarize themselves with both if they are to develop effective characters.

Getting access to legal cases is fairly simple with the Internet. Sites such as www.findlaw.com provide summaries of cases—especially landmark cases—and also offer the full text of the court proceedings. It would be a good idea to become familiar with the way judges write their opinions and the way a given case gets treated. Besides the Internet, there are law libraries associated with most universities and law schools, and cases from every state will be found in bound volumes. Courthouses, too, have law libraries, but you may need permission to access them.

There are four types of law in the American governmental system: constitutional, statutory or legislative, administrative, and judicial (case law). Most legal resource materials offer information on one of these types, so the writer needs to decide which type of resource will best serve the purpose.

1. Constitutional law is related to federal or state constitutions.
2. Statutory law is derived from legislative bodies, such as congress or local governments.
3. Administrative law is about regulations, such as tax regulations or the issuance or revocation of licenses.
4. Judicial (case) law involves cases that have been decided by the courts, all of which together form the history of judicial decisions, with each court building on the decisions made by prior court rulings.

Each state has its own common law history and its own case laws, and justices frequently rely on precedents. Each court also has a defined jurisdiction, both geographically and by subject. Writers will have to make decisions in all of these categories before doing research.

A typical case will include the title, such as *Oncale v. Sundowner Offshore Services, Inc.* or *Powell v. Alabama*. It will be dated and will include the name of the judge or judges who heard the case. Then there will be a summary of the events that took place, along with a description of the "ultimate issue" (the actual legal issue at stake): "This case presents the question whether workplace harassment can violate Title VII's prohibition against discrimination because of sex when the harasser and harassed employee are of the same sex." The researcher can find out who the parties were, what happened and where it took place, the defense to the action or issue, precedents cited in the decision, and how the case was resolved. If remanded back to a lower court, the researcher will have to trace its path.

Note: Some legal issues have Web sites devoted to them that will put the issue in perspective. Sites devoted to the battered woman syndrome or abortion, for example, may include a brief history of legal decisions.

How a Forensic Mental Health Professional Gets Hired

There are basically two ways forensic mental health professionals can be called into a case: through connections or because of expertise.

- If the mental health professional has presented herself in a certain jurisdiction as a neutral fact finder, then the court may hire her to perform a court-ordered evaluation for assessing such things as competency or criminal responsibility. That means she is not working for either side but is expected to just deliver a professional report.
- If the mental health professional knows an attorney, she might be called into that person's cases where psychological assessments are necessary. That means she will be helping support a particular side of a case, within ethical guidelines.
- If the mental health professional works at a forensic hospital for the criminally insane, he may have to give court testimony about someone in his care. Any notes he takes or observations he might make can be subpoenaed.
- If he has special expertise in an area that often involves litigation, such as neonaticide (the suspicious death of an infant), he may acquire a reputation and get called into cases around the country.

In general, mental health professionals are brought in to testify on two general areas—competency and some type of diminished capacity, such as insanity. Each of these will be examined at length in chapter seven, but the next two sections provide a brief description.

Competency Hearings

These legal procedures take place in both criminal and civil cases. Most often, we hear about competency to stand trial—whether or not a defendant understands the legal process and can contribute to his or her defense. However, there are other competencies relevant to the criminal process: competency to waive one's Miranda rights (right to silence and to legal counsel), to confess, to understand the nature of the crime committed, to testify, to refuse an insanity defense, and even to be executed. (Charles Singleton murdered a sixty-two-year-old store owner and was given the death sentence. At some point during his appeals, he developed paranoid schizophrenia and had to be given psychotropic drugs. His psychosis went into remission, but then he decided to stop taking the drugs, making it difficult to carry out his sentence.)

In civil cases, competency screenings cover such things as parenting capability in child custody suits, guardianship, and consent to treatment.

Insanity Assessment

Most people believe insanity is a psychological term, but it's actually a legal one. Briefly, it means a lack of responsibility for one's actions at the time of the crime due to mental disease or defect, which diminishes criminal intent. Admittedly, there is room for interpretation, and various states have differing responses to the idea of cognitive or volitional impairment.

Steps in a Typical Case
1. Referral

Psychologists generally get drawn into a court case through an attorney. They may have done some networking to notify attorneys of their availability, but they might also be called upon because of expertise in some specific area. An attorney (or the court) will call, describe the case, and offer to set up an appointment with the client. The psychologist must then return a written acceptance with a schedule of fees and arrange to meet the client. He then informs the client—especially if working for the prosecution—that anything said or written is for the court and may be entered into the legal process. Mental health professionals should not get caught up in confidentiality issues, because they act as court officials not therapists. They should also restrict their client encounters to the referral issue.

Many people think that mental health experts are only used in cases where the insanity defense is being considered and that such situations become a matter of dueling experts, with each expert paid to say whatever that attorney wants him to say. While it is true that attorneys may pressure psychologists to enhance or downplay certain behaviors in order to strengthen the case, the psychologist is better off giving an impartial report of what he or she has found. That may even mean declining to give testimony and returning the fee.

Most often, this referral will be for a competency hearing or a "mental state at the time of the offense" determination. Unabomber Ted Kaczynski, for example, was evaluated for his ability to defend himself, as he insisted he wanted to do, and was found mentally unable to do so. If a person suffers from schizophrenia, as with one man who pushed a woman onto a subway track, then he must be assessed for his mental state at the time: At the moment he pushed her, did he know right from wrong and could he conform his actions to the law? It must also be determined whether or not he was taking medication, what his reactions to the medication were, and whether the type of medication was appropriate. It actually is rare that anyone gets an NGRI—not guilty by reason of insanity—but these cases get media scrutiny, so they seem more numerous than they are. However, when used, they rarely convince a jury—even when they should!

2. Building a File

The first thing a psychologist must do is collect information. An assessment or basic interview with the subject is generally not sufficient to make a decision. Fortunately, the psychologist has the attorney's resources at her disposal, so she provides a list of what she needs, such as school and hospital records, work appraisals, military records, crime scene photos, autopsy reports, and witness statements. The attorney must do his best to get or arrange for them. Mental health professionals also gain information from their own clinical interviews on family background. Information known to have been illegally acquired must be avoided because it will jeopardize the admissibility of the entire report.

Then, psychologists perform tests. Forensic assessment involves intelligence, personality, projective, and motor skills assessment tests (all detailed in chapter five). The most common battery includes the following tests:

- Wechsler Adult Intelligence Scale
- Minnesota Multiphasic Personality Inventory
- Rorschach
- Thematic Apperception Test

- Millon Clinical Multiaxial Inventories
- Bender-Gestalt
- Halstead-Reitan Battery

When testing a defendant who is using any sort of diminished mental capacity or insanity plea, one important function is to check for malingering—faking symptoms of amnesia or psychosis. Several tests include scales that indicate lying, exaggeration, and falsely presenting a good or bad impression. Psychopaths are con artists and can fool even the best behavioral experts. However, those who attempt to fake psychosis often get caught on the tests because their ideas about symptoms are based on popular misconceptions.

With all diminished capacity cases, writers need to check the state law. New York has a defense labeled "extreme emotional distress" (which does not have a clear definition), while some other states make no provision for diminished capacity except in the case of outright insanity. Often there is little uniformity from one jurisdiction to another.

3. Providing a Psychological Report

This psychological report must be a written summary of the psychologist's findings specific to the referral issue, which will include the following elements:

- the referral source
- a reason for referral
- sources of data on the client
- a confidentiality waiver
- the test scores and interpretations
- significant client background
- collateral information
- a mental status examination
- a diagnosis from *The Diagnostic and Statistical Manual of Mental Disorders: DSM-IV*
- observations during sessions
- a summary
- recommendations for treatment

Anything in this report is discoverable (available to both sides) and open to cross-examination, although a certain amount of lawyer/client privilege on the defense extends to the psychologist's examination.

4. Observing Courtroom Protocol

Like any expert witness, a mental health professional must be fully prepared when going into court. Generally, he has done an assessment for the court based on psychological tests, crime scene photos, clinical interviews, public records, witness interviews, and hospital or prison reports. Whatever he has written has been made available to the other side, and he must be prepared to defend or explain his opinion. In addition, if he has published other material relevant to his testimony, such as a book on situational homicides, then he may have to defend or explain any statements in those reports as well. I knew a psychologist who had written a book that criticized what she called "designer defenses" and then was hired to offer support to a defense that seemed to undermine her position. She had to explain herself so the jury would not feel that she was playing both sides.

The idea is for the mental health professional to be credible, confident, and competent. In other words, trustworthy. Court etiquette demands that a mental health professional dress conservatively, have all relevant data on hand, act professionally, and address either the judge or the jury, depending on the type of legal proceeding (bench or jury trial). He answers only questions he is asked, and if he feels something should be brought out in the trial that has been neglected, he makes that suggestion to the relevant attorney (unless hired specifically by the court as a neutral witness). Impression management is the key. The more clear (free of jargon), composed, and convincing the mental health professional is to a jury, the more likely it is that his testimony will make a positive difference.

5. Making Recommendations to the Court

Generally as the mental health professional's testimony wraps up, she is pressured to give an expert opinion on the legal issue of guilt or innocence. This is beyond her field of expertise, and she should be aware of that. Even so, the attorney can get around this by asking what the chances are of an offender repeating his or her offense. Historically known as the analysis of "dangerousness," it is now referred to as risk assessment (more will be said about this in chapter six). The mental health professional needs to know the boundaries of expertise and maintain them.

Let's look at an early use of psychiatry for forensic purposes: the case of Charles R. Starkweather, a young man who went on a killing spree with his girlfriend in Nebraska in 1958. This shocking case inspired several movies, including *Badlands* and *Natural Born Killers*. We can clearly see how the five steps play out.

On December 1, 1957, nineteen-year-old Starkweather held up a gas station, abducting the attendant and driving him into the countryside to shoot him in the head. Six weeks later, Starkweather shot and killed the parents of his girlfriend, Caril Ann Fugate, and murdered her two-year-old sister. Fugate stayed with him, and they took off. He next killed a family friend and two teenagers who gave them a ride. (He forced them into a storm cellar and shot them.) Then Starkweather and Fugate invaded a home where they murdered three people, including a deaf maid. Their final act before they got caught was to kill a man for his car.

Due to the shockingly explosive nature of these crimes in such a young man, the case was referred to an expert on criminal behavior. Dr. James M. Reinhardt, professor of criminology at the University of Nebraska, spent about thirty hours interviewing Starkweather before making his report.

To make a full assessment, he spoke with people who had known Starkweather throughout his life. Reinhardt ultimately described Starkweather as having a suspicious, unrealistic assessment of the world around him. The third of seven children, Starkweather had grown up in abject poverty. He was short, myopic, redheaded, bowlegged, and had a speech impediment. Taunted by classmates as "Redheaded Peckerwood," he lapsed into "black moods," developing "a hate as hard as iron" against anyone who humiliated him. When in 1956 he watched James Dean play a nihilistic adolescent named Jim Stark in *Rebel Without a Cause*, Starkweather found his hero.

There was no apparent abuse in his background, and his murderous rage seemed rooted in the cruelties inflicted on him by peers. For Starkweather,

Charles Starkweather Led to Courtroom

Charles Starkweather, who murdered his girlfriend's parents in 1958, is shown here being escorted to court by Sheriff Merle Kamopp and Chief Deputy Les Hanson. Starkweather's story is an interesting case study of how psychological examinations began to play an important role in trials.

the world had become an intolerable place where the symbol of power was the gun.

When he was tried for murder, his attorney attempted to show that Starkweather could not have premeditated those killings because he was either insane or had an organic brain disorder. Other psychiatrists who assessed him said Starkweather had a paranoid assessment of the world around him, a consuming hatred, and a delusional quality to his responses. Since he'd given several different versions of what he and Fugate had done, the psychiatrists interpreted this as a processing disorder. In short, they felt he was not entirely responsible for his actions.

The jury rejected the expert opinion, and Starkweather was found guilty and sentenced to die.

From the beginning, the case involved experts in abnormal psychology in both the fields of criminology and psychiatry. Referrals were made, files were developed to give context to the rampage, a report was written that synthesized the information for the court, court protocol was followed in terms of offering testimony in line with the attorney's defense strategy, and recommendations were made regarding the defendant's state of mental health.

While this sums up how a mental health professional is used in court, it doesn't yet address the fundamental issues involved in getting such testimony to conform to legal expectations. It also does not speak to why it seemed irrelevant to the jury that Starkweather had been viciously harassed as a child or that he appeared to have some neurological difficulties. To see what these defense experts were up against (which often still holds true today), it's instructive to understand how the goals of psychology and psychiatry can actually conflict with what lawyers and judges seek.

The Psychology of the Courtroom— The Basic Dilemmas

The use of mental health experts in the courtroom has generated a lot of controversy. The public believes that such testimony is subjective and easily manipulated and that psychology tries to undermine notions of free will. Psychologists, on the other hand, can feel that offering expert testimony within legal boundaries compromises their values. This creates tension in the courtroom, even on the same team. Most of the issues revolve around differing philosophies.

Free Will vs. Determinism

The law assumes that a person is free to make decisions and that the act of committing a crime generally arises out of free agency. As such, that person can be punished. Psychology (aside from the more humanistic theories) tends to view behavior as being determined by certain factors like upbringing. Psychologists are geared toward explaining those factors and showing a causal relationship between the factors and the behavior in question.

For example, if a woman kills her husband outside circumstances of immediate duress, it would seem that she acted freely. She could have left or found help, but she didn't. However, an expert on battered woman syndrome might try to convince the court that the woman's behavior is similar to post-traumatic stress disorder (PTSD), which involves flashbacks and the fear of a threat against one's life even when not imminent. The woman was acting under a compulsion that overwhelmed her free will, and thus she cannot be held fully responsible. While she may not be acquitted, such testimony can have a mitigating effect on sentencing. It also has the effect of setting precedent and allowing other such defenses to be introduced.

Truth vs. Conflict Resolution

Behavior scientists are dedicated to promoting mental health and resolving conflicts. In contrast, the legal arena's adversarial approach tends to sharpen conflict. It's designed to uncover facts and ensure that justice is done, and that may mean using intense pressure to get at the truth. An attorney may want to force conflict on whoever is testifying to get that person to crack. Many clinicians find this difficult to tolerate.

Mental health professionals may also feel that the legal process distorts their findings because attorneys present only the evidence they want to use. However, the nature of a trial involves each side putting its best foot forward. Because of this, some mental health professionals may feel exploited.

Probability vs. Certainty

The conclusions of social science rest on statistical probability and inference, while the court seeks degrees of certainty—such as certainty beyond a reasonable doubt. Either the defendant knew that what he was doing was wrong, or he did not. There's no room for quibbling. The facts must be interpreted clearly because people's lives are at stake. A mental health professional tends to speculate about a range of possibilities rather than pinpoint only one, but the court expects him to give a clear statement.

Mental health professionals who understand their roles in the legal arena will fare better than those who attempt to make it more conducive to their profession. Attorneys tend to hire experts who know what's expected and who perform.

The Initial Clinical Interview

After a mental health professional is hired for either side, the first step is to arrange to see the defendant. We get a good example of this in Gerald DiPego's screenplay, *Instinct*, based on a novel called *Ishmael* by Daniel Quinn. It's about a famous primatologist named Ethan Powell who's been found living with gorillas in Rwanda for two years. He killed two game wardens, so he's arrested. He remains mute, even when transported to a prison for the criminally insane in Florida.

A young psychiatric resident, Dr. Theo Caulder, is assigned to do an evaluation for competency. (They don't say what kind of competency, but it's probably competency to stand trial.) There's little time, so Caulder must first prepare a complete biography of Powell—in twenty-four hours. This may seem far-fetched, but in fact mental health professionals can get such last-minute assignments and have to work around the clock to prepare.

Caulder goes to Harmony Bay Correctional Facility to meet with Powell and must interview him in the presence of guards and the prison psychologist. The circumstances are less than ideal, but psychiatric forensic facilities generally have little to offer in terms of amenities. He sits face-to-face with the prisoner across a bare table. He turns on a recorder (not always used because attorneys worry about what may get into court) and offers paper and a pencil, but must follow the prison rules about how it gets used. He asks for Powell's name, gets nothing, and has to figure out a question that will provoke the man to speak. He notices that Powell is heavily medicated, so Caulder's challenge is even greater. Just because he wants and needs an interview does not mean the subject will cooperate.

While most forensic mental health professionals don't have assignments this tough, the movie shows the tension that can enter into this face-to-face assessment. Often, a psychologist is called on by the prosecutor to interview a resistant defendant. A mental health professional who must enter a prison to get information from a defendant needs to have some street savvy. When the FBI's Behavioral Science Unit was formed, the special agents involved went from prison to prison interviewing inmates to get experience about which procedures worked best, what to expect, and how to deal with a recalcitrant (or overly verbal) subject. To them, no amount of clinical knowledge could replace learning on the job—even though it was unsettling at times to be alone with a serial killer.

A typical case might involve the following: A man commits a homicide and claims he did it but could not stop himself. He behaves erratically in police custody, but it is several months before attorneys can get him assessed. By that time, he may even be on medication. The initial clinical interview involves a mental health professional trying to determine for the attorney if at the time of the offense the man was delusional and acted on an irresistible impulse.

The type of information likely to be gathered would include the following:

- the results of a mental status examination, which provides an assessment of the subject's current level of functioning
- information about the subject's pre- and post-offense behavior, including responses during the initial questioning by police
- information about the subject's behavior while in prison (patient's statement and jailhouse records)
- physical state during the interview, including attire, unusual movements, and grooming
- extreme mood or emotional shifts during questioning
- evidence of memory impairment
- thought content and belief system
- overt or covert threats to self or others
- quality of speech (volume, pace, distinct patterns)
- personal history (vocational, religious, military, academic, psychiatric, family support systems)

The Mini Mental Examination

A psychiatrist developed a quick assessment device to help mental health professionals make partial but efficient determinations of mental status. It consists of the following ten questions, with a scoring scale to rank the level of mental impairment or clarity.

1. Where are we right now?
2. What is the location of this place?
3. What month is it?
4. What day of the week is it?

5. What year is it?
6. How old are you?
7. When were you born?
8. Where were you born?
9. Who is the president of the United States?
10. Who was the president before him?

Once this assessment is done, arrangements can be made for a longer interview or for a series of interviews, depending on how much information is needed and how much time is available. All of this information is used in a formal report that the clinician must prepare for the attorney.

The Forensic Report

Upon accepting a case and getting a written agreement for the type and cost of services to be rendered, the mental health professional must keep track of all records for what will become the final report for the attorney. He might write a preliminary report of his clinical interview with the subject and estimate what he will need to do from there, or he may save all the information for one summary report. In short, he is documenting all aspects of the evaluation. The substance of the report may become public knowledge, which means that the psychologist must minimize invasions of privacy.

The guiding factor in any report is the referral question: Is this about competency, a character disorder, psychosis, or sentencing guidelines? It's easy to get distracted by other issues, but the reason for the referral should be the organizing factor. The examiner needs to weigh all the factors, find an organizing theme, point out limitations, and consider alternatives. This report not only gives the attorney an idea of what can be used in court but offers the examiner a summary of his own testimony. It is also possible that the report, if concise and convincing, may trigger settlement talks or even satisfy both parties and avert a trial altogether.

One case I worked on involved a middle-aged man whom I'll call Jackson. He was charged with the second-degree murder of his wife after beating her so badly that she died of her injuries. He actually stomped on her. The couple's two adult children overheard the violence but failed to intervene. Jackson woke his daughter to tell her there was something wrong with her mother, as if he did not understand what had happened. He exhibited aspects of paranoid schizophrenia, because he claimed that his extreme beatings often arose from jealous suspicions about his wife's loyalty.

The forensic report was based on the following documents:
- the statement of fact (felony complaint)
- the arrest report and indictment
- a waiver of rights
- case evaluation from the district attorney (including all notes)
- the autopsy of the victim
- the toxicology report on the defendant
- all relevant police statements
- the hospital incident report
- the child protective services report
- the grand jury testimony
- the mental health services report
- any appellate decisions on domestic violence relevant to the case
- the physician examination
- the defendant's voluntary statements/clinical interview
- employment records for the defendant
- Minnesota's Multiphasic Personality Inventory profile and assessment analysis
- interviews with the children

With all of these documents, the case file was over one hundred pages, which was a lot of material to summarize for a report of ten to fifteen pages. Part of the reason for the brevity is ease of reading for busy people, but it is also to avoid offering the opposing side ammunition for cross-examination. Basically, the report itself needs to offer brief statements on the following:
- circumstances of the referral
- the date and nature of any clinical contacts
- all data sources (police reports, employment records, etc.)
- relevant personal background information about the client
- clinical findings (from interviews, assessments, observations)
- psychological formulations—integration of all data to answer legal referral questions

It needs to avoid:

- gratuitous comment
- inferences and theory
- psychological jargon
- strategy advice

So if your character is involved in any way in a courtroom assessment, you need to know how such a report would be structured—even if you don't actually write the contents. Something in the contents may even become part of the plot.

Expert Testimony

Experts should have a pretrial conference with the attorney to make sure the expert testimony is consistent with the attorney's strategy. The attorney may also be able to describe characteristics of the judge and the opposing counsel, anticipate the types of questions in cross-examination, and fill in any final details. If deposition transcripts are available, he might have the mental health professional read over any relevant parts. At this meeting, the mental health professional can provide details about the database, assessment, and any potential weaknesses in the position—in particular regarding the standard of "reasonable medical certainty." The mental health professional and attorney should also discuss the attorney's full expectations and the mental health professional's ethical obligations.

Potential experts must first qualify as such with the court, so they generally get questioned by both attorneys and even by the judge. This is known as part of the *voir dire*, or the procedure for evaluating a trial participant, and it is usually conducted while the jury is present. Qualified experts may then offer testimony, including expert opinions. The *voir dire* establishes the boundaries of their expertise—that is, if the mental health professional is there to talk about the adverse psychological effects of sexual harassment, he or she cannot also address the viability of repressed memories.

If the witness is impressive, the opposing side may stipulate to their qualifications—in other words, not ask a lot of questions—to avoid having the jury hear about the witness in detail. Basically, the questioning elicits a history of the witness's education, certifications, publications, and experience. There may also be questions about prior court experience and fees. Sometimes the opposing attorney will use the opportunity to say what the witness is unable to do or to undermine the witness's credibility.

One thing experts need to know well is what they've said in their own research. I met a forensic psychologist who, on the witness stand, offered an opinion of a client that was contrary to something he had stated in a published paper several years earlier. The cross-examining attorney had done her research, and she caught him in an embarrassing contradiction that threatened to discredit him. He had not even recalled that he'd made such a statement in that paper.

Even experts get anxious about being in court, because many attorneys are committed to winning via methods of persuasion rather than to getting at the truth. They hire experts merely to support their positions. Those experts who can adjust to the attorney's position fare better than those who want to get their own agenda across.

Credibility relies on three things:

- expertise
- trustworthiness
- charisma

The mental health professional needs to know the results of the assessment on the defendant, as well as the recent research on any theories or diagnoses put forth. She needs to come across as honest, and it's generally best in court to rely on a conservative appearance. She's also better off if she is somewhat animated and stylish rather than dull, because jury members will pay more attention.

The first step is the direct testimony, which means the attorney who has hired the expert will lead him or her through the relevant testimony. This includes evaluation procedures and results, as well as the clinician's conclusions. If personality, intelligence, or other types of tests were used, the clinician must be prepared to state their validity in terms that laypeople can understand. The idea is to provide sufficient information to make the point, without overwhelming the jury with too much information, and to keep it as free of jargon as possible.

Some background is important for understanding the admissibility of expert testimony. Several court cases have challenged and refined admissibility procedures. Mental health professionals face the perception that their data and interpretations are not hard science and thus are not facts. A tire tread expert who uses measurements and plaster casts may have more persuasive force with a jury than a psychiatrist. Nevertheless, the complexities of some documented psychological syndromes are beyond the knowledge of laypeople, so problems can arise when unfamiliar information is presented. Juries may find it difficult to evaluate for accuracy and relevance to the case. In part, that's why there have been landmark court decisions about expert testimony.

In 1923, the District of Columbia Court of Appeals issued an opinion that became the first guideline for the admissibility of scientific evidence. In a case known as *Frye v. United States*, the defense counsel tried to enter evidence about a device that measured blood pressure during deception (a forerunner to the polygraph). The court decided that the thing from which the testimony is deduced must be "sufficiently established to have gained general acceptance in the particular field in which it belongs." It also had to be determined that the information was beyond the general knowledge of the jury. This *Frye* test became general practice in most courts for many years. It saved the judge from running minitrials about the scientific evidence itself.

However, critics claimed that it excluded theories that were unusual but well supported by evidence. Several attempts were made in the courts to rephrase the *Frye* test, but they generally had problems of their own.

Most relevant for mental health professionals (and for writers using mental health professionals), the *Frye* test was replaced in many states by a standard cited in 1993 in the Supreme Court's *Daubert v. Merrill Dow Pharmaceutical, Inc.* decision, which emphasizes the trial judge's responsibility as a gatekeeper. The court decided that "scientific" means having a grounding in the methods and procedures of science and claiming to have "knowledge" must be stronger than subjective belief. The judge's evaluation has only to focus on the methodology, not on the conclusion, and also on whether the scientific evidence applies to the facts of the case. In other words, when behavioral science evidence is presented, judges have to determine

- whether the theory can be tested
- whether the potential error rate is known

- whether it was reviewed by peers and has attracted widespread acceptance within a relevant scientific community
- whether the opinion is relevant to the issue in dispute

Because of *Daubert*'s emphasis on testing, falsification, and validation, it heavily impacts the admissibility of social science evidence. Much of that evidence is controversial, particularly when new syndromes are offered. Experts must be prepared for a *Daubert* challenge, even though it was strictly meant for unusual or controversial methodologies. There is still much debate in journals about policy and law, so writers should consult the latest developments when considering a defense based on social science testimony.

Once a mental health practitioner is accepted, he serves as an expert, which means his role specifically is to educate. Expert opinion is most effective if it is

- within a discipline known to reach reliable results
- communicated objectively
- autonomous
- consistent with professional values
- respectful
- able to take into account alternative explanations
- clearly associated with the issues
- aimed at making complex matters accessible but not oversimplified

Although the opposing attorney may make a few objections during direct testimony, he will generally wait until he gets his turn for cross-examination. At this stage, he will challenge the expert's credibility from every angle and attempt to downplay or distort any information in direct testimony that is damaging to his side. He may also point out errors or omissions during the evaluation process. Attorneys actually have access to strategies for cross-examining mental health experts, but mental health professionals have access to the same material, as well as to published papers on how to cope with the attack.

Attorney strategies will follow one of these routes:

- suggestion of witness fallibility
- boxing into a corner with yes/no questions

- lack of scientific certainty in the findings
- using part of direct testimony to "load" a question as a setup
- using published professional reports to contradict oral testimony
- using hypothetical situations or leading questions to try to trap the expert
- using complex questions to which a simple response is insufficient

Above all, the witness who is well prepared need only maintain composure and consistency in her testimony and to keep good eye contact with the jury. Hopefully, the attorney who hired her will object when certain strategies become obvious, but in any case, she has qualified as an expert and can feel confident about her data.

A mental health professional can increase her credibility, despite what an attorney might do, with a little impression management. She should

- dress professionally for a low-key image
- show her familiarity with courtroom procedure
- speak directly to the jury when answering questions and use language the jury can understand
- develop a conversational tone
- avoid becoming defensive
- make sure she has given the case professional attention
- be prepared to testify about any aspect of the evaluation

In a survey, court participants noted that clarity, familiarity with the facts, and impartiality outweighed education and personality in terms of witness credibility.

The "Ultimate Issue"

The ultimate issue is the conclusion that the fact finder(s) must ultimately draw. It's the legal issue to be decided, such as whether or not a defendant was insane at the time he committed the crime. The ultimate issue can be about competency, insanity, dangerousness, or even parental fitness. A mental health professional may provide diagnostic or prognostic data, but she cannot decide how it meets legal requirements for conviction or sentencing. The judge and jury decide conclusively on all legal issues. Nevertheless, a clinician is often pressured to draw this conclusion, and ethical standards notwithstanding, may have to make a pronouncement of some type that addresses the ultimate issue in her reports or in court.

Judges seem to prefer such testimony, and if it serves an attorney's agenda, they want it to be made as explicit as possible by an expert. Some jurisdictions even have rules of evidence that require it. Nevertheless, the professional stance is that mental health experts ought to resist making statements on matters of law.

How These Concepts Influence Character Development

While much of this information is pretty straightforward, there is room for character development, particularly when a mental health professional finds that he or she does not fit well with the role imposed by the court. For example, going back to the movie *Instinct*, Dr. Caulder was to assess whether Powell could be judged sufficiently competent for a court hearing on his case. Caulder became attached to Powell and began to consider him a friend. He was no longer interested in "competence" but wanted Powell to be free to return to the lifestyle he had adopted while living with the gorillas. Caulder's mentor warned him several times against forgetting his professional duties, but he decided that it was personally worth the risk of his career to ditch the formal assessment and get closer to Powell's heart. Thus, his role as forensic evaluator not only conflicted with his role as therapist but also with his inner evolution as a person who saw something in his client that others did not—could not—see. What had been a court case became a matter of his own humanity.

Given the ethical, philosophical, and professional tensions inherent in the interface between law and psychology, there's plenty of room for personality conflicts that can create character depth.

3

Theories of Criminality

Providing the Context

After a mental health professional has answered a question such as why a defendant would cover the face of a murder victim, he or she may be asked to explain it in the context of a theory of criminality. For example, if a neuropsychologist has testified about the statistical correlation between crime and brain injuries, then she may have to discuss how neurological deficits appear to weaken impulse control. Whether or not this theory is made explicit in court, all expert witnesses need to be clear about the theories that gives their claims context.

Almost every scholarly field, from anthropology to economics to genetics to psychology, has offered at least one theory about the causes of crime, and many individuals have made their careers on some unique variation. None seems to explain all instances of criminality, and some are built more firmly on political ideology than on facts and empirical data (e.g., it is politically preferable to claim that crime will occur more frequently in the inner city than in a quiet middle-class neighborhood). Some theories focus on character disorders and mental illnesses, while others examine situational factors or else group crime into certain types of categories.

Many theories contradict others in the same field. Let's compare, for example, a socioeconomic theory with one that is more centered on the individual.

In identifying what has caused the recent increase in crime, social scientist Elliott Currie describes the general erosion of social responsibility: When people think first of personal acquisition (which they do in a society that emphasizes material gain), they feel less inclined to extend themselves to others. In contrast, Myron Magnet, another social theorist, argues that it is pointless to blame social conditions; those values more relevant for crime prevention are located in the individual. Crime has increased, Magnet says, with the diminished emphasis on personal responsibility and restraint.

Currie blames the economic climate. The year 1990, which followed eight years of a conservative Republican government, showed a substantial jump in homicide and institutionalization. The policies of the political right, he insisted, moved the culture toward a way of life that destroyed institutions that sustain social order. The 1980s government encouraged private gain and thus evolved us toward a "market society." Individuals, families, and communities increasingly looked to the free market to provide for their needs. Yet, a market society only increases poverty, inequality, and feelings of deprivation; erodes the capacity of local communities for provision and socialization; withdraws public services; and subjects families to the increased stress associated with domestic violence and child abuse. It also creates pressure to meet high economic standards that many cannot meet without resorting to crime, which in turn weakens the value of human life when measured against personal gain. Thus, it promotes the potential for crime, especially among urban minority youth.

Magnet views this tendency to blame pervasive social forces as sidestepping the real issue, which is personal responsibility. He cites a failed experiment in the early sixties run by George Cadwalader, who had taken a group of delinquent boys to an island to teach them survival skills. Believing that bad environments create bad boys and good environments have the opposite effect, Cadwalader had hoped that they would learn self-reliance and teamwork. Instead, they appeared to be impossible to rehabilitate. Thus, he concluded that his founding belief was idealistic and unsound. Even so, Magnet points out, that same discredited theory is used by people today to excuse criminal behavior, and it has infected the criminal justice system with the tendency toward leniency. The idea that crime is the product of poor social conditions, he claims, became dominant in the sixties, along with an attitude that reframed the crimes of underclass racial groups as a heroic rebellion.

Magnet then locates the causal factors of crime in human nature, which he says is inherently violent. Through police agencies and prisons, society must actively restrain aggression and instill in each person a social contract—an internal restraint system based on respect for others. Criminals act out because they have not been adequately socialized and because they have been encouraged to see crime symbolically as resistance to social oppression. However, those who buck the system of the "Haves" are also harming the "Have-nots," because the collapse of the social order spreads crime into all neighborhoods.

So which is the most crime-generating or criminogenic factor: social forces or the individual's unrestrained inner violence? The evidence can be interpreted either way.

Even within a category of theories there can be contradictions. When evaluating which personality constructs lead to aggression, for example, many theorists proposed that low self-esteem is a key factor. Bullies and rapists were thought to be men who did not value themselves. However, another researcher said that there is increasing evidence that high self-esteem is instrumental in aggression. Many violent types have an inflated, albeit unstable, sense of self. If challenged or criticized, they react with violence to reestablish their self-esteem. Researchers who support this theory believe that studies of incarcerated offenders that measured a significant proportion with low self-esteem are a result of the offenders being locked up. The low self-esteem supporters counter that the so-called high self-esteem factor is actually narcissism, which is based on perceived superiority, not a healthy regard for self.

Whatever the case, the theory proposed in court should be clearly defined and well supported. While I cannot offer all the possible philosophies on crime, what follows is a basic survey of types of theories.

Types of Theories
Sociological

Most sociological theories tend to fix the causes of crime on some social or cultural force or circumstance. The cause generally has to do with something independent of individuals that nevertheless affects them. The idea is that the individual is a member of a group that is affected by the force or circumstance in such a way as to be more likely to commit a crime. For example, poverty, the lack of opportunity to enhance status, or the feeling of powerlessness due to membership in a stigmatized social class can contribute to a criminal act.

Criminal defenses generally rely on sociological factors like these to try to mitigate a crime when guilt is obvious or to try to deflect responsibility onto a larger group. The reason an eleven-year-old boy shot a man, one mental health professional claimed, was because the system let him down. He needed psychiatric help during a certain period of his life and didn't get the proper attention. The decisions of social workers are to blame, but more importantly, it's the fault of a bloated bureaucracy in which individual cases get only the most superficial attention.

There was a time when such theories were popular because people wanted to blame society, but as more people want to see crime punished, some of these theories have fallen into disrepute.

Biological

Biological theories stress some factor arising from the body as the cause of crime. Perhaps the person had a genetic predisposition to do this and happened to be living in circumstances that triggered it. Maybe certain crimes like rape are ancestrally based, more functional for primitive population expansion but now considered a violation. There are also theories that have cited chromosomal abnormalities, body type determinants, and biochemical factors. The "Twinkie defense," in which Dan White claimed to be high on sugar from junk food when he shot down San Francisco mayor George Moscone and supervisor Harvey Milk in 1978, actually got him a diminished capacity verdict of manslaughter. For a while afterward, all kinds of people came forward to admit to such things as sugar-induced shoplifting and spousal abuse. "My body made me do it."

It is true that if certain personality types such as psychopathy are hardwired in the brain, and if psychopathy is highly correlated with crime and recidivism, then biology may play a part.

Donald Black, author of *Bad Boys, Bad Men: Confronting Antisocial Personality Disorder*, believes that antisocial personality disorder affects up to seven million Americans. He claims that evidence strongly suggests that some people are just born bad. The warning signs in these people include the following

- they've had reactions since childhood against every type of regulation and expectation

Suspect Dan White Being Taken to Jail

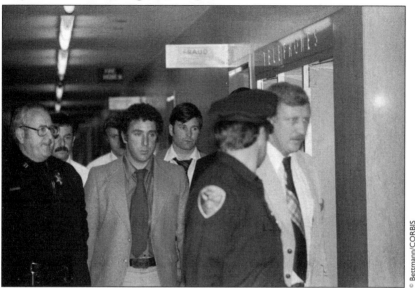

Dan White became famous for using the designer "Twinkie defense." He claimed his diet of too much junk food was the reason he killed San Francisco Mayor George Moscone and supervisor Harvey Milk.

- resistance appears to be their driving force
- they fail to understand or care about the difference between right and wrong
- they lack empathy
- they show no remorse

Black claims that antisocial personality disorder is eight times more common in males than females, a fact that suggests biological factors.

However, to argue that a person cannot make decisions about what is right and wrong because of the way his or her brain processes environmental stimuli or because of certain physiological features involved in gender requires strong physiological proof, not just supposition. It also requires explaining why people who share those factors do not commit crimes.

The fact that many personality dispositions respond to pharmaceuticals implies that physiology is indeed involved in certain mood disorders, but there is still no evidence that something like schizophrenia actually causes someone to become violent against another person. Why would one schizophrenic push someone into the path of a train while most others would not?

Some neurological studies indicate that many serial killers have experienced some form of brain damage, which indicates that there may be something wrong with their neural circuitry. Stephen Dinwiddie, a psychiatrist at the Washington University School of Medicine in Missouri, supports the idea from his survey of twin, adoption, and family studies that biological factors play a role in repetitive antisocial acts. Antisocial recidivists show unique EEG patterns and hormonal and metabolic levels.

Again, there is no evidence that this causes them to be killers. What it may mean is that their inhibitions are diminished, which allows anger or aberrant behavior to be expressed in certain circumstances that might otherwise lie dormant or be controlled through restraint.

Writers who develop neuropsychologists as characters have to be careful not to confuse correlation studies with causal factors, but this is an area where a lot of criminal theory is currently being developed. Make sure you read the latest research in journals devoted to neuropsychology and crime or on professional Web sites like the American Psychological Association (www.apa .org) before preparing a theory.

Psychological

Psychological theories look at personality factors to try to determine if certain personality types or traits are more likely to be generative of crime. They include psychoanalytic, behavioral, and trait theories. Many psychologists have written books on the "criminal personality type." Once again, however, there is no evidence that certain traits cause someone to commit a crime.

J. Reid Meloy, an expert on psychopathy and on stalking behavior, offers an example of psychoanalytic thinking. The psychopath has only low levels of empathy or an absence of it altogether. His relationships tend to be sadistic, based in power over others rather than in attachment to anyone. This has to do with poor attachment to others in the family, which starts at a young age. Meloy proposes a dual-track orientation, claiming that psychopaths are biologically predisposed to antisocial activity because they have a hyperreactive autonomic nervous system. Crime or exploiting others excites them. In addition to that, they are motivated by "primary object" conflicts—they just don't bond. That means they're motivated to do things that heighten their nervous systems, and they have no real conscience about hurting others.

Stanton E. Samenow, an authority on the criminal personality and a former member of Reagan's task force on crime victims, dispels several myths about criminals. He cites the failure of rehabilitation systems that are based on erroneous assumptions about crime being caused by society, broken homes, alcoholism, television violence, and unemployment to indicate that these are not in themselves causal forces. He insists that the criminal's way of thinking is vastly different from that of responsible people and that the "errors of logic" derive from a pattern of behavior that began in childhood. Criminals, he says, choose crime by rejecting society and preferring the role of victimizers. They are in control of their own actions, but they assign the blame for their behavior to others. They devalue people and exploit others insofar as they can be manipulated toward those ends to which the criminals feel entitled. The excitement of crime, they believe, staves off emptiness.

Diverging from individualistic psychology, social psychology theories attempt to study individuals in an environment; for example, a young black male in a neighborhood that pressures people to join gangs. Criminality is learned through social interactions and exposure to certain role models. Some people believe that human nature is inherently prone toward anarchy and has to be restrained by social institutions and socialization in families. Others believe that people learn to be criminals because crime appears to offer more short-term reward or to be the only way out of a situation.

Social psychologists Craig Haney and Philip Zimbardo did an experiment in the early 1970s at Stanford University in which they randomly assigned students to be prison guards and inmates. The circumstances in which these students became colder and more brutal to one another seemed to support the idea that environment had a strong influence on aggression. In the mid-1990s, they looked back and found that throughout the 1980s, society had evolved away from the notion of rehabilitation and toward an increasingly hard-nosed and dehumanizing attitude toward criminals. That, coupled with sensational media attention, turned the justice system into a "runaway punishment train." More people were being incarcerated and for longer periods of time, even though the crime rate itself had decreased. Haney and Zimbardo indicate that brutal attitudes of criminal containment, punishment, and retribution will influence prisoners to become more demoralized and hardened than if they were treated with a rehabilitative attitude. The shift away from rehabilitation, they claim, has created a social environment that has a negative effect on character development. The prisoners themselves then become criminogenic agents. Department of Corrections data showed that about one-fourth of those initially imprisoned for nonviolent crimes were sentenced a second time for committing a violent offense. They learned in prison to be more violent.

Another example of social learning theory is developed by Lonnie Athens, author of *The Creation of Dangerous Violent Criminals*. He takes the approach that antisocial behavior results from a series of evolutionary stages. People start off benign, he believes, and violence is therefore preventable. In an attempt to discover why some people in a crime-vulnerable environment turn violent while others do not, he interviewed violent criminals to find out what they had in common. He came up with the idea that people become violent through a process he calls violentization, which involves the following four stages:

- brutalization and subjugation
- belligerency
- violent coaching
- criminal activity (virulency)

First, the person (usually a child) is the victim of violence and feels powerless to avoid it. Then, he is taught how and when to become violent (often by the person who was violent to him) and how to profit from it. It's not long before he's had sufficient exposure to act on it. According to Athens, if someone from a violent environment does not become violent, it's because some part of the process is missing. Athens seems not to include psychopathy or an inherent tendency toward violence and shallow emotion as part of the antisocial scenario.

Mixed Theories

Most mental health professionals accept that there may be a complex organization of factors that lead to crime. It's difficult to ignore the neurological and twin studies, but it's also difficult not to notice how certain situations seem to bring out a criminal act. Additionally, there's no doubt that some people with character disorders such as antisocial personality disorder are more prone to acting out aggressively. Thus, a mixed theory, while not as tidy, may be a more accurate assessment.

One interesting approach, for example, looks at crime through a spectrum of motivations that arise from a variety of factors. Forensic psychologist Louis B. Schlesinger and forensic psychiatrist Eugene Revitch believe that there are motivational stimuli that lead up to a crime, with environmental and sociological factors on one end of the continuum and psychogenic (internal or personality) factors on the other. According to them, 75 percent of crime is triggered by a situation. For example, a man loses his job and panics over how he will support his family, so he kills them. Schlesinger and Revitch also acknowledge that certain organic or toxic factors contribute. Someone under the influence of an intoxicant may act out in ways that would not occur during normal functioning. Paranoid schizophrenics may behave strangely under the influence of a delusion. Thus, they group the motivation spectrum for offenses into these five categories:

1. social (the environment or a certain group of people have the largest influence in a crime)
2. situational (a set of stressful circumstances is most obviously the cause)
3. impulsive (generally sexual, sometimes psychotic)
4. catathymic (sudden explosive act from a buildup of tension)
5. compulsive (part of a character disorder or fantasy obsession)

While most people are familiar with social, circumstantial, impulsive, and compulsive influences, few have heard of catathymic behavior. This notion comes from the work of Fredric Wertham, who described catathymia as the urge to carry an idea through to a violent act. The person imbues the violence with symbolic meaning, and his thinking acquires a delusional quality, marked by rigidity and incoherence. Then, extreme emotional tension from some situation culminates in the violent crisis. After it's over, he returns to superficial normality and freedom from tension.

In the first two categories listed on this page, repetition of the crime is least likely. In numbers three and four, repetition depends on circumstances, while repetition is most likely in the last category because the motivation is more clearly located within the person. A compulsion motivates behavior beyond the person's control. This mixed theory, then, is based primarily on diverse motivations.

Another mixed theory comes from David T. Lykken, author of *The Antisocial Personalities*. He thinks that upbringing plays a part with some types, while biology is the primary factor in others. While some people may be inherently prone toward behaviors that contribute to the crime rate, Lykken believes that not all who have antisocial tendencies are born that way. Most antisocial personalities are caused by poor parenting—an absent father and an inadequate mother. He cites several twin studies that support the view that criminality has a substantial heritability factor but claims that traits like fearlessness, aggressiveness, and sensation-seeking can be properly channeled away from antisocial behavior.

It seems that some criminals are predisposed toward crime regardless of social factors, while for others any of several possible social influences plays a role. There appears to be a multiplicity of potential factors involved in criminal behavior, and no one factor is either necessary or sufficient in itself to cause an increase in crime. Social trends may precipitate some crimes but ought not to be the exclusive focus of those interested in decreasing crimes.

Why a Clear Theoretical Position Matters

An expert witness is hired to give clear testimony and to help the jury understand certain psychological factors in a case. Most "facts" are interpreted through a theory. A mental health professional who attempts to offer explanations from more than one theory—"Well, twin studies show A, but I'm more inclined to think that the explanation is B, which arises from a weak ego structure"—is going to confuse everyone and weaken the case for whoever hired her.

In addition, she leaves herself open to cross-examination that could completely dismantle her credibility. A good attorney has done some research on the mental health professional and will be prepared with questions not only about her credentials but also about any theories she has proposed. The aim is to get her testimony thrown out. The more clarity a mental health professional has in her position, the more able she will be to both explain and defend it, particularly if the other side has their own theory to establish.

It isn't important that the theory have some prominent name attached to it, but the mental health professional should know the basics of the theory—who founded it, how it has evolved, and what the most recent version is. It's also important to have statistics that back up any claims made for the theory and to indicate which prominent professional journals recognize it. The point is to show that the theory is established in the field and not some fly-by-night idea made up to fit the case.

For example, when psychologists were first testifying about the battered woman syndrome, it was difficult to get juries to understand why some women remain with an abuser. Many of those cases were lost. However, when it was associated with Martin Seligman's groundbreaking theory on "learned helplessness," it was much easier to explain how women may not only stay with abusers but even participate in their crimes. Learned helplessness was a concept derived from empirical studies with dogs that showed that when shocked enough times with no escape, they gave up. Human beings can suffer from the same pattern. Thus, a well-grounded, clearly stated theory with research support can go a long way with a jury.

4

Types of Character Disorders

The Code Book

For diagnosis, billing, and treatment, mental health professionals of all types rely on the codes found in *The Diagnostic and Statistical Manual of Mental Disorders: DSM-IV*. It conveys information about clients' conditions to insurance companies and managed care organizations and provides common reference points for referrals and professional articles. It also contains a standard diagnostic system and goes through changes as the profession evolves in its consensus on mental illnesses. Each new edition has reclassifications, additions, and deletions. For example, homosexuality was once listed as a mental illness but was eventually removed. In 1987 the *DSM-III-R* (third edition, revised) listed twenty-seven new categories.

It all started back in the 1920s when a movement developed to standardize medical terminology. By 1952 the first edition of the *DSM* was ready for use. Having a standard reference manual improved the reliability of diagnostic judgments. There was also an *International Classification of Diseases* manual, and the first revision of the *DSM* aimed at coordinating the two references. Another impetus for change was the way the *DSM* seemed to stigmatize mental illness. Critics attacked the lack of research and then went after the medical model of mental illness, so revisions kept coming out.

Now in its fourth (but not last) incarnation, the *DSM* can be implemented in a wider variety of settings than before. The coding and classification relies on a system of the following five axes: three are diagnostic and the other two cover areas other than clinical syndromes:

1. clinical disorders and conditions that elicit clinical attention
2. personality disorders and mental retardation
3. general medical conditions
4. psychosocial and environmental problems
5. global assessment of functioning

There are seventeen major sections, from mood disorders to dementia, and writers are urged to pick up at least the pocket-sized *Diagnostic Criteria From DSM-IV*. Proper use requires clinical training and skills, because diagnosis relies on a clinical interview, observation, and other forms of assessment. If characters who are mental health professionals are going to sound realistic, then writers need to be familiar with the terms and criteria.

COMMON PSYCHIATRIC TERMS
Character Disorder
A personality disorder that shows a chronic, maladaptive, and inflexible pattern of reaction that often provokes things in the environment that the person wants most to avoid; also called a character neurosis.

Personality Disorder
An enduring maladaptive pattern of perceiving and relating to the environment, causing significant hindrance to one's functioning. The *DSM-IV* groups them into these three "clusters":
1. paranoid, schizoid, schizotypal
2. antisocial, borderline, histrionic
3. avoidant, dependent, obsessive-compulsive

To make a diagnosis, clinicians need to determine that there is a combination of the following:
- the chief complaint
- long-term symptoms
- known childhood difficulties
- medical conditions
- the person's support system
- psychosocial stressors
- defense mechanisms

- reality testing
- IQ
- current mental status

With this information, clinicians can make at least an initial diagnosis and check incoming information against it. They can also decide which assessment devices might be most helpful. Whereas one type of disorder may warrant neurological tests, another might call for the Minnesota Multiphasic Personality Inventory. The assessment tests are discussed in detail in chapter five.

The current official coding system is based on the *International Classification of Diseases*, ninth edition, and most of the disorders have a related numerical code. Schizophrenia, paranoid type, for example, will be 295.30. Schizophrenia itself will be characterized by a list of symptoms, from which two or more are selected that have endured for a significant percentage of a month's time. The symptoms list includes delusions, hallucinations, disorganized or catatonic behavior, flat emotional affect, and disorganized speech. If schizophrenic is diagnosed, then the next step is to look over the list of symptoms in the subtypes categories and decide which is the best fit. Once that's established, then a diagnostic code is assigned.

Sometimes a specific disorder had a different name in the *DSM*'s third edition, and the fourth edition will include that name. Psychopathy, for example, has gone through several classifications, including sociopath, and currently is diagnosed under antisocial personality disorder (although that classification is under dispute from those who work with psychopaths).

Many major disorders are subtyped. Schizophrenia, for example, is broken down into subtypes like paranoid or catatonic. Each has its own diagnostic code and set of criteria.

The diagnosis is generally applied to an individual's present condition. It includes specifying the severity and course of an illness.

Prior to making any psychiatric diagnosis, a physical and neurological exam is important to eliminate those medical disorders that mimic psychosis. Viral encephalitis, a brain infection, often resembles schizophrenia, as does Huntington's disease or a brain tumor on the pituitary gland. HIV infections cause dementia. Temporal lobe epilepsy can produce delusions and hallucinations.

Since the *DSM-IV* reflects a consensus of current formulations from the evolving knowledge in the field, writers should keep up with revisions, especially regarding medications. *Diagnostic Criteria From DSM-IV* (which explains how to use the manual) and the *American Psychiatric Glossary* both provide ample information on all of this in a fairly condensed and accessible manner. The psychiatric glossary lists neurological deficits, a table of psychological tests, and defines all of the disorders used in the *DSM-IV*. The *Pocket Handbook of Clinical Psychiatry* is also helpful.

Those mental disorders that most often occupy forensic psychologists and psychiatrists in criminal cases include psychopathy, character disorder, and psychosis.

Psychopathy and Antisocial Personality Disorder

Given how poorly understood this category is, it will be beneficial to writers to learn how it has evolved and who the major players are in making assessments.

In 1941 Hervey Cleckley published *The Mask of Sanity*, a groundbreaking approach to the notion of the psychopath, and he outlined a brief history of the concept: In the early part of the century, "constitutional psychopathic inferiority" was a catchall for most mental and physical deviance and defect. Then, brain damage and physiological conditions were separated out, but there was still a diverse body of problems grouped under one heading. The next step was to remove "constitutional" from the classification, leaving the unworkably broad "psychopathic personality." For the percentage of people not psychotic or psychoneurotic, but who were unable to lead normal lives and who caused distress in the community, the most common designation was psychopath.

Coming up with sixteen distinct clinical criteria for assessing psychopathy, Cleckley described psychopaths as follows:
- hotheaded
- manipulative
- exploitative
- irresponsible
- self-centered
- shallow
- unable to bond
- lacking in empathy or anxiety

- likely to commit a wide variety of crimes
- more violent, more likely to recidivate, and less likely to respond to treatment than other offenders

Cleckley's work proved to be a valuable contribution, but as the concept of psychopathy continued to evolve, the emphasis in assessment moved toward specific behavioral manifestations.

Stedman's Medical Dictionary defines psychopaths as people whose lives are dominated by some abnormal sexual, criminal, or passional instinct. Other sources cite their antisocial nature and moral irresponsibility.

In 1952 in the official psychiatric nomenclature, the word "psychopath" was officially replaced with "sociopathic personality" and eventually came to be used interchangeably under the heading of "personality disorder." Then, with the second edition of the *DSM* in 1968, "sociopathic personality" yielded to "personality disorder, antisocial type." Those persons exhibiting an antisocial personality were described as unsocialized, impulsive, guiltless, selfish, callous, and failing to learn from experience. However, there were no criteria for using the construct of psychopathy in a test for meaningful assessment.

During the seventies, many researchers attempted to do this, yet it was still difficult to generate replicable research findings. The publication of *DSM-III* shifted things when it introduced a list of explicit criteria for psychopathy as antisocial personality disorder. It was retained as a construct in the *DSM-IV* revision as a pervasive pattern of disregard for the rights of others, evident since the age of fifteen, and indicated by three of the following:

1. failure to conform to social norms and observe lawful behaviors
2. deceitfulness, repeated lying, use of aliases, or conning others
3. impulsivity or failure to develop long-term plans
4. irritability and aggressiveness
5. disregard for safety of self or others
6. consistent irresponsibility
7. lack of remorse and indifference to harming, mistreating, or stealing from another

However, researchers who focused on psychopathy weren't satisfied. While psychopaths do exhibit many of the listed behaviors, only around 90 percent of them fit the criteria for antisocial personality disorders, while the vast majority of people with an antisocial personality disorder are not psychopaths. The *DSM-IV* wasn't viable for those who wanted to focus on the original concept of psychopathy as defined by Cleckley.

Then came Robert Hare, a Canadian psychologist who had access to prison populations. He and his associates came up with a set of diagnostic criteria that offered a practical approach to both assessment and treatment and which also influenced how juvenile antecedents are identified and measured. Based on Cleckley's work, Hare devised a list of traits and behaviors for his Psychopathy Checklist (PCL). He listed twenty-two items (twenty in the revised PCL-R), to be weighted from 0 to 2 by clinicians working with potential psychopaths. The instrument, with items grouped around the two basic factors of narcissistic personality and antisocial behavior, was tested extensively with prison inmates. Refocusing antisocial personality disorder, psychopathy is now redefined as a disorder characterized by the traits that Cleckley had listed, with a few more included as follows:

- lack of remorse or empathy
- shallow emotions
- manipulativeness
- serial relationships (multiple marriages)
- lying
- egocentricity
- glibness
- low frustration tolerance
- parasitic lifestyle
- persistent violation of social norms

A person who was evaluated according to the PCL or PCL-R didn't need to have all of the traits to be diagnosed a psychopath. He or she just needed a score that fell within a certain range, and that score could be derived from manifesting a number of the traits so strongly that they each rated a "2" on the scale. The PCL-R proved to be a useful, accurate, and practical clinical tool that surpassed evaluation according to the *DSM-IV* criteria.

Other researchers noted evidence to suggest that psychopathy emerges early in life and persists into middle age. The "prototypical psychopaths" were shown to be responsible for particularly heinous offenses. Childhood indicators include the following:

- early drug abuse
- incidents of theft or aggression
- truancy
- general problem behavior
- lying
- poor educational achievement

Yet not all children who exhibit these behaviors go on to commit adult crimes, suggesting that (1) not all psychopaths become criminals, (2) some behavior changes with age, and (3) some intervention may help redirect behavior. This supports Cleckley's suggestion that many psychopaths either do not commit crimes, or they commit them too cleverly to be caught.

Probably the most famous psychopath in fiction is Hannibal Lecter in Thomas Harris's *The Silence of the Lambs*. For years, he got away with killing people. He was glib, egocentric, charming, manipulative, deceptive, and without remorse. He implied that he was simply evil, without cause or reason. Many people believe the person closest to evil is the psychopath.

While the voluminous literature on psychopathy focuses primarily on males, the question arises: Are female psychopaths different? Recent estimates indicate that severe psychopathy among women is rare, about one-third of the estimated prevalence for men. Looking at the personality profile of a thirty-year-old woman who was believed to be a psychopath, it was clear that there was early onset of antisocial behavior, evidence of sexual aggression, poly-substance abuse, and sexual perversion. Her score on Hare's PCL put her in the ninety-fourth percentile of a normative group of male prison inmates. She also showed fluctuating levels of reality awareness, but no deficits in impulse control.

Standing trial for murdering a cellmate while serving a four-year sentence for armed robbery, this woman appeared to be emotionally shallow. She had suffered sexual abuse in her family home, was removed at the age of six, and lived in foster homes over the next three years. She had numerous short-term relationships with sadomasochistic tendencies and only completed school through the ninth grade.

Her crimes included breaking and entering, auto theft, assault, armed robbery, and substance abuse. She acknowledged a history of mutilating animals. Half of her life was spent in prison, and all of her immediate family members had been incarcerated at some point.

Based on this case study, it may be that psychopathy in females shows up as a manifestation of a hysterical personality, which is different from the way that males behave.

The Other Personality Disorders

Personality or character disorders are enduring and rigid patterns of experiencing, perceiving, relating to, and processing the environment that fail to adjust to social norms. These disorders manifest in the way people think, feel, control their impulses, and function with others. They are generally maladaptive and cause a significant amount of distress to the person and to others. A disorder of this nature may contribute to a breakdown of the family and an inability to function at a job. Sometimes disorders are "comorbid"—that is, they overlap. One may have caused the other, or the person was simply vulnerable to both. There are many types of personality disorders, but only a few will generally come into the legal arena in the context of a crime. Let's discuss those specific types.

Narcissistic Personality Disorder

This disorder is characterized by a pattern of grandiosity and an excessive need for admiration. Such people can achieve great things because they think so highly of themselves, but often the people around them suffer. People with narcissistic personality disorder

- have an exaggerated sense of being special such that they limit their associations only to others they deem worthy
- freely exploit others to advance their own ambitions
- are too caught up in their self-importance to develop empathy
- typically believe that others envy them
- are preoccupied with fantasies of unlimited power and success
- believe they are deserving of ideal love

- have a sense of entitlement
- engage in arrogant behaviors

One episode of the television show *The Practice* dealt with this type of disorder in the extreme. A gay politician hired the legal firm featured on the show to defend him in a murder trial. Because the lawyers did not understand the dynamics of narcissistic personality disorder, they were vulnerable to his manipulations. They fought hard to get him off and succeeded, and he then let them know that he was indeed guilty but could not now be retried. He had disposed of a man who was in his way and had figured out a way, through lies and manipulation, to avoid being convicted. He then could not resist letting his attorneys know how clever he was and how they had been duped. (In another episode, he murdered someone else, but this time the defense team was more savvy about the narcissistic personality.)

One reason people with narcissistic personality disorder make good fiction characters is that their manipulations are finely honed, but they have a bit more humanity than psychopaths, so their character disorder can provide numerous intriguing plot twists. They also tend to be intelligent and clever, two qualities which never fail to engage an audience.

Psychologist Phyllis Beren names four primary characteristics that alert an evaluator to a narcissistic disorder:

1. a disturbance in the regulation of self-esteem (constant need for admiration or devaluing others, excessive grandiose daydreaming, controlling others, feelings of worthlessness, idealizing others, or excessive lying)
2. a compelling need for things that mirror their perceived ideal self
3. a lack of self-awareness that can manifest as a lack of empathy for others (precarious friendships, sadistic behavior)
4. overdevelopment of one area of the personality at the expense of others

Needless to say, someone who values himself above all others, who has little empathy, who becomes preoccupied in grandiose fantasies, and who has little self-awareness may not flinch from committing a crime to achieve his goals. He is like Raskolnikov's extraordinary man—in Dostoevsky's *Crime and Punishment*—he's above the laws that "lesser" people should follow. Narcissism is the beating heart of psychopathy.

Borderline Personality Disorder

The name for this disorder was derived from the belief that someone suffering from borderline personality disorder was at the borderline between neurotic and psychotic. However, the conception of it has evolved to being viewed more as a disturbance in the regulation of emotions.

According to the *DSM-IV*, borderline personality disorder is characterized by the following:

- instability in one's relationships
- poor impulse control
- volatile affect
- a self-image that fluctuates between empty despair and grandiosity
- black-and-white thinking
- self-mutilation

They're known to overidealize the very people upon whom they might suddenly turn with terrible accusation. Their impulsivity is generally damaging, involving them in reckless sexual or substance addictions. They fear abandonment but also fear being engulfed within a relationship, so they offer mixed signals that wear out those closest to them. People with borderline personality disorder can become intensely paranoid or experience transient psychosis or dissociation. They also show intense anger and make frequent threats of suicide.

While borderline personality disorder is listed among the other personality disorders, there is a movement afoot to turn it into a medical disease that can be treated the way any organic disorder is treated. That is, the potential for psychosis can be minimized, and if there is no character disorder per se, then the person can live functionally. By some estimates, borderline personality disorder affects one in fifty people, and one in five of those are admitted to psychiatric units. It seems to have a strong genetic factor, with a 20 percent chance that a mother with the disorder will pass it on to her children. One in every ten of these people will die by suicide. Many mental health practitioners believe that borderline personality disorder is highly resistant to treatment because, like vampires, these people just drain a therapist and then move on to the next one.

The female character, Anna, in Josephine Hart's novel *Damage* displays many of the characteristics of someone with borderline personality disorder.

She gets involved with a young man, Martyn, and then she draws his father into a heated sexual liaison behind Martyn's back. She needs the attention of both to feel good about herself—knowing that this may come at their expense. Because of her machinations, Martyn dies and his father's marriage and career end, but Anna walks away unscathed. Earlier in her life, her own brother had killed himself over her, and she had used men to help herself heal. She had told her tale of sorrow to draw each of them into her turmoil and then had inflicted on them her inner damage. She had grown to accept that she causes agony in the lives of everyone around her. That was just the way it was. Since pleasure was her main emotion, she freely used them up to get what she needed. Anna was a "catalyst for disaster," a damaged woman who could not be broken but against whom others could break.

Histrionic Personality Disorder

People with a histrionic personality disorder show excessive emotional instability, which means they are unpredictable and often theatrical. Since one study indicated that female psychopaths tend to show more consistency with histrionic personality disorder, I have included this on the list. These people desperately seek attention, and they will emphasize their physical features to get it. When not the center of attention, they may cause significant trouble. Their emotional constitution is shallow and shifts rapidly. They may exaggerate their role in a situation just to create an impression, and they may believe that a relationship is more intimate than it actually is. If they refuse to face reality and persist in their patterns of seeking immediate gratification, they can become stalkers.

In the movie *Blue Sky*, Jessica Lange plays Carly Marshall, a woman with repetitive mood swings that indicated an unstable sense of self, similar to the person with borderline personality disorder. Her husband is a patient man who works in the military as a radiation detection technician. To get attention, Carly keeps changing her hair color, keeps overspending, throws tantrums, makes up fantastic stories, and uses her body to manipulate others. She recklessly puts her husband's career at risk and makes a deal that forces him to be confined in a mental hospital. When she finally helps him get back on his feet (because she needs him), she starts her needy behavior all over again.

Personality Disorders Depicted in Movies

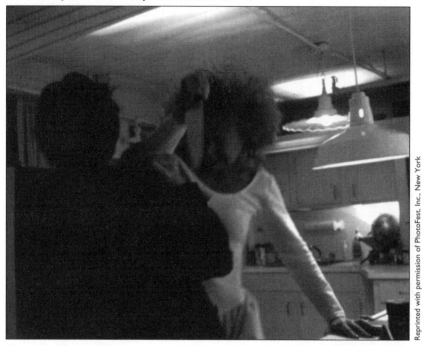

Throughout the movie *Fatal Attraction*, actress Glenn Close offers a terrifying portrayal of someone with symptoms of either a borderline personality disorder or a histrionic personality disorder.

Reprinted with permission of PhotoFest, Inc., New York

The female killer in *Fatal Attraction* likely suffered from either borderline personality disorder or histrionic personality disorder. She had an affair with the main character and then demanded all of his attention. When he moved to break off the relationship, she became aggressive. She lured him and provoked him, and when she could not get her way, she broke into his home and tried to kill him.

While many people who suffer from these disorders would see that as a dramatic and unfair representation, stalkers who fixate in this way on a person and who must have that person's attention to feel okay about themselves generally get desperately addicted. Some have been served with restraining orders and even been taken to court, and that still does not stop the behavior.

Post-Traumatic Stress Disorder

Post-traumatic stress disorder is not so much a character disorder as a reactive state to a past trauma. It is considered an anxiety disorder in which exposure to an extremely stressful event results in a persistent reexperiencing of the event, disturbed sleep, hyperarousal, numbing, and avoidance of anything associated with the trauma.

It has been used as a defense of temporary insanity. Generally, diagnosis relies on a personal report, which has its drawbacks. Post-traumatic stress disorder has mixed results in criminal defense but does get used where symptoms seem to merit it. Unfortunately, it is an easy illness to malinger, so it can get a bad rap. Post-traumatic stress disorder was first associated with Vietnam veterans, but it has also been linked to incest, rape, and abuse survivors. In court, mental health professionals have been allowed to explain to juries a person's reaction to rape to help prove that sexual intercourse was not consensual. However, this kind of testimony is vulnerable to challenge, since the victim has something to gain by faking the symptoms. When used as a criminal defense, the causal link is always shaky because it must be made between the symptoms and the stressor event and also between the symptoms and the criminal act. If secondary problems like drug abuse can be located in the defendant's behavior, post-traumatic stress disorder is a difficult defense.

Psychotic and Mood Disorders
Schizophrenia

The most prevalent of the psychotic disorders, schizophrenia is often misunderstood as a split or multiple personality. In truth, schizophrenia is an illness marked by a confusion of thinking and speech that is at times chronic and at times marked by intermittent attacks. It occurs equally in men and women, generally appears between the ages of fifteen and thirty-five, and affects about 1 percent of the population. There appears to be a significant genetic component in that a person may inherit a tendency toward it that can be triggered by some outside stressor.

Schizophrenia can cause the sufferer to withdraw from the world and retreat into delusions and fantasies. The person's perception and thinking about reality can be so impaired as to become dangerous. The research evidence suggests that the cause of schizophrenia is either a chemical or structural abnormality of the brain. Some researchers believe there may be a connection to complications during pregnancy or birth. Initial symptoms include a mild feeling of tension, sleep disturbances, and loss of interest in things. In its worst phases, people experience delusions, hallucinations, or disordered speech. Some people with this disease do develop violent tendencies, although there is a misperception that all schizophrenics are potentially violent. More often than not, they withdraw into themselves. They may be paranoid, but not everyone who is paranoid is schizophrenic.

There are four types of schizophrenia.

1. Disorganized—the person is incoherent
2. Catatonic—the person is withdrawn and mute and may lie around in unusual positions
3. Residual—the person is past the delusions and hallucinations but has no interest in life
4. Paranoid—the person feels persecuted, suspicious, and grandiose

Of these four, the one of most concern in criminal work is paranoid schizophrenia because voices have been known to command a person to kill or take his own life, damage property, stalk someone, or otherwise cause havoc. (Also see Comorbid Disorders on page 81.) People with this illness are difficult to medicate because they suspect others of poisoning them or trying to control their minds.

This is a lifelong illness with no known cure. Antipsychotic drugs may help stabilize brain chemistry but must be taken under close supervision. There are many criminal cases in which a person stopped taking his or her medication. For example, a fatal tragedy in New York involved Andrew Goldstein, who had been treated for schizophrenia but had stopped taking his medication. He walked up to a woman waiting for the subway train, and as it approached, he pushed her into its path.

Writers who want to work with this illness in character development need to pay attention to the ongoing research, as new developments happen rapidly, particularly in the realm of psychopharmacology. Traditional antipsychotics control hallucinations and delusions, but have side effects (blurred vision, muscle control, spasms, shuffling) that can deter a schizophrenic from taking them. New antipsychotics treat more symptoms with fewer side effects, but the best medications are the most expensive.

A good example of how the two sides in a legal arena deal with this illness can be seen in the case of Angel Maturino Resendiz. This forty-year-old drifter, known as the "Railway Killer," claimed that it was his duty to rape and kill nine people in three states because they were evil. The defense was insanity. A neuropsychiatrist testified that Resendiz was delusional and disordered in his thinking. He interviewed and tested the man for over ten hours before concluding that Resendiz was a paranoid schizophrenic who had rigid, irrational beliefs and trouble relating to reality. Another forensic psychiatrist bolstered this finding after interviewing the accused and reading his letters, and both witnesses were pressed to describe how someone with such disordered thinking can still perform seemingly normal everyday tasks. "This is the most illogical disease known to mankind," Dr. Larry Pollack insisted. "We can't impose logic on it." He concluded that Resendiz believed that what he was doing to his victims was right. Resendiz also believed that he could travel while asleep, be invisible, and affect weather patterns. He thought that the reason he had evaded the police for two years was because of his superhuman speed and God's protection. Police tracking dogs, he said, didn't want to confront a "wolf-tiger angel with a dinosaur look."

Resendiz's mother offered testimony that he had been dropped on his head as an infant and had been in several violent fights during childhood, one of which gave him a serious head wound. He had also been sexually assaulted.

On the other hand, a court-appointed psychiatrist who also tested the killer said that Resendiz suffered from serious personality disorders and had strange beliefs, but was not insane at the time of the offense. Magical thinking (the idea that by thinking he can make it so), he indicated, is not necessarily psychotic. The key issue was whether his mental disease prevented him from discerning right from wrong. This expert doubted that.

As it turned out, the jury rejected the insanity defense (which happens much more often than not). They deliberated for ten days before deciding that Resendiz was aware that he was committing a crime when he broke into his victim's home and assaulted and killed her. They did not buy that Resendiz thought he was compelled by an evil force into doing God's work, nor that he thought he was half angel with supernatural powers. He was convicted of first-degree murder. Schizophrenia, a psychiatric diagnosis, is not the same as insanity, a legal definition.

In television, an episode of *Law and Order* took on a similar case in which three forensic mental health professionals were involved. It involved a young man who repeatedly stabbed his foster parents and claimed he had no memory of it—that he had done it in a psychotic state. The defense was not guilty by reason of insanity.

The prosecution had psychology professor Dr. Elizabeth Olivet interview him. She concluded that he might have amnesia about the murders and be suffering from drug abuse, but she could not see any sign of psychosis or schizophrenia that might provide an insanity defense. A psychiatrist was hired by the court—not by either side—to put him under hypnosis. The defense objected by calling on the case of *Rock v. Arkansas*, an actual case that essentially stated hypnotically refreshed testimony (or testimony brought out under hypnosis) could not be used in court. However, the prosecutor allowed that he wanted to use it only to help the defendant and would not use any harmful testimony in court.

Under hypnosis, the boy seemed to retrieve a repressed memory of abuse by his biological mother, which was corroborated by her and by yet a third mental health professional. The defense hired a psychologist, who counseled abused children for the Department of Social Services, to testify to the consistency between the defendant's behavior and that of other abused children. The plea was changed from insanity to self-defense but failed to win the jury because the boy's father could not corroborate the abuse stories told by the mother. Nor did the defense's expert convince the jury that two sleeping people who had never abused the boy constituted a threat in his mind.

Again, psychosis is not equivalent to insanity. While a person may have been psychotic while committing a crime, it doesn't follow that suffering from a psychosis robs a person of the ability to know right from wrong at the moment of a crime or of the ability to resist a compulsion. The complexities of this defense will be considered in detail when we look at the psychologist as expert witness in chapter six.

Bipolar

Also called bipolar affective disorder or manic-depressive disorder, this is a cyclical disturbance characterized by dramatic mood swings. People suffering from it may have intense periods of high energy in which they seem superhuman. They go without rest for long periods of time, have grandiose ideas, and seem to accomplish an astonishing amount. However, they may then swing into serious depression, accompanied by delusions fed by low self-esteem. They may hear voices during either phase, but between phases they may feel normal. Sometimes a bipolar disorder consists of major depression with brief periods of feeling "hypomanic" or periods of euphoria and unrealistic optimism.

When a woman was found raped and murdered on an episode of *Law and Order*, a deranged homeless man named Bauer was arrested. The defense attorney said it was obvious from the man's mental condition, which was close to raving, that he would get off on a not guilty by reason of insanity plea. The prosecutor was not so sure. He hired his psychiatrist, Emil Skoda, to examine Bauer and scrutinize Bauer's complete medical and psychiatric history. Skoda concluded that since Bauer's illness was more pronounced in winter months, he was not schizophrenic, but bipolar with psychotic features. That meant he could understand that what he was doing was wrong. The fact that Bauer covered his victim with her coat afterward indicated remorse.

The defense attorney then opted to go the competency route, attempting to prohibit the prosecution from putting her client on antipsychotic medication and effectively preventing the trial from going forward. (Unfortunately, there was no indication of who she had hired to make a mental health assessment of her client.) "He might have known what he did," she said, "but that doesn't mean he's not crazy." Since Bauer had a history of manipulating the mental health system, the court ordered him to undergo drug therapy so he could be restored to competency. It turned out not to be a case of first-degree murder but of mercy killing of a young woman who also suffered from mental illness and who needed someone to help her end it. He had loved her, so he had helped.

Dissociative Identity Disorder (Multiple Personality Disorder)

Dissociative identity disorder is not really a psychotic condition, although it has been confused with schizophrenia as a split identity. Two or more subpersonalities develop in a single human being, each with its own identity. Each takes turns controlling the personality and behavior. The "core" person generally experiences periods of memory loss and may even find herself in a foreign place with no idea how she arrived. This is called an amnesic barrier between identities. One "person" may have full access to the memory bank, while others get only partial access. In some cases, the subpersonalities know which one the controlling or core personality is. People with dissociative identity disorder often develop it from an early childhood trauma, such as sexual abuse or violent beatings. They learn to dissociate—to mentally remove themselves from full awareness of the situation—and this form of psychological flight becomes a survival mechanism. This then disturbs the normal integrative functions of identity and memory. Poly-fragmented dissociative identity disorder may involve several hundred different identities in a single body.

Experts on this personality disturbance talk about how a memory that is not recalled may still have the energy to emerge in symptoms like depression, numbness, hypersensitivity, and reactions to certain environmental triggers that may touch on that memory. There may also be flashbacks that are maddeningly vague, or the memory might return many years after the incident (although repressed memory testimony in court has become suspect). These people may "trance out," feel out of touch with reality, ignore genuine pain, and experience sudden panic attacks. They may also act out with eating disorders, abuse of others, self-abuse, or addictions. Generally, they have trouble with intimacy in relationships and may experience any number of sexual dysfunctions and sleep disturbances.

A mental health professional trying to determine whether this disorder is present would begin with a clinical interview to check if there is any memory of childhood abuse or stretches of time that the subject cannot recall. The questions should include ways to assess the presence of symptoms. Some type of structured diagnostic test might be utilized, such as the Dissociative Experiences Scale (DES) and the Dissociative Interview Schedule (DIS). It is also important to try to collect data from people who have seen the subject in an altered personality state. While other personalities can be elicited through hypnosis, it's also possible to affect a suggestible person with hypnosis in such a way that he will act as if he has different personalities—especially if he has something to gain. This is a tricky diagnosis under the best conditions, and authors of fiction tend to underestimate its complexity.

Dissociative identity disorder is difficult to fake well, although people

The Hillside Strangler is Caught Lying

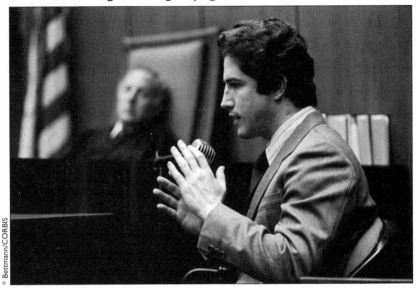

Ken Bianchi, one of the two Hillside Stranglers, fooled several mental health professionals by pretending he had multiple personality disorder. Knowing the symptoms of a disorder—as well as how they can be faked—is key for a writer who wants to create realistic court settings. Here, Bianchi testifies against his accomplice, Angelo Buono, to avoid the death penalty.

certainly have tried. The most notorious case was that of Ken Bianchi, one of the two Hillside Stranglers at work in Los Angeles in the mid-1970s. Under hypnosis, Bianchi revealed that he had dual personalities, one good and the other ("Steve") a brutal murderer. He convinced several experts with his performance, although one psychiatrist felt he was faking it. As a test, he suggested to Bianchi that a true case of multiple personality disorder involved three personalities, and suddenly Bianchi developed yet another one. At one point, Bianchi himself suggested that he might be faking it, which made his testimony against his partner suspect. He also said he wasn't sure that he was telling the truth in anything that he said. The court decided to try him as a legally sane defendant. Finally, he entered into a plea agreement that he would confess and testify against his partner, Angelo Buono, to avoid the death penalty.

A fictional account of a similar situation is seen in *Primal Fear*, a movie based on a novel by William Diehl and starring Richard Gere as Martin Vail, an arrogant defense lawyer who takes the case of an altar boy suspected of murdering the archbishop of Chicago. Neuropsychologist Molly Arrington (a psychiatrist in the novel) believes Vail's client has multiple personality disorder. To her, it's a textbook case. Why? Because the guy seems to suffer headaches and then go through a shocking personality change. The shy, stuttering Aaron becomes the aggressive, foul-mouthed "Roy." It's hardly a textbook case, but as we soon learn, Arrington has no real experience. She's an academic who has read about this in books. Nevertheless, she herself raises the issue of malingering—of faking symptoms. Because she fails to test this, she is deceived along with everyone else. Aaron, it turns out, has been performing all along.

James Patterson uses multiple personality disorder as a defense in *Along Came a Spider*, in which a kidnapper/murderer apparently manifests two different personalities—a good guy and a bad guy. This is a little too simple, and it gets worse when the detective-psychologist Alex Cross fails to do a full workup to make a reliable determination, but at least everyone realizes that a clever sociopath might be manipulating them into believing that his primary personality is innocent of the crimes.

Writers have overused the multiple personality syndrome as a plot twist to the point where it is no longer unique and is generally presented in a stereotypical manner. A writer would be hard-pressed to come up with an original story using this psychiatric disorder.

Schizoaffective Disorder

Schizoaffective disorder involves a group of disorders in which major mood disturbances (anxiety or depression) and psychotic symptoms (hallucinations, delusions) coexist for at least part of the time. Major depression, manic episodes, and schizophrenia are present together for at least a month, with two weeks or more of hallucinations in the absence of prominent mood symptoms. While a defense might focus only on the psychosis, where mood problems occur simultaneously, a mood disorder might be the more accurate diagnosis.

Comorbid Disorders

A personality disorder often has manifestations of several other disorders. You can have bipolar with psychotic phases, a borderline-narcissistic disorder, a mood disorder like depression with paranoid tendencies, and any number of other combinations. One interesting study found that someone with schizophrenia that was comorbid with psychopathy or antisocial personality disorder tended to have an increased risk of committing a crime. In fact, they found that the prevalence of antisocial personality disorder was higher among schizophrenics than in the general population. The possibility of comorbidity means more plot complications for writers. Just imagine all the permutations of personality!

Rare Disorders With Forensic Implications

Without going into these disorders in detail, mental health professionals are likely to be called into unique cases involving assessment of behavioral manifestations. For writers who want something that hasn't been worked over, research on the following disorders may yield some provocative material.

- **Capgras' syndrome:** Capgras' syndrome is the delusion that others (or one's own self) have been replaced by imposters; it is often reported in paranoid schizophrenia and organic brain disease and can lead to violence against the supposed imposter.

- **Morbid jealousy or erotomania:** This is when someone becomes so enamored of another that he resorts to stalking and even to violence to keep the connection constant; it may involve delusions that a partner is unfaithful and generally involves some level of aggression.

- **Pseudologia fantastica:** This involves constant lying without any discernable purpose that is created by an underlying pathology; a certain amount of this behavior occurs in factitious disorders (disorders in which symptoms are feigned for attention or gain), antisocial personality disorder, and psychopathy. It has numerous implications in court, from assisting in one's defense to perjury.

Designer Defenses

Many of the so-called designer defenses arise from the notion of temporary psychosis or from a twist on one of the disorders listed previously. In the 1970s, a young Vietnam vet killed a fifteen-year-old girl, tied her up, and left her in a closet in an abandoned apartment. His defense: post-Vietnam syndrome. He was triggered to recall his commando-type activities in Vietnam, he said, by the Asian features of his victim. Part of him "watched" while the other part went into action as a "killing machine." Even the prosecutor's psychiatrist bought it, and the man was found not guilty by reason of insanity. (However, it was determined later that he had never served in any commando units or performed any such activities.)

In 1989 Lyle and Erik Menendez murdered their parents with shotguns. They then claimed that they had found their parents slaughtered, but Erik eventually confessed. To escape convictions, they created a scenario of sexual and emotional abuse, contributing to a defense of post-traumatic stress disorder that made them hypersensitive to imagined threats. They got a hung jury . . . at first. The second trials were run differently, with guilty verdicts for both.

This psychological strategy bleeds into television. In one episode of *Law and Order*, an FBI special agent and former marine was charged with shooting a female writer who was having an affair with his wife. The defense psychologist claimed it was a case of "extreme psychosexual panic," retranslated as "gay panic," which entailed such a collapse of the ego structure that the defendant could no longer handle stress. This amounted to temporary insanity.

Another episode dealt with the murder trial defense of "cyberspace obsession," where a kid spent ten hours a day online. He supposedly became confused between what was real and what was fantasy.

Such defenses often are devised when full-blown psychosis cannot be proven. They generally tap into some social force, such as guilt over Vietnam, to sway a jury. The idea that people can just "snap" has become popular. When Susan Smith shoved her car with her two seat-belted sons into a lake to their deaths, her attorney claimed that "she just snapped like a twig." She was a victim of depression, molestation, and numerous social factors.

Whether or not a defense can win an acquittal, it can result in a hung jury or mitigate the severity of the punishment.

Creating a Believable Criminal Without Stereotyping

Creating a character about whom a psychologist would testify means resisting oversimplification. One way to do that is to look for a real-life case. Professional journals are full of case histories, and it's easier to spin a character from that than to devise one based merely on a *DSM-IV* diagnostic category.

The following professional journals can be found in many university or law libraries:
The Journal of Social Psychology
The Journal of Clinical Psychology
Psychological Bulletin
American Journal of Psychiatry
Journal of Abnormal and Social Psychology
Journal of Interpersonal Violence
Journal of Personality Disorders
Criminal Behavior and Mental Health
The American Journal of Forensic Psychology

The more life details you can find, the more believable the character will be.

Another way to create a believable character is to study a type of crime you want to work with—mass murder, serial crime, spree killing—and make the character consistent with the kind of person who tends to engage in that type of crime. Patterns do emerge. The more of this type of crime you study, the more likely it is that you will develop a feel for the nuances.

Let's say, for example, that you want to write about women who get involved with violent men to the point where they actually help those men find, torture, rape, and even kill the victims. There are several cases on record of such women (although when caught they tend to resort to the defense of battered woman syndrome). A comprehensive look at such stories reveals a startling sociopathic streak in these women that defies social expectations of what women are like. It then becomes easy to develop a character as a "victim" who in fact has the capacity to torture and kill. (Karla Homolka in Canada actually helped her husband rape and kill her own sister.)

There is also a study made by former FBI profilers on the wives and girlfriends of sexual sadists that goes into how women from a seemingly normal background can become involved in such horrific behaviors. Former FBI Special Agent Roy Hazelwood published his interpretation of the study in his book, *Dark Dreams.* The study involved extensive questioning of twenty women, so there is plenty of material from which to develop a character.

Immersing yourself in a different kind of psychology can make for some interesting plot twists that arise from a truly deviant female. It will also mean engaging a psychological expert who can explain how such a personality develops. For additional drama, it can also mean dueling experts, one of whom uses a battered woman syndrome defense and the other who must make a convincing argument using the rare cases of female psychopathy.

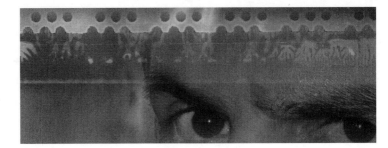

5

Psychological Assessment

The Function of Measured Assessment

Mental health professionals use psychological assessment tests as an objective method for answering specific questions about a person in order to solve problems or make certain decisions about treatment. Often tests will measure strengths and weaknesses with respect to various traits. The idea for this developed through psychometric analysis in which traits were key to understanding a personality. However, these tests have been shown to be most accurate for the assessment of skills, mechanical ability, and neurological deficits. When it comes to mood, dependence, avoidance, or many other personality traits, tests have to be supplemented with clinical observation, interviewing, and personality history.

In psychological assessment in forensic work, a mental health professional may be appointed by the court or hired by one of the attorneys. Whoever hires him is the one asking the question for which the tests must offer some answer. A court may need a competency or insanity assessment, as well as some sense of whether the defendant is malingering (faking) his or her symptoms. Some tests measure personality traits, some neurological deficits, some IQ levels. Generally more than one test is performed—called a test battery—and some clinicians tend to prefer a certain battery of tests over others. For example, in the trial of Robert E. Kleasen for the murder of two Mormon missionaries in 1974, the examining psychologist used an IQ test, a neurological test, and several tests that reveal personality patterns to make the determination that Kleasen was depressed, evasive, rebellious, and paranoid.

Kleasen's IQ score also contradicted his claim of a post-graduate degree, which indicated a tendency to deceive.

Direct examination will elicit basic information about the tests, but cross-examination will elicit the purpose of the tests, the scores, the significance of those scores, and other factors. Mental health professionals who use tests need to be familiar with test construction and statistical information on reliability and validity. They should also know the main interpretive hypotheses, and for each assessment test, the types of items on a test and what that particular instrument was developed to assess. If controversy surrounds the use of a test for a particular diagnosis, such as with IQ tests, clinicians need to be able to explain the normative samples and why their use of the test circumvents the criticisms. It may also be relevant to know information about the inclusion of minorities in developing the test, especially if the defendant is a member of a minority. The more clearly this information can be presented, the better.

Considerations when choosing a test or test battery involve how long the test is (time might be limited), how long it might take to get results back, whether it requires the examinee to be able to read (and if so, at what level), and what the testing conditions are. Also, the mental health professional must know whether the salient issue is cognitive, neurological, emotional, intellectual, memory, or thought process functioning. In some cases, there may also be a need for assessing suicidal and malingering potential.

Tests Used in Patient Assessment
- Minnesota Multiphasic Personality Inventory (MMPI-2)
- Millon Clinical Multiaxial Inventories (MCMI-III)
- Wechsler Adult Intelligence Scale-Revised (WAIS-R)
- Rorschach
- Thematic Apperception Test (TAT)
- California Psychological Inventory
- Beck Depression Inventory
- Bender Visual-Motor Gestalt (a.k.a., the Bender Gestalt)

Following are descriptions of the most commonly used tests in a court of law, although the tests don't always go unchallenged and generally must be thoroughly explained in layperson's terms to the jury. (These tests stand apart from competency screenings and crime-specific inventories, which are covered later.)

The Assessment Interview

Before any tests are given, the mental health professional interviews the subject to glean valuable data by way of behavioral observations, reactions to his or her life situation, and eccentricities. This interview can also establish rapport for a better transition into the testing situation. The interview is guided by relevant themes that should contribute to the established goals, such as achieving a deeper understanding of the situation that requires a standardized evaluation. The interview may also be organized in a way to trigger problem behaviors in a controlled environment. These interviews may be structured or unstructured, depending on the type of information the mental health professional is seeking and what kind of rapport she is trying to establish. In other words, a mental health professional may choose to use an item inventory or a standard question and answer or just go with her own personal style. This kind of question-and-answer situation also aids in interpreting the test data later, particularly in issues of malingering. Certain aspects of the clinical interview also help predict future behavior. The primary problems involved with such interviews are the inconsistency in standards among practitioners and the potential for interviewer bias.

The interview should elicit some or all of the following types of information:

- family and personal history
- history of the problem
- self-concept
- memory problems
- general mood
- reactive tendencies
- personal fears

An interviewer must introduce himself, state the purpose of the interview, state for whom he is doing the interview, ascertain the subject's understanding of the purpose, explain the instruments to be used, and go over confidentiality issues, which differ depending on whether the interview is for the prosecution or defense.

In normal clinical practice, what people say to a therapist remains confidential unless they threaten harm to a specific person or group in a way that offers details about how and when the threat will be carried out. When a mental health professional does a defendant evaluation for the prosecution, anything the defendant says will be disclosed to a third party—the lawyer who orders the examination—and may be turned over to the defense attorney. If the evaluation is done for the defense, it may become a matter of "work product," which does not have to be disclosed unless the attorney raises the issues in court, in which case whatever the mental health professional discovered becomes part of the defense. That means that what the person said to the mental health professional might be expressed in open court and even reported in the media. All notes may be examined by the prosecution.

By advising a client of these factors, the mental health professional risks not getting as much information as she might need, in which case she must tell the attorney or court that her report is limited, qualified, or partial.

At the initial interview, the mental health professional must also obtain a signed release.

An example can be seen in the movie *Primal Fear*, where a psychiatrist interviews a boy accused of a brutal murder. She asks about his childhood, his girlfriend, his psychiatric history, his criminal record, and his association with the deceased. She lets him know that her videotape of the interview is for the attorney and thus is not wholly confidential between her and him. She does not go on to test him, but her questions provide a model for achieving both rapport and information that would help her decide on which tests to use.

Minnesota Multiphasic Personality Inventory (MMPI-2)

The Minnesota Multiphasic Personality Inventory assessment device is commonly used in the courtroom as a standardized way to categorize people over the age of eighteen according to personality types. It is fairly well supported for the assessment of malingering and may be used by the defense for detecting certain personality factors or by the prosecution for rebuttal in mental incapacity claims. In whatever way it is employed, it must remain within its assessment boundaries.

The MMPI-2 uses a questionnaire format with limited response choices (true or false). Examples are:

"I work under a great deal of tension."

"At times I think I am no good at all."

There are 567 such questions, and it takes about ninety minutes for the average person to finish this test. The end result, based on adding the way the person responded to the questions, is a revelation of such things as an individual's level of emotional adjustment, his attitude toward taking the test, and whether or not he is trying to make a false impression or even outright lying.

The primary scales for which T scores (scores based on averages and standard deviations) are obtained include the following:

- L scale, for lying
- K scale, for correction
- F scale, for deviance

It is suggested that clinicians who give this test for legal purposes score it by hand, using clinical observations to assist with interpretation. Many clinicians do rely on computer scoring, which is more standardized, but they have little awareness of the nuances of the test the way someone who scores by hand does.

Once the major scales are scored and laid out for a profile, the subscales for such things as ego strength, addiction potential, and marital distress are scored. There are more than a dozen of these, and scoring them all can make for a complicated profile. The overall score based on the thirteen primary scales may be sufficient, making reference to only those subscales that clarify a point of information. It is important that the defendant taking the test answer as many questions as possible, because leaving a large percentage blank invalidates the results.

The scoring procedure is as follows: The L scale is checked first for the possibility that the test subject lied (because a high score could invalidate the test altogether). Within a more qualified range, the L scale also indicates defensiveness. A high K score indicates that one is defending oneself against the test, "faking good," or responding "false" to most of the questions. Scores on this scale are used to adjust some of the other scores that might have been higher without the defensiveness. Low K scores indicate the possibility that they responded "true" to all of the items, and this must be checked because it also invalidates the test. It may also mean the test subject is exaggerating problems. The F scale was designed to detect when an individual takes a different approach to the test than that of the test authors (and normative groups). A large number of deviant responses may invalidate the test results or may predict a high degree of psychopathology. Such a person may also be "faking bad," or pretending to be sick. Scores within a certain range on this subscale are suggestive of malingering. A few of the subscales reveal inconsistent responses and need to be checked before proceeding to the clinical scales.

The personality-based clinical scales are numbered across the top of a graph from 1 to 10 (which is actually called scale 0) and then the scores for each scale are mapped with a connecting line to offer a visual profile that shows the high and low scores. It ends up looking something like a child's drawing of mountains with pointed peaks, although it may slope upward or downward.

To go over the individual scales first, briefly:

1. Hypochondriasis involves a preoccupation with one's body.
2. Depression measures hopelessness and dissatisfaction.
3. Hysteria involves disorders in response to stressful situations.
4. Psychopathic deviate is an indication of rebelliousness and difficulty with social standards.
5. Masculinity/femininity is an outdated gender orientation scale based on stereotypes.
6. Paranoia is about grandiosity and feelings of persecution.
7. Psychasthenia is an obsessive-compulsive measure.
8. Schizophrenia reveals a general disturbance in mood and thought processes.
9. Hypomania is about impulsivity and restless energy.
10. Social introversion is self-explanatory.

Subject's Adjustment Level and Overview

Subject's T score of 61 on the F scale does not indicate serious psychopathology, although it may suggest nonconventional thinking. Her mean T score on the clinical scales (excluding scales 5 and 0) is 47.5, suggesting a fairly average response. Only scale 5 (T=69) was higher than 65. The slope of the profile is slightly negative, which indicates functioning but with reduced efficiency. High scores on the Dom scales (66), TPA (69), and FAM (65) indicate a dominant personality with a competitive drive (64) that conflicts with family members. Family alienation was higher (77) than family discord (62). The antisocial subscales, both attitude and behavior, were moderately high (61 and 61), along with an inability to disclose (60), although none of these factors were alarming or exaggerated. Subject's endorsement of the Lachar-Wrobel critical items [a subscale] reveals an unsatisfactory adjustment to her gender, a high degree of work-associated anxiety, fitful sleeping patterns, deviant thoughts and experiences, an admission of excessive use of alcohol, and areas of problematic anger.

In summary, subject seems to have a hypomanic, Type-A, dominant personality that alienates her from family, may contribute to her dissatisfaction with submissive gender expectations, and may produce tension in her life. Her anger and deviant thoughts indicate areas of concern, as do her antisocial and problematic anger, although no T score is elevated to an extreme that indicates the need for treatment. Code type: 49/94

More important than results on an individual scale are the grouped profile configurations. Two-point code types, which result from combining the two highest scale scores from the clinical scales, offer a general picture of the personality. The most likely types to be found in the courtroom involve scales 3, 4, 6, 8, and 9. For example, "4-6" types are immature, narcissistic, and self-indulgent. They are resentful and make excessive demands on others. They have poor histories with both work and relationships and tend to be suspicious of others. They also deny that they have problems. "4-9" types are generally antisocial and frequently in trouble. They have poorly developed consciences, fluctuating values, and tend to abuse substances—a key contributor to many crimes.

Part of an MMPI-2 report for court might read like the example printed here. It will give writers some idea of how complicated the scoring and analysis can get. Any scales mentioned that aren't among the thirteen primary scales are subscales.

While much more can be written, the point of a court report is to be succinct. Say only what needs to be said to address the legal issue. However, many books, such as *MMPI-2: Assessing Personality and Psychopathology* by John R. Graham, are devoted to interpretations of this test. There are many charted profiles in this book to show what they look like and how they get interpreted. (Note: For fiction about juveniles, the MMPI-A was developed for adolescents.)

Millon Clinical Multiaxial Inventories (MCMI-III)

Like the Minnesota Multiphasic Personality Inventory, this is a standardized self-report assessment device, although much shorter. It is designed for adults with basic eighth-grade reading levels. It has 175 items, scored to produce twenty-eight scales that grow out of a combination of Theodore Millon's theory of personality and the *DSM-IV*. Accordingly, the mental health professional who tests an individual gets readings on such things as Clinical Syndromes, Severe Personality Pathology, Severe Syndromes, and Personality Patterns. It covers a wide range of adult pathology, particularly certain disorders from the *DSM-IV*.

Administering the test takes twenty to thirty minutes and offers information to assist in diagnosis of personality disorders such as avoidant, schizoid, histrionic, and narcissistic. It is especially good at detecting personality styles that may otherwise be overlooked. This test assesses personality dysfunction, although its true accuracy is hard to judge. An attorney opposing a mental health professional's testimony could easily attack it on those grounds. That's why it should never be used alone or as a purely diagnostic tool.

Test results from the MCMI-III have been ruled admissible in many courts for certain issues: generally, for malingering and deception, prediction of behavior, and the use of computer-assisted test results for forensic interpretation.

Given how complex the interpretations of this test can be, writers are again referred to Theodore Millon's *Inventories MCMI-III*, second edition, to get a sense of how different profiles are measured and interpreted.

An Example of a Millon Clinical Multiaxial Inventories Report

Subject completed the test in the average amount of time and omitted no items. She has a valid profile. She expressed interest in taking this test since she was aware that it had updated scales and a focus on personality disorders, but she said afterward that she was disappointed at the transparent nature of many of the questions.

Subject's self-report of a recent problem with work in the past three to twelve months is likely to take the form of an Axis I disorder. Her responses are those of a well-functioning adult facing minor stresses, or she is trying to present a socially acceptable appearance.

Her BR [base rate] score of 44 on the Disclosure scale suggests an underreporting of difficulties.

The Debasement score is 0, which is very low.

She has a high score of 84 on the Desirability scale. Client is either self-confident and conscientious or resists admitting shortcomings. She is inclined to view such problems as a sign of weakness and is possibly concerned with being appraised negatively by others. Her scores are adjusted to compensate for defensiveness but may fail to reveal her character or her disorders.

The highest BR score is on the Histrionic scale, with an 89. Such people are dramatic and emotional. They have a low tolerance for boredom, so they constantly seek new situations. They become highly invested in friends, at least as long as the excitement is high. They make good first impressions, but their independent appearance hides a strong dependency need. They need support but seek it in an extroverted manner. They avoid focusing on painful feelings. Typically, they have a good sense of humor and an engaging manner. They adapt easily to new situations and have little difficulty interacting with others.

Frequent code types with this character style include high scores on Anxiety (although client's is 0), Somatoform Disorder (client's is 0), or Alcohol and Drug Dependence (client's scores are in the average range).

- **Severe personality pathology:** No scores are elevated, and both Borderline (8) and Paranoid (0) are extremely low.
- **Clinical syndromes:** Only the Drug Dependence scale had any degree of elevation at BR 65, but not high enough to be of concern.
- **Severe syndromes:** No elevations in this area and extremely low on Major Depression (0).

Wechsler Adult Intelligence Scale-Revised (WAIS-R) and Wechsler Intelligence Scale for Children-Revised (WISC-III)

Both the WAIS-R and the WISC-III are intelligence tests in a battery format, but one is designed strictly for children. (There is also a scaled-down version for an even younger population: the Wechsler Preschool and Primary Scale of Intelligence, or WPPSI-R.) Each of the subtests assesses different aspects of intellectual abilities to yield three different IQ scores: a verbal, a performance, and an overall score. The verbal and performance scores are averaged from eleven subtests. IQ tests are controversial but can prove valuable when trying to determine if a defendant is of severely limited IQ and may thus fail to appreciate the wrongfulness of an act.

An IQ is a standard score with a mean of 100 (average). The scores indicate how a person compares with others of similar age. The basic idea of "intelligence" on the Wechsler is that it is a global capacity that involves thinking rationally, acting with purpose, and dealing effectively with situations. This involves logical abstract thinking, problem-solving, fluid and crystallized intelligence, making adjustments, rote recall, range of factual knowledge, dealing with novelty, achieving a goal, exercising memory, and learning from experience.

The Verbal-Performance IQ score is about perceptual organization, short-term memory, degree of focus, verbal comprehension, and processing speed. Some of the subtests are timed, and the amount of time required translates into a score, with speed being more meaningful than just correctly answering a question like "Who wrote *Faust?*" There may be fluctuations in performance among the various subtests, so a decision by the tester as to whether to weigh those fluctuations significantly in the overall impression has to be made.

The Full Scale IQ score determines how the defendant ranks relative to her peers and provides an estimate of her abilities. It is the most reliable score and the one most frequently noted. A score of 115 is 95 percent accurate, and the actual IQ of someone getting 115 may fall anywhere from 110–120.

These tests can also be used to assess brain damage. Skills like problem solving, spatial organization, memory, and abstract learning can be adversely affected by brain damage. The tests are not sufficient for diagnosis but may indicate a need for more sophisticated neurological tests.

In court work, the significance of IQ is most relevant to cases where mental retardation is suspected. The IQ range is 50–70, mild retardation; 35–50, moderate; 20–35, severe, below 20–25, profound.

Delinquent adolescents generally score higher on Performance subtests (Object Assembly, Picture Completion, and Picture Arrangement) than on the Verbal tests, while tests of academic achievement are likely to have low scores. This population will show a pattern of problems with adapting to structure.

Rorschach

The Rorschach test is considered to be projective, meaning the subject "projects" unconscious material outward onto unstructured items or tasks, and it's highly subjective in interpretation. However, a standardized interpretation method has been used so that the Rorschach test is acceptable in some courts (see John E. Exner's *Rorschach: A Comprehensive System, Volume 1*). Some studies claim that the Rorschach test has rarely been challenged in court, but it has been shown to be unreliable for insanity evaluations and for malingering. There is some support that it's useful for diagnoses of psychopathology.

The Rorschach test consists of ten symmetrical inkblots on individual cards, and subjects tell the examiner what each configuration brings to mind. Mental health professionals then use the various responses to determine how personalities are structured. This test is commonly utilized in psychiatric hospitals and is included in many test batteries. It is easy to administer and takes about fifty minutes to complete. However, scoring and interpretation can take two or three times as long and is best done by someone with experience—especially if it's for the court.

The idea behind the Rorschach test is that people have defined perceptual "sets," or ways of processing information that are organized by their needs, inner conflicts, and experiences. For example, someone might feel a strong need to be organized, and that will be reflected in her responses to the ambiguous stimuli. To talk about the inkblots, subjects have to draw on their personal imagery and relationships, and the ambiguity of the inkblots supposedly exaggerates their mental sets. Their responses represent how they confront other ambiguous situations that require them to organize their thoughts and make judgments.

A subject is then scored along the following three categories:

1. the location of her focus on the inkblot
2. which properties of the inkblot she used to make her judgments
3. the general class of objects that would include that response

Some people feel the Rorschach gets past a person's conscious processes to reveal the inner workings of the personality. It may reveal underlying pathology that is otherwise covered by a confident façade. People who perform deceptively well on structured tests may show an entirely different side on a more ambiguous test. Also, thought disorders may be more likely to appear when judgments have to be made. Research literature indicates that the Rorschach is highly sensitive to underlying schizophrenic processes and will also show certain coping deficits and obsessional styles.

Scoring the Rorschach is highly complicated (there are six major scoring approaches), and defending an interpretation in court is even more difficult since there is no universally accepted coding system. Even slight differences in wording and rapport during the test administration can significantly alter the results. Exner's scoring system is the most psychometrically sound, and some of the other scoring systems have been incorporated into it, but it is not the only one in use. Writers who want to use Rorschach interpretations are urged to consult a manual devoted to it.

Thematic Apperception Test (TAT)

The Thematic Apperception Test is a projective technique that consists of pictures about which the subject has to create a story. Like the Rorschach, this test is designed to reveal the beliefs, thought patterns, emotional conflicts, and stable personality features of the examinee—particularly underlying repressed complexes. Consisting of twenty cards with ambiguous depictions of various life events, the TAT is one of the most widely used psychometric devices as a complement to other tests. The cards are structured and require organized thinking.

The following are examples of the types of pictures featured on the cards:

- a boy sitting at a table looking at a violin

- a woman at a door looking downcast
- a woman grabbing the shoulders of a man turning away from her
- a boy looking away from two men performing surgery on a patient on a table
- a naked man climbing down (or up) a rope

In telling a story about each picture, the subject has to describe the feelings and situations of the characters featured on the card. His response is rated on a score card according to such items as intensity of reaction, how long the story is, and how frequently he speaks of particular needs or impressions. Each card is scored separately, but they're organized together to come up with such overall results on things like reality testing, ego function, thought processes, defensive functioning, and mastery. Using a standard TAT analysis sheet, a list is made of each category; a score of high, moderate, or low is assigned; and notes are written about the subject according to these three levels:

1. descriptive
2. interpretive
3. diagnostic

According to Gary Groth-Marnat in the *Handbook of Psychological Assessment*, third edition, the test developers, Christina Morgan and Henry Murray, were concerned with the assessment of how people interacted with their environment through their individual needs, attitudes, and values. In particular, the Thematic Apperception Test was designed to measure the strength of someone's needs. A distinction is made between primary needs (water, food, sex) and secondary (recognition, autonomy, achievement). Any of these needs may conflict with, fuse with, or subsidize another need. These needs become the most significant determinants of behavior, especially when "pressed" by some environmental influence such as deprivation, restraint, danger, or affiliation.

Problems occur in court when presenting TAT results because projective responses and their interpretations appear to be highly subjective and therefore suspect as official evidence. To use this instrument well requires an extensive amount of training. Even at that, clinical intuition still plays an important role.

Using this test in court (which would likely involve legal objections) would mean focusing on certain patterns of responses that imply violence, significant needs, or personal conflicts. However, the TAT is not presented as a diagnostic device for insanity evaluations. Its forensic value is more often associated with acquiring clinical information that could help interpret more standardized tests.

California Psychological Inventory (CPI)

The California Psychological Inventory is a self-administered test made up of 462 true/false statements, aimed primarily at young adults and completed in approximately one hour. It collects information about behavior patterns, opinions, and attitude and plots the results on twenty scales. There is approximately a one-third content crossover with the MMPI-2, but the CPI focuses more on interpersonal behavior like self-control, social presence, empathy, tolerance, dominance, and achievement in normal populations. Scores fall into quadrants that offer descriptions of a personality type, such as a socially conforming extrovert, a socially conforming introvert, a rebellious extrovert, and a rebellious introvert.

Since this test is aimed at normal populations, it may not be relevant to writers seeking more dramatic material. However, mystery and crime writers ought to be conversant with it as part of a test battery.

Beck Depression Inventory

The Beck Depression Inventory is a self-report format designed to assess thoughts associated with depression. It's often used with a person who has recently been arrested to see how depressed he is—especially if there's some reason to suspect he'll make a suicide attempt.

The test items were derived from observing the behaviors and symptoms of depressed patients. Respondents rate the intensity of each of a list of twenty-one symptoms on a scale from 0 to 3. The general areas involve guilt feelings, apathy, change in habits, fatigue, and social withdrawal. This inventory requires a fifth-grade reading level for comprehension and takes no longer than ten minutes to complete. The higher the score, the more severe the depression.

Neurological Tests

There are several different types of assessment instruments for determining if a person suffers from neurological impairments such as information processing, memory deficits, motor performance, and visuoconstructive abilities. Neurological tests can help attorneys prove that their clients have thought-processing disorders that might make them incompetent or unable to recall details accurately. (Recall how Charles Starkweather's inconsistent stories inspired psychiatrists to check for neurological dysfunction.)

The Halstead-Reitan Battery (HRB) contains a variety of subtests, such as Trail Making, Finger Tapping, Tactual Performance, Aphasia Screening, and Speech Perception. There is also the Luria-Nebraska Neuropsychological Battery (LNNB) and the Michigan Neuropsychological Test Battery (MNTB). Some of the subtests from the WAIS-R, such as Block Design and Digit Span, can point to neurological problems as well. Following are the tests most frequently used, no matter which battery is chosen.

Neurological Symptoms Checklist

The neurological symptoms checklist is a standardized listing to help the mental health professional take a focused history of behaviors and symptoms that might point to a specific impairment. It covers speech, thinking, perception, motor, and academic skills.

The Bender Visual-Motor Gestalt
(a.k.a., the Bender Gestalt)

The Bender Visual-Motor Gestalt test is used extensively to screen for neurophysiological deficits and fine motor control. It has also been used as a nonverbal intelligence test. The subject has to copy onto a blank piece of paper a total of nine designs that are presented sequentially. The subject's copies are rated for their degree of accuracy to the originals. The scoring checklist involves twelve assessment criteria, such as simplification, perseveration, cohesion, and angulation difficulty. Other items noted include completion time, omissions in any drawing, scribbling, frustration, and increase in design size as the test progresses. Scores are checked for degree of brain damage vs. normal functioning.

Trail Making Test

For the Trail Making Test, the test subject draws lines connecting numbered circles, first in sequence and then in alternating numbered and lettered circles. The time it takes to complete these tasks correctly is the basis for the score. The Trail Making Test assesses attention and orientation, as well as speed of visual processing and eye-hand coordination. Problems may indicate specific areas of brain impairment.

Rey Auditory Verbal Learning Test (RAVLT)

In the Rey Auditory Verbal Learning Tests the client has about fifteen minutes to memorize a list of fifteen unrelated words that are repeated over five separate trials. Next, another list of fifteen words is presented, with the intention of memory interference. Then the subject tries to recall as many of the words from the first list as possible. The functions of short-term memory, learning strategies, information retention, and differences between learning and retrieval from memory are assessed.

Finger Tapping Test

Subjects are instructed to tap their dominant index fingers for five successive ten-second trials. They repeat this with their nondominant index fingers, and scores are compared. This is a test of simple motor speed.

Forensic-Only Assessment Instruments (FAIs)

There are numerous questionnaires and scales for various forensic issues, such as the Rogers Criminal Responsibility Assessment Scale (R-CRAS) and the Sexual Violence Risk-20 (SVA-20) for sexual violence. The Rogers Criminal Responsibility Assessment Scale will be addressed in chapter seven.

Fictional Scenarios

In a novel or screenplay, the standardized assessment part of a clinical interview can illustrate malingering, psychosis, calculated deception, or interesting projections. Since a testing scenario is not typically dramatic, it may serve best as backstory. For example, the way testing was used in *Law and Order* to more dramatically show the cold-blooded responses of a little girl who had murdered a boy younger than herself: As she answered questions, it became clear that something was frighteningly wrong with her and that she would probably murder again. Her cold-bloodedness was better shown in a situation like assessment than in a court statement.

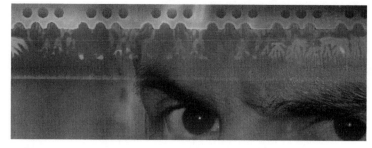

6

The Psychologist as Expert Witness

Legal Objections to Mental Health Professionals as Experts

Lawyers often object to mental health professionals coming into legal cases on one (or all) of these three grounds:

1. irrelevance
2. intrusion
3. information that fails in credibility

Lawyers feel that mental health professionals are often ignorant of the court procedure and of their role in it. When mental health professionals fail to understand legal definitions, they sometimes think a psychiatric problem is tantamount to incompetence. They may also use the wrong legal criteria or believe that an incompetency assessment is for the purposes of treatment.

Some lawyers feel that mental health professionals try to psychologize the law, first by trying to get the idea of legal competency to conform to psychiatric constructs and second, by trying to answer the ultimate legal question, which only the court can answer.

As to the third charge, it can be the case that a mental health professional does not spend sufficient time with a defendant to speak to the issue or else may bring in theories that are not well supported. Even if he does, the research is based on probability, not absolute certainty. It is also the case that a mental health professional gets placed in the role of advocate for one side, despite his avowed neutrality, and the lawyer for the other side will be resentful.

Nevertheless, the mental health professional does have a place in the courtroom.

Witnessing for the Defense vs. the Prosecution

In both cases, the mental health professional should maintain objectivity and seek to provide the truth about the client from her assessments. She should request all material relevant to that goal and reserve her opinion until she has made a thorough investigation. She should also avoid pressure to tailor her diagnosis toward some specific bias. All arrangements should be put into writing, and a full workup of the mental health professional's expertise should be provided to the attorney.

With the client, the mental health professional must go over the limits of confidentiality. Anything written or recorded could become an issue in court. She must describe the nature of her services beforehand and declare to whom the evaluation results will be revealed. She must avoid any impulse to do therapy. The following information differs in various states, but in many places, if a mental health professional reaches a conclusion that is not helpful to the defense, the results are shielded as attorney-client privilege. (Some states insist that any psychiatric information must be turned over to the government.) If a mental health professional is retained by the government, then any material must be turned over to the defense. If the court orders the evaluation, then there is no privilege and the information is made available to all parties. Writers must know the state's laws on this issue in order to provide accurate information. In any event, the subject being evaluated must be told that what he says to the mental health professional is certainly going to be shared with the attorney. The mental health professional should be prepared with a statement about the limits of confidentiality for the client to sign. A copy of that must go to the attorney.

Whatever conclusion is derived, the mental health professional must know her chain of reasoning for reaching her conclusion from the available data, including making all assumptions within a theoretical system sufficiently clear to a layperson. A cross-examining attorney will probe the logic for any weak link.

Before the trial, the mental health professional should prepare the attorney with her testimony and find out the most critical issues in which she plays a part. She can help the attorney with questions that will best elicit her testimony, and she can ask what legal challenges she ought to expect. During the trial, she should look at the jury when she responds to the questions and refrain from getting into an argument with the cross-examining attorney. If her data is challenged with other scientific studies, she can note problems with those studies or agree to look further into the matter.

Mental health professionals who go from trial to trial harm their credibility, because people tend to view their motives as financially driven and wonder how they have time to be experts when they're always in court. It's also the case that if they've made statements either in print or in trials that contradict what they might say in other trials, they will have difficulty convincing anyone of their sincerity. And it goes without saying that if they testify to the harmful effects of an alcoholic parent but have an alcohol problem themselves, they lose the jury's trust.

A mental health professional who agrees to assist the defense needs to be aware that he may be suspected as a hired gun to try to free a guilty person. It is likely that a prosecutor will have a mental health professional on his own team to refute whatever is said. The more objective and prepared the mental health professional is, the better the impression made on the trier(s) of fact.

A mental health professional can also serve in a consulting capacity— although he may get called as a rebuttal witness if needed to counter damaging testimony. As a consultant he may do the following:
- assess trial strategies
- assist in jury selection
- evaluate case notes on a defendant
- prepare lay witnesses
- help select experts
- make suggestions for cross-examination
- provide research for rebuttal of the other side's experts

Such mental health professionals may never have met or examined the defendant.

The following sections discuss some of the outstanding issues about which mental health professionals have testified. (Insanity is such a complex issue that it rates its own chapter, which follows.)

Competency

Whether or not a defendant is mentally competent is a frequent issue in a trial and an issue that can occur at several different junctures. As mentioned earlier, there are many types of competencies at issue. In the criminal arena, there is the competency to

- waive the right to silence and to legal counsel
- agree to search and seizure
- confess
- stand trial
- testify
- plead guilty
- conduct one's own defense
- refuse the insanity defense
- be criminally responsible
- serve a sentence
- be executed

In the civil arena, the issues involve competency to

- consent to treatment
- be a guardian
- take care of a child

Those competency issues that require psychological evaluation most often involve standing trial, waiving rights, and criminal responsibility. Any time the defendant is thought to be unable to perceive the situation realistically, he or she may be tested for competence.

Unabomber Ted Kaczynski initially refused to undergo any type of psychiatric evaluation, although his ability to adequately assist in his own defense was questioned. When he decided to defend himself, it was clear that he probably did not perceive his situation realistically, so the judge refused his request unless he agreed to a competency evaluation. He begrudgingly

Unabomber Found Competent to Stand Trial

Although a therapist believed that Unabomber Ted Kaczynski suffered from paranoid schizophrenia, he insisted on not pursuing a mental illness defense. Kaczynski was sentenced to life in prison for the murder of thirteen people.

submitted. Dr. Sally Johnson, who had also evaluated President Reagan's would-be assassin John Hinckley, spent twenty-two hours conducting the evaluation. To make her assessment, she used collateral information that included Kaczynski's extensive writings and photos of the contents of his cabin. She then reported that he was an intelligent man who was socially withdrawn and whose mental decline was attributable to paranoid schizophrenia. Yet he did not want to pursue a mental illness defense. Nevertheless, Kaczynski was found competent to stand trial. (His wish to defend himself became moot when he pleaded guilty to thirteen counts of murder and bombing to avoid the death penalty.)

Either attorney may make a motion for a judicial order of examination. The judge evaluates the facts to decide whether or not the accused understands the court proceedings and can assist counsel in his own defense. The judge then determines whether the defendant should be placed in a treatment facility. The landmark case on this issue was *Dusky v. United States* in 1960. In that case the standards were set for a rational and factual understanding of the charges on the part of the defendant. According to the guidelines set forth, to be judged competent a defendant must

- have the present capacity to understand the criminal process
- have the ability to function in that process
- have the present ability to consult with counsel

Thus, to be judged mentally incompetent by federal statutes, there must be a preponderance of evidence that the defendant has a mental defect or condition that prevents him from understanding the charge, the pretrial and trial procedures, his rights, what will happen if he is convicted, and how to cooperate with an attorney. This does not mean incompetence depends on being mentally ill. Incompetence can derive from organic or toxic impairments as well. A mental health professional makes the examination, but the judge makes the final decision.

Anyone judged incompetent to proceed will have the trial postponed indefinitely, pending the results of a psychiatric examination. The defendant may be held in a facility for years. Or, the defendant may be restored to competency, such as in the case of schizophrenics whose conditions can be controlled with medication. Yet a competency hearing is not an insanity defense. It is a procedure to ensure that the defendant is mentally fit to continue to exercise the right to due process.

Each state makes its own regulations about competency that can be checked with a criminal attorney, a forensic mental health professional, or at a law library. You could also call a law professor at a local college. Some are elaborate, some are simple. Writers are advised to find out the specifics for their settings. For example, in some states, in addition to the federal standards, the defendant must be able to have a psychological presence (be mentally focused) in court.

Of course, a defendant can always try to fake it if she thinks being in a hospital will be superior to being in prison, but incompetency is a tough thing to fake as a way of life. One must be pretty far gone to be incompetent, and those who try faking it will have nurses and doctors watching them and retesting them.

There is no standard way to evaluate competency, although such a procedure should not be confused with an evaluation of mental state at the time of the offense (MSO). The first thing to determine is how the defendant views his present situation. That simply means to ask and see if it's consistent with what's actually happening. From there, the mental health professional can ask him the following questions:

- what he understand about the charges
- what his understanding of the procedures are
- who represents him
- what he thinks of that person
- what he understands about the jury's role
- what he knows about plea bargaining
- what will occur if he is found guilty

If the responses are clear and show an understanding of the issues involved, the competency exam can be concluded at that point. (In general, however, people who can answer these questions well are not even sent for such evaluations because it's fairly evident that they are competent.)

If not, the mental health professional may use an IQ test to measure intellectual deficiencies or one of several competency screening devices that are available. There must also be some assessment of malingering in cases where a defendant might prefer a postponed trial. (In other words, he may pretend to be mentally ill.)

One more consideration is that the defendant must appear able to make a presentable court appearance. If there is some mental defect, such as shouting compulsively or giggling inappropriately, that might make a bad impression and thus compromise the defendant's best interests, the judge needs to know.

One way to measure intellectual deficiencies is with the Competency Screening Test (CST), developed at Harvard Medical School in 1970. This test consists of twenty-two incomplete sentences about court procedures that the defendant must finish. For example:

"When I prepare to go to court with my lawyer . . ."

"When the jury hears my case, they will . . ."

"When I think of being sent to prison, I . . ."

The responses are scored on a three-point scale and compared to what others have said in various stages of competence and incompetence. The idea is to check for the defendant's intellectual capacity, neurological status, and personality. The mental health professional should never probe the issue of guilt or innocence.

Even if using screening devices, it may be imperative to do a full psychological workup with a clinical interview and an assessment battery that will provide information about the defendant's intellectual abilities, neuropsychological condition, and personality structure. Any defense of insanity or diminished capacity may start with the competency screening.

A written competency report will include the following details:

- the defendant's response to the evaluation
- any difficulties he had
- all clinical observations
- scores of any testing instruments used
- personality factors such as coping mechanisms
- an overall opinion about how well he might be able to participate in the legal proceedings

Kaczynski's competency evaluation was far more complex than most, but the report handed to the judge and made public included these factors. (A copy can be viewed on the Court TV Web site at www.courttv.com.)

Evaluating Confessions: Forced or Voluntary

Although a confession is an important factor in criminal cases, a coerced or false confession must always be considered. False confessions can lead to erroneous convictions. This is why a confession is generally excluded from testimony when it was elicited by means of any of the following:

- brutality
- prolonged isolation or deprivation of food or sleep
- threats of harm or punishment
- promises of leniency
- without first notifying the accused of his rights

The legal system assumes that these conditions adequately protect the rights of those confessing. However, this does not take into account the fact that the police use deception to get confessions from innocent people, nor does it block juries who erroneously hear such confessions from considering them as part of the evidence. A psychologist as expert witness can help educate juries about some of the problems involved in confessions. The entire defense of four young men arrested in the early nineties for the murders of four girls in Austin, Texas, rested on the problems with confession testimony. Two of the boys appeared to have confessed, but their attorney used the top experts in the field to put this testimony into doubt. There was no other evidence that tied them to the murders, and a videotape of one of the confessions indicated how untenable it was.

The purpose of police interrogation is to get a confession and to elicit information that can be used as evidence. Since they are not allowed to brutalize a suspect, police may resort to psychological techniques like sympathy, false statements about evidence or informants, outright lies, or appeals to religion. Police interrogation manuals give advice on how to heighten tension, weaken a suspect's sense of control, and break down resistance. The point is to get suspects to feel more anxious about deception and less aware of the negative consequences of confessing. In a case on the television series *The Practice*, the district attorney pretended to an adolescent who had killed her baby that she, too, had once found herself pregnant. She assured the girl that if she were to just admit what she had done, things would be much better. The district attorney also promised to help. It was later revealed that everything the district attorney said was a deception to get the girl to confess—and it was within the bounds of the law.

However, there are extreme cases of outright deception and manipulation that must be considered. Police misled murder suspect James Jackson to believe that his shoes matched footprints at the scene (they didn't) and that the victim's blood was found on his pants. They also told him that a witness had seen him and that his prints were found on the murder weapon. Jackson inferred that he would be convicted and that things would go easier for him if he confessed, so he confessed. Then he retracted it, saying he'd been coerced. The North Carolina Supreme Court ruled that since Jackson was not physically coerced or offered leniency, his statement would be considered voluntary. It soon became clear to police that although the court did not think well of trickery and deceit to get confessions or evidence, the court did not prohibit it. Unfortunately, this implicit permission can be stretched too far.

While many people believe such circumstances are quite rare, in fact numerous cases can be found where evidence was misinterpreted, suspects were pressured in the extreme, and false confessions were gained. The fact that over seventy men have been exonerated in the past three years whose "airtight" cases had put them on death row indicates problems with the way cases can be handled.

The film *Gone in the Night* was based on the real-life 1988 kidnapping and murder of seven-year-old Jaclyn Dowaliby in Chicago. The kidnapping quickly became a high profile case and put tremendous pressure on the police and city officials to solve it—and made it easier to overlook, reinterpret, or manipulate evidence. When early evidence handling was botched and no suspects surfaced, the police turned their focus on the parents. Nothing was found to be amiss in a background check, so they created some things. In short order, they took away the Dowaliby's young son, claiming that he had been physically and sexually abused (although photos showed no evidence of this). The police detectives then developed a theory that the Dowalibys were part of a satanic cult. When Cyndi Dowaliby had another baby, they took that child from her as well. Their next step was to try to turn the couple against each other. Failing that, they worked on the couple's friends and relatives. Even worse, they leaked distorted information to the press and drew out the legal process to force the couple to continue to raise money for legal expenses. When a single piece of evidence was found that contradicted the official theory, the investigators quickly reinterpreted it to make it work.

In terms of confession evidence, David Dowaliby had hired a psychic who told him the body would be found in a field. When police did find the girl, Dowaliby asked, "Was she in a field?" The prosecution later claimed that he was admitting evidence of the crime scene, and he was falsely convicted of first-degree murder.

Since the police were working on a single theory, they failed to turn up evidence of a mentally disturbed relative who had lied about his whereabouts that night—and who in fact had abducted and killed the child. A private detective, along with a reporter, discovered how police had abused the system, and they managed to get David Dowaliby out of prison. The Dowaliby case is not the only one in which parents have been accused and abused by the system.

Types of Confessions

Some people are compulsive confessors or have some psychological reason for giving voluntary confession. When Lindbergh's baby was kidnapped, for example, over two hundred people confessed—none of whom did it. In another case, the shocking 1947 murder in Los Angeles of Elizabeth Short, a.k.a., the Black Dahlia, there were numerous confessions from males and females alike. Among them was Corporal Joseph Dumais who told another soldier that he had known Short and had been out with her on the day she was last seen. Investigators found bloodstains on his clothes and a batch of newspaper clippings about the crime in his possession. Dumais made a statement that allegedly ran to fifty pages, and he admitted that when he got drunk, he got very rough with women. However, his story failed to check out against the facts, and he was sent to a psychiatrist. Then, a young woman walked into the police station and announced, "Elizabeth Short stole my man, so I killed her and cut her up." She, too, stumbled over essential details about the location and method of killing, so then she confessed that she had made up the story. In fact, some people who claimed credit for the deed were not even born at the time Short was murdered!

Motives for this kind of strange behavior range from protecting someone else to wanting a piece of the fame. Others believe they are guilty of *something* and seek to be punished, even if it's for something they did not do. Some people confess to impress others. In a few cases, confessions are forthcoming in one state to avoid being prosecuted for a crime in a state with stiffer penalties. Some just want attention or a way off the streets.

Another type of confession, according to psychologist Saul Kassin, is the "coerced-compliant confession." This results from intense pressure. The interrogatee complies to gain relief or avoid something aversive. The person secretly knows he is innocent but pleads guilty to cut his losses. For example, three black tenant farmers were beaten in Mississippi in 1936 and were told the beatings would stop only when the men confessed to a murder. In cases

Rough Sketches of Possible Lindbergh Suspect

F. B. I. -18-1
SKETCHES OF "JOHN", WHO RECEIVED THE LINDBERGH KIDNAP RANSOM MONEY. DRAWN FOR THE FEDERAL BUREAU OF INVESTIGATION, UNITED STATES DEPARTMENT OF JUSTICE, IN JULY, 1934, BY JAMES T. BERRYMAN, OF THE WASHINGTON, D. C. EVENING STAR FROM A VERBAL DESCRIPTION GIVEN BY DR. JOHN F. CONDON.

Police were overwhelmed with information about the famous Lindbergh kidnapping case. Along with over two hundred people confessing to the crime, they also had this drawing of "John," who received the ransom money for the kidnapped baby. This photo was drawn for the Federal Bureau of Investigation, United States Department of Justice, in July 1934, by James T. Berryman.

with inexperienced adolescents, long hours of interrogation and sleep deprivation can frighten them into confessions. Four young men confessed to the massacre of six monks in Arizona. One of them, a boy with psychiatric problems, implicated the others. They were then subjected to threats and unrelenting interrogation until they confessed. Not long after, the real murderers were found, and the four boys were released.

There are also "coerced internalized false confessions," in which the suspect believes his own confession after a certain amount of interrogation and persuasion. The suspect's memory might even be altered, making the truth difficult to determine.

A rather shocking case, and one in which false confession became a major court issue, was that of Paul Ingram in Washington. In 1988 one of his two daughters, pressured by youth workers at a church retreat to admit to abuse in her background, accused him of sexually molesting her. He was astonished and vehemently denied the charges. Then, his other daughter made a similar accusation. Between the twenty-three police interrogations, his minister's insistence on a confession, and learning about repressed memories from a police psychologist, he began to wonder if he might be guilty after all. Eventually, he confessed and was soon pouring out detail upon detail of a satanic cult in which he was involved—which included the murder of babies. He was convicted and sent to prison for twenty years, where he continued to insist on his guilt.

In preparation for the trial, sociologist and cult expert Richard Ofshe was asked into the case to "prove" that the memories matched the facts. Ofshe carefully interviewed the girls and then Paul Ingram. He sensed that the girls were not truthful and wondered if Ingram had been manipulated into a confession.

Ofshe tried an experiment. Over two days, he caused Ingram to recollect events that Ofshe picked out at random—including events that no one had described. At first Ingram did not remember the fake incidents, but after prayer, he began to. He offered a written confession, in embellished detail, of events that Ofshe knew had never occurred. From what he could see, the entire confession was probably false. However, to his surprise, Ingram refused to budge on his position that he had done these things. Ofshe concluded that it was all a product of social influence rather than a true memory.

However, the prosecution refused to turn Ofshe's report over to the defense. Only when Ofshe complained to the judge did the defense get to see it.

Characteristics of Confessors

People who are prone to internalize false confessions are generally vulnerable in some way (youth, trust, suggestibility, low IQ, or fatigue) and are shown false evidence, such as a rigged polygraph or statements supposedly made by an accomplice. It has even been shown that false memories can be implanted with suggestion by a powerful authority who uses reinforcement. In an experiment with college students typing on a computer, 69 percent signed confessions that they had hit a key they were not supposed to have hit, even though they did not. Twenty-eight percent internalized their guilt, and 9 percent manufactured details to fit the alleged event. The simple fact that the computer had stopped responding (it was rigged) and a confederate had accused them of being at fault made them believe in their guilt, although they had no memory of doing what they confessed to doing. In fact, all participants initially had denied the charge. Unfortunately, it seems that some people can be induced to accept responsibility for things they did not do, especially if false evidence is produced. Since most people believe that no one would confess to something they did not do, expert testimony on this phenomenon can be crucial in court.

Writers who wish to develop such a scene in court need to understand the ramifications of the *Daubert* ruling (see page 47), however, because empirical evidence is weak. Writers should consult the work of Richard Ofshe and Richard Leo, who have documented over sixty cases of police-induced false confession, twenty-nine of which led to false convictions. They offer valuable details of how false confession is done and how it affects the suspect.

Any psychologist who deals with the justice system needs to understand that suspects may be vulnerable to the kinds of deceptions and pressures used by police to obtain confessions. There have also been many efforts to preclude testimony about false confessions, so a psychologist being hired as an expert needs to understand the legal history of this issue, i.e., the landmark cases. The important thing is to get triers of fact to understand the totality of circumstances leading up to confessions, especially the interrogation techniques, both coercive and rewarding. (One suspect in Michigan was thrust naked into an unlit, cagelike cell in a basement where he lay for days on a concrete floor without blankets or any sense of what was going to happen to him—all of this before any hearing. After a few days, he was offered a steak dinner to confess. He didn't accept, but hungry as he was, he was sorely tempted.)

Lie Detection and Malingering

In *Primal Fear*, a neuropsychologist, defense attorney, prosecutor, and judge all fall for the act of a boy accused of murder who acts out a dissociative identity disorder. The mental health professional actually had raised the possibility of malingering before she met with him but had failed to follow through with any of the tests that might have picked it up. She did not even notice his long pauses before answering questions, which is one sign of deception. She assumed it was part of his personality since he was shy. Yet she ought to have tested him anyway. When she didn't, she contributed to the decision to send him for treatment and eventual freedom rather than to death row.

Lying and malingering are two different aspects of what a mental health professional may need to deal with, but they both come under the theme of deception detection.

Detecting when a defendant is lying is a source of endless research and debate. Technological lie detectors like polygraphs have their defenders and detractors and should be administered only by a very skilled and experienced administrator. Often, they're not used at all, which means that mental health professionals must rely on other means of noting when words or behavior are false.

One idea is that lying is a more complicated activity than truth-telling and thus produces certain physiological reactions such as a heightened pulse rate, dilated pupils, and certain behavioral manifestations. This is especially true if the stakes are high, such as going to prison. However, people telling the truth under conditions like that may also display emotions. They may be anxious about whether they are believed or may be embarrassed to be there under those conditions. To further complicate the problem, psychopaths and pathological liars are very good at lying, and their skills make the typical modes of detection irrelevant. They appear to have lower levels of autonomic nervous activity and are not as adversely affected by the idea of punishment.

In general, the conditions under which people tend to be apprehensive about lying include when the target person has a reputation for reading lies, when the target person is suspicious, when the deceiver has little experience lying, and when the consequences of being found out are serious.

The types of behaviors that may signal deception include the following:

- language that includes more negative than positive statements, over-generalizations, deflections away from the self, increased pitch
- uninterrupted talking with slower speech rate
- speech hesitations and pauses, taking longer to respond to questions, appearing to think through what they will say, answers that seem too long or are irrelevant, no apparent spontaneity
- increase in number of shrugs
- blinking and an increase in nervous habits like stroking
- increased leg and foot movements
- eye contact increases
- decreased number of specific verbal references; fewer sensory details
- hyperventilation, blanching, flushing, breath holding, sighing
- asymmetrical, miserable, or fearful smiles
- reduced use of hand gestures
- lack of head movement
- unusual body movements
- increased behavioral clues when feedback appears positive (interest and encouragement)
- inconsistent information

It should be noted that none of these behaviors is a definitive sign of deception, but they show up more often in those with the greatest motivation to deceive—possibly because they're trying hard to plan and control what they say. It may also be that paying attention to their verbal communication minimizes their guard over their behavior. However, those people who appear to be the best liars under pressure have experience with lying (probably have lied since childhood, are comfortable with attention, are confident, and are physically attractive).

As I've already pointed out, malingering is a deliberate attempt to create the impression of being mentally ill, and in this context, it's often done to avoid a charge of criminal responsibility. We'll now take up the subject in detail and see what mental health professionals do about it.

Many people believe that psychosis is the same thing as insanity, so if they can fake something like schizophrenia or dissociative identity disorder, they will incur no legal penalties. Mental health professionals have spent a great deal of time researching malingering and deception, specifically to refine their techniques at detecting them. It is paramount to detect malingering in order to avoid sending a sane person to a psychiatric hospital with the possibility (though rare) of getting released for failing to meet the requirements of confinement.

To detect malingering of psychiatric symptoms, mental health professionals need to gather quite a lot of information. Otherwise, they can be easily deceived, as was one mental health professional who interviewed Lyle Menendez in prison for over sixty hours. Accused of killing his parents, Lyle claimed to have been sexually abused to the point that he was operating under a sort of "learned helplessness" feeling of pervasive threat. He affected a convincing façade of shame and a reluctance to talk about such an embarrassing thing. However, he later told someone he had "snowed" everyone with this story. Some people are very good liars—or else some experts are not such good lie detectors.

To detect malingering in cases like this, mental health professionals are looking for one or more of the following:

1. an exaggerated presentation
2. inconsistent information
3. a deliberateness of manner
4. an attempt to display obvious (and stereotypical) symptoms
5. an inconsistency with past psychiatric diagnoses of the same person

The mental health professional may check the defendant's past history of psychiatric confinement (if any) and any statements from witnesses (friends, family, prison guards, hospital staff) as to the person's current and past condition. She may also have to observe the subject in various settings over a period of time. In forensic assessment, time is limited, so other means must be found. Key to an assessment will be discrepancies in the person's ability to focus and talk rationally with people other than the mental health professional.

Another way to assess malingering is to compare the symptoms presented by the defendant with those that fit a typical clinical profile. Schizophrenia generally manifests in auditory hallucinations, but someone trying to fake this illness may "see" visual hallucinations, which are more likely to be the result of toxic conditions from drugs or alcohol. If the person knows enough to talk about auditory hallucinations, then he should be asked what the voices are saying. They ought to be more along the lines of belittling the person than of commands to do things. "You're bad" rather than "Go kill the dog."

Hearing commands is generally part of a delusional structure, so a mental health professional must determine that this delusion is evident in other parts of the personality structure. Generally, mentally ill people will have developed some strategies for trying to diminish the voices. The person being questioned should be able to spell out what those strategies are and say how well they have worked.

Some assessment instruments, such as the MMPI-2 and Rorschach, are highly sensitive to psychotic conditions, so it's important to use them on malingerers for a more objective check. The MMPI-2 not only picks up schizophrenia but also has a scale for "faking bad" (trying to appear ill).

For specifically distinguishing a real from a faked illness, mental health professionals may use the Structured Interview of Reported Symptoms (SIRS), which contains 172 items that involve questions from a variety of other instruments. Its eight primary scales include descriptions of improbable symptoms, rare symptoms, psychiatric problems that almost never occur at the same time, blatant symptoms, and subtle symptoms. Responses are evaluated as (1) honest, (2) indeterminate, (3) probable malingering, and (4) definite malingering. The SIRS is widely used in forensic assessments, is empirically testable, has a low error rate, and meets the *Daubert* standard (see page 47).

Malingerers make a point of ensuring that people pay attention to their illnesses while most truly mentally ill people would rather not be the focus of attention. If they say the delusions or hallucinations were sudden, this is inconsistent with the clinical picture of mental illness, except for drug-induced psychosis. Malingerers often tend to overact.

Malingering the disorder known as dissociative identity disorder, as happened in *Primal Fear*, is another popular ploy, but such people tend to believe that this involves a split personality between a good and bad person. That's generally not the case, as pointed out in chapter four. (Dissociative identity disorder is also a controversial diagnosis that has been disputed by some mental health professionals and overdiagnosed by others. While the jury is still out, it's probably much more rare than has been stated in recent literature.)

Mental health professionals who do work with dissociative identity disorder should be on the lookout for the following

- defendants who have a hard time retaining the voice and personality of the one they want to blame for their crimes
- defendants who appear not to be confused by the criminal behavior, as would be likely in an authentic case of multiple personality
- lack of evidence of a history of the kind of fragmenting and amnesia characteristic of dissociative identity disorder in the defendant's background

Lying of any type appears to be a complex task that involves the whole body. Emotional cues can be valuable, although most people still cannot detect deception that way. Liars who know they need to control their behavior may end up overcontrolling, which makes their voices sound strained or distinguished by a greater number of pauses, more fluency, and a higher degree of eloquence.

One study indicated a problem with professionals who felt confident that they could easily detect a liar: Not only were they wrong, but many professionals actually showed decreased abilities. However, since they were confident about their abilities, they did not realize how often they were mistaken. Degree of confidence was inversely related to true ability. All mental health professionals need to take note of that. The same is true for police interrogators, who can as easily be mistaken but believe they are not. What happens then is that they fall into relying on stereotypes. (The best human lie detectors, it turns out, are secret service agents and highly skilled poker players.) A person's success at the detection of deception or malingering depends on his experience with a symptom or a described situation. The more experience, the greater the chance he can detect deception. He will also be experienced with people who make clear attempts to influence him.

Eyewitness Testimony

In October 1999, the U.S. Department of Justice released the first guide for collecting and preserving eyewitness testimony. Psychology played a significant role in the guide's development; it was psychologists as expert witnesses who focused on the many deficiencies in the legal arena and on cases in which DNA exonerated someone positively identified by an eyewitness.

Psychologists led the way in research that showed eyewitnesses can be completely convinced of their identifications but can nevertheless be mistaken: There is no correlation between confidence and accuracy.

Psychological research on this issue has developed over the past thirty years on two main issues: "event memory," in which a witness describes something that happened, and "identification memory," which involves a witness's ability to recognize the perpetrator in a lineup or photo spread.

Both types of eyewitness accounts are affected by misleading questions, which means that such memory is malleable—shaped by events occurring after the event witnessed. In other words, if a witness saw a man assault someone and run, and then was shown a photo of someone who resembled him, the witness's memory might actually shift toward the photo, and the witness would be vulnerable to identifying the wrong person. Witnesses will incorporate new information and testify about it with all confidence as if they had actually seen it during the event.

One study with three hundred subjects explored conditions that produce faulty eyewitness testimony. It turned out that a key part of the process was to mislead an eyewitness and then elicit information in a way that committed that person to what he or she said. The subjects viewed a slide containing a crime and then heard a narrative about the crime that contained misinformation (which can happen when police officers try to tell witnesses what they think happened). The results showed that memory gets impaired not so much by the misinformation, but by the act of retrieving it to write a statement. Retrieved misinformation can actually block accurate information about what was witnessed.

Another problem was that police procedures often corrupted the eyewitness testimony, either with subtle cues or spoken affirmation, and even by showing a photo of the person police felt was the perpetrator before a lineup. Researchers also found problems in their basic techniques: They asked too many close-ended questions, asked them in a rigid order, and interrupted witnesses in a way that shifted the focus of attention. Eyewitnesses became confused and passive and often did not deliver information that was useful or failed to offer as much as they actually knew.

What the Research Says

More than two hundred people per day are identified by eyewitnesses as participants in crimes. It was not until the 1970s that such testimony was examined in research for accuracy, and the results were dismaying. Psychologists began to identify those conditions that affected the chances of mistaken identification.

- Surrounding an innocent suspect in a lineup with people who do not resemble the details from the witness statement increases the likelihood of identifying that person as the perpetrator.
- Failing to instruct witnesses that the actual perpetrator might not be in a lineup increases the pressure to pick someone.
- Lineups encourage relative judgments in which witnesses compare the possibilities, whereas a procedure in which the lineup "suspects" are presented sequentially encourages a more absolute judgment of "This is or is not the guy."
- The judicial system has endorsed the belief that a confident eyewitness implies greater accuracy, but research has shown that accuracy is a perceptual and memory issue, whereas confidence is a function of social variables.

The recent work with DNA evidence to exonerate people on death row has brought the problems with eyewitness testimony to light. DNA testing had freed sixty-two people as of the year 2000, a surprising number of them from death row. Mistaken identification was involved in thirty-six of the first forty cases, with fifty separate incidences altogether of mistakes. In another study of all sixty-two people, fifty-two were found to be based on faulty eyewitness identification, with seventy-seven mistaken eyewitnesses. In 205 cases that were shown to be wrongful convictions without the use of DNA testing, nearly half were attributed to mistaken eyewitness accounts. Even in lineups, there is a 20 percent rate of mistaken identifications.

It becomes clear, then, that the research psychologists offer can help predict and minimize the error rate or can point out where juries should be cautious. The Department of Justice has acknowledged this research and has urged the following reforms:

- better methods of questioning witnesses
- better instruction before a lineup
- cautioning against guessing
- how to select appropriate lineup fillers
- avoiding postidentification suggestions

Psychologists are still hoping to encourage a double-blind procedure in which the officer conducting the lineup does not know who the suspect is. They also suggest using sequential lineups rather than simultaneous lineups to avoid relative judgments.

It is important to note that some courts still do not accept expert testimony on eyewitness data, believing that the trier(s) of fact can decide if there are errors. However, research shows that people fail to adequately understand the problems with biased lineups, even when brought to their attention by the defense attorney, and the use of eyewitness testimony heightens the degree of scrutiny in which police officers have interviewed witnesses and conducted lineups.

Forensic Hypnosis With Eyewitnesses

A landmark appellate case in 1968, *Harding v. State*, involved a request to allow the admission of testimony that had been "refreshed" (enhanced) through hypnosis. Prior to that, hypnosis had been considered too unreliable for lawful admissibility. Yet things shifted somewhat with the *Harding* judgment. The victim of a shooting and attempted rape identified her assailant only after she was hypnotized. The Maryland Supreme Court decided that hypnosis was like any other memory aid device and allowed it without much qualification, but jurors were instructed to evaluate its credibility. More such cases followed, and soon courts were forced to devise guidelines. However,

Ted Bundy Reacts to Jury Verdict

In this photo, Ted Bundy responds strongly to the jury recommendation that he receive death by the electric chair for the murder of two Chi Omega sorority sisters. The jury's verdict of guilty was determined after examining a great deal of evidence, including Bundy's hypnotically refreshed testimony.

© Bettmann/CORBIS

a number of courts opted for the *Frye*-based decision (see page 47) in *State v. Mack*, in which the Minnesota Supreme Court ruled that hypnosis had not been generally accepted by the scientific community, and therefore, recall from hypnosis was inadmissible. Today, courts are still divided.

Due to the foibles of human memory, hypnosis has been utilized as a tool to try to fill in gaps, add detail, and ensure accuracy in eyewitness testimony. The most popular techniques involve past-memory regression and memory enhancement. A hypnotist exploits the subject's suggestibility in order to induce a trance that produces a relaxed mental state. The subject becomes attentive, focused, and less prone to critical judgment that can block memory. Going into a trance purportedly allows the heightening of imagination with the hope that some detail, such as a license plate number, might be recalled that would otherwise remain inaccessible. Hypnosis apparently bypasses the individual's psychological defenses and allows repressed material to surface. It was used in such high profile cases as the Boston Strangler and the Sam Sheppard murder investigation. Even Ted Bundy was convicted in part with hypnotically refreshed testimony. He appealed to the U.S. Supreme Court on this basis but lost.

The first use of hypnosis to solve a crime was in 1845. A clairvoyant was put into a trance to try to identify a thief. She described a fourteen-year-old boy, who subsequently confessed. Some other cases involving hypnosis went to court, and by 1897, the California Supreme Court had ruled that evidence discovered through hypnosis was inadmissible.

Problems with using hypnosis include the following:

- the possibility that a recovered memory is incomplete, inaccurate, or based on some leading suggestion
- hypermnesia or confabulation, in which the subject fills in the gaps with false material that supports his or her self-interest
- hypnotic recall, in which a posthypnotic suggestion of something that did not happen gets retroactively integrated into the subject's memory as if it did
- personal beliefs and prejudices may influence how an event was initially registered and/or the person interprets it during recall
- "memory hardening," which occurs when a false memory brought out through hypnosis seems so real that the subject develops false confidence in it
- a false memory, once articulated, can be difficult to distinguish from genuine memories

All of these problems have been documented in experiments. Unfortunately, jurists are generally unaware of these errors. One study showed that jurists tended to attribute a higher rate of accuracy to hypnotically refreshed testimony than is warranted by the evidence.

A more restrictive approach, based on guidelines, arose from trial cases in the early eighties, notably *State v. Hurd.* In 1978 in New Jersey, Jane Sell was attacked with a knife while sleeping in her bedroom. She escaped but afterward could not recall the details of the attack. Under hypnosis by psychiatrist Herbert Spiegel—who did not interview her prior to the procedure—and with considerable leading, she identified her attacker as her former husband, Paul Hurd, with whom she had had two children. The evening before the assault, Jane's current husband, David Sell, had engaged in a heated phone conversation with Paul Hurd regarding visitation rights.

In her posthypnotic state, Jane Sell expressed mistrust about her thinking, but Dr. Spiegel and the investigating detective encouraged her to accept her identification to protect her children. She gave a statement identifying Paul Hurd as her attacker, and he was indicted and charged with assault with intent to kill. Defense counsel argued on the basis of *Frye v. United States* (see page 47) that hypnotically refreshed testimony is inadmissible *per se* and that Jane Sell's testimony was tainted by suggestion and coercion. The case went to the New Jersey Supreme Court in 1981.

Justices Pashman, Clifford, and Sullivan reviewed the issue of whether Sell's testimony was true recall or confabulation. In reaching their decision not to admit the testimony, the court came up with the following state guidelines.

- witnesses must use a psychiatrist or psychologist trained and experienced in the use of hypnosis
- the hypnotist should be independent of, and not regularly employed by, the prosecution, police, or defense
- information given by any party to the action to the hypnotist should be written or recorded and made available to all parties
- the hypnosis session(s) should be video- or audiotaped, including pre- and post-interviews
- only the expert and the witness should be present during all phases of the hypnosis
- the subject's prehypnosis memories for the events in question should be carefully recorded and preserved

The court determined that Sell's testimony had failed to follow any of the proposed safeguards.

Also in 1980, in *State v. Mack*, there was a ruling because of numerous errors in the testimony that a witness who has been hypnotized cannot testify about either pre- or post-hypnotic recollections in prosecuting a case. The victim initially recalled nothing about her attack, but under hypnosis, she remembered her male companion, who had ordered her to remove her clothes. He had threatened her with a knife, she claimed while in a trance, and had stabbed her repeatedly. She also remembered that she had danced with a man. However, when compared to the facts, her testimony proved problematic: She remembered eating at a restaurant that did not serve the meal she recalled, she described the defendant's maroon motorcycle as black, she actually had danced with someone else the night of the attack, and she had suffered only a single wound. These discrepancies and her confidence in the hypnotically restored "facts" caused the Minnesota Court of Appeals to rule that hypnotically refreshed testimony was too inaccurate to be accepted in court.

Yet in 1987, the U.S. Supreme Court reviewed the *Rock v. Arkansas* case in which hypnotically refreshed testimony had been rejected *per se*, as dictated by state law. Mrs. Vickie Lorene Rock shot her husband in 1983 during a fight and claimed it was an accident, but she could not recall the details. She had wanted to leave their apartment, but her husband had prevented her and had begun to choke her. She picked up a gun, and while he hit her again, she shot him. She believed that her finger was on the hammer not the trigger, but that the gun had gone off anyway. At her attorney's suggestion, Rock twice underwent hypnosis by a trained neuropsychologist, Dr. Bettye Back, who first interviewed Rock for an hour. The sessions were recorded. Rock recalled that her gun had misfired when her husband had grabbed her arm. A gun expert testified that the Hawes .22 Deputy Marshall was indeed faulty and was prone to fire if dropped or hit, even if the trigger was not pulled. However, the prosecutor filed a motion to exclude this testimony, and the trial court ruled that hypnotically refreshed testimony was inadmissible. The only statement Rock was allowed was what she had told the doctor prior to hypnotic treatment. She was convicted of manslaughter and sentenced to ten years in prison and a ten-thousand dollar fine.

The Arkansas Supreme Court affirmed the conviction and restated that testimony derived through hypnosis is inadmissible because it is unreliable. Yet grounds for further appeal rested on whether a state law could so restrict a defendant's right to testify by excluding material parts of the testimony.

The U.S. Supreme Court ruling, delivered by Justice Blackmun, vacated the Arkansas decision on the basis that a total ban of such testimony restricted Mrs. Rock's Fourteenth Amendment right to due process and her Sixth Amendment right to call witnesses. Arkansas's law seemed to have followed other states in a ruling that excluded this type of testimony, yet those other states had not applied this to defendants but to other witnesses. Hypnosis has its weaknesses, the Court stated, but to totally exclude it is arbitrary, and no state's judicial rules may be arbitrary or disproportionate to the purpose for which they were designed. "Arkansas's *per se* rule excluding all hypnotically refreshed testimony infringes impermissibly on a criminal defendant's right to testify on his or her own behalf." Since the hypnotic procedure has been credited with obtaining certain types of information, such as investigative leads and identifications later corroborated, and since inaccuracies can be reduced with safeguards, the state's interest in barring such testimony does not justify an exclusion just because the case involved hypnosis. In this case, the tape recordings indicated that the doctor did not suggest responses, and there was expert corroboration regarding the defective weapon. The trial court should have considered these things when evaluating admissibility. The Arkansas Supreme Court was instructed to review the case again in a manner "not inconsistent" with the U.S. Supreme Court ruling on allowing the hypnotically refreshed testimony.

That same year, 1987, the U.S. Court of Appeals for the Eighth Circuit ruled in *Little v. Armontrout* that an indigent defendant was entitled to a court-appointed expert to assist him in challenging hypnotically refreshed testimony used against him. On the evening of August 13, 1980, the victim, M.B.G., was raped in her apartment. The assailant wore one of her blouses wrapped around his head and another around his torso, but she noticed his hands were black. When the blouse on his head slipped, she glimpsed a partial profile. A policewoman interrupted the attack and the assailant fled through a window. M.B.G. gave a description of her attacker to police.

Two days later, M.B.G. was hypnotized for two hours by a police officer who had been to a four-day training workshop. An audiotape was made, but subsequently erased. However, M.B.G. was unable to recall further details under hypnosis. Four months later, she was again hypnotized to assist her in sleeping better. The case was not discussed, as the officer later testified, and no tape was made. Soon thereafter she looked through photographs of suspects and picked out Leatrice Little, who had recently become a suspect, and then successfully identified him in a lineup. He was convicted of rape and burglary. He appealed on the basis of the court's violation of his Fourteenth Amendment right to due process.

In reaching their decision, the circuit court reviewed two central theories of hypnosis: the retrieval theory proposed by Dr. Martin Reiser and the construction theory proposed by Dr. Martin Orne. The retrieval theory (in which the police officer who hypnotized the victim was trained) holds that all experiences are recorded and stored in a memory bank, and hypnosis aids in recalling details. The subject is encouraged to "watch" the event as if watching television, with the hope that more details will emerge. The construction theory holds that a memory of any given event is "constructed" by many factors, particularly the person's perception of the event relative to other experiences. Proponents of this theory believe that the past is continually remade in the interest of the present, which entails serious problems with accuracy in hypnotically induced recall.

In evaluating M.B.G.'s testimony, the court determined that some of the testimony was suspect and that the hypnosis sessions did not adhere to any of the safeguards cited in *State v. Hurd* (no recordings, no written prehypnosis interviews, the hypnotist was an amateur and not impartial, and others were present). M.B.G.'s original physical description of the suspect did not match the defendant, and some suggestion could have planted during the second session (closely following the time when Little came under suspicion). The lack of record of the session deprived the defendant of a means of attacking its credibility. Since M.B.G.'s was the only testimony that placed Little at the crime scene, and fingerprints found on a windowsill where the assailant escaped did not match Little's, there was no corroborating evidence. The state was ordered to begin a new trial within three months or release Little from custody.

Hypnosis, when used with proper procedure and precautions, can generate information that can be helpful in a police investigation, but which may be suspect when taken into court. Given the potential difficulties involved in hypnotic recall, it seems best that courts adopt conservative measures and evaluate the probative value of this technique on a case-by-case basis.

In light of this complex history, it is absurd that James Patterson in *Along*

Came a Spider had his police detective being asked in court to put a defendant into a hypnotic trance. Just because Alex Cross was also a psychologist did not mean he was an expert hypnotist. Even worse, this kind of maneuver would have been questioned at once by the other attorney and probably by the judge as well. Undoubtedly, it would not have been allowed in the courtroom, but would have been videotaped under court-ordered conditions that followed strict guidelines.

Writers should not assume that whatever psychologists can do in their practices they will be allowed to do in courts. There are many reservations about certain types of procedures and testimony, so be very clear on the legal precedents and arguments about any psychological procedure.

Books on the subject include the following:
Psychological Evaluations for the Court
The Handbook of Forensic Psychology
The Psychologist as Expert Witness

That said, under the right conditions hypnosis can be a powerful tool. It has been successfully used to help solve crimes and even to ascertain false confessions and a mental state at the time of the offense that led to acquittal. It ought only to be used by a well-trained professional. Memories are malleable and can be forged with suggestions and leading questions. Hypnosis can actually turn people into better liars than they would otherwise be and can supplant real memories with false ones. Extreme care must be taken to avoid all clues, and even at that, hypnotically assisted memories ought only be used to find more conventional evidence.

Being an expert witness means much more than simply being skilled in some area and being prepared. The courtroom is highly political, defendants may lie, eyewitnesses may be mistaken, and even the most sincere confession may be false. Knowing what can happen in a case and having some awareness of legal precedents on psychological issues will aid experts in achieving their best presentation.

7

Mental States at the Time of the Offense

Evil vs. Ill

Two young men in New Jersey were bored one evening, so they decided to commit a crime. They called a restaurant and ordered a pizza for delivery. When the deliveryman arrived, they shot him, saying they simply wanted to know what it would be like to kill someone.

Another young man turned eighteen. He had told his girlfriend that he was going to get a certain make of car for his birthday. He didn't, so when he spotted a woman driving one, he forced his way in, killed her, and stole her car, passing it off as his birthday present.

Some people have no trouble calling an act evil. Others prefer not to use that term; rather they interpret "evil" as a symptom of imbalance or dysfunction. Philosophers, theologians, psychologists, and even biologists have all grappled with the concept of the irredeemable person. The idea is that certain people freely choose to do heinous things and know precisely what they are doing.

Can we really determine how the malignant personality forms? Many theorists have tried, yet their answers have not contributed to treatments that could eradicate malfeasance from our midst. Perhaps we don't want it gone; perhaps it feeds a hunger that we fail to acknowledge. It may be that our focus on *Pulp Fiction* sociopaths and mothers who drown their children to get men diverts us; stories about people who perpetrate horrendous crimes provide a degree of arousal that we miss in our safety-conscious culture.

The problem with calling an act evil rather than considering it an illness

Evidence in the Jeffrey Dahmer Case

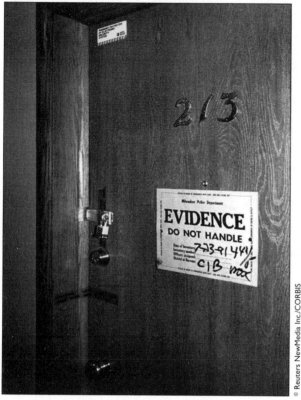

Behind this door is the apartment where police arrested cannibalist and necrophiliac Jeffrey Dahmer. The evidence they found in the apartment helped the jury decide that Dahmer was evil, not insane.

© Reuters NewMedia Inc./CORBIS

is that it often overlaps with the insanity issue and taints it. If people decide that some behavior is "evil," they don't want to believe that a mental defect was responsible; they want the evil person to be supremely punished.

Let's say you want a character to be an expert witness in a high profile murder trial where insanity is the issue. For example, in Wisconsin in 1993, Jeffrey Dahmer stood trial for killing fifteen young men. He also cut them open, had sex with body parts, ate body parts, and tried to turn some of his victims into lobotomized zombies. He thought he might acquire some sort of special power, and his victims would be able to live through him. At his trial, Dahmer pleaded not guilty by reason of insanity (NGRI). Psychiatrists were called in for both sides. The defense said that his necrophilia—a mental disease—made him commit these kinds of crimes. The prosecution said he was aware that it was wrong, and he was able to prevent himself from doing it.

The issue was not whether he was a necrophiliac—no one questioned that—but whether his mental illness controlled his behavior. The jury concluded that he was evil, not ill. They decided that he certainly knew right from wrong at the time of his acts and that he was breaking the law. It's possible, but does that mean he was *not* mentally ill? Or that his illness was not instrumental in the kind of crimes in which he engaged? There are some complex questions here that the courts have failed to address. They seem to have difficulty dealing with the difference between an impulse that one cannot resist and an impulse that one chooses not to resist.

Before a mental health professional can offer testimony, he must come to terms with the ultimate issue: whether he can infer the legal notion of insanity from the diagnosed mental illness. He should not necessarily testify on it, but he needs to know how the chain of reasoning would work for a jury. Typically, such an expert wants only to present the results of an assessment and interview, but lawyers and judges generally pressure for a more definitive stance: "Doctor, in your expert opinion, is this person insane?" That means the mental health professional must have done a careful analysis of the actions and ideas leading up to the crime.

The legal system relies on a belief that people are generally rational and that they make decisions based on their desires and beliefs as a result of their own free will. They are not victims of mental conditions or social forces. Thus, they are responsible. Mental health experts generally undermine this folk psychology with explanations that show hidden factors that make it more difficult to blame a person who has committed a crime while in an unbalanced state of mind. Courtroom tensions regarding psychiatric testimony generally arise out of a conflict between paradigms. That's why it's important to understand how the insanity defense (and others related to it) got its start and what it's all about.

Criminal Responsibility

The law recognizes that responsibility for committing a crime depends on two things.

1. *Actus reus*: evidence that the accused engaged in the act.
2. *Mens rea*: the accused had the required mental state to have intended to commit the act or to have foreseen its consequences.

Triers of fact must consider excusing someone's behavior in those without *mens rea*, because acts of deranged people are not to be judged in the same way as the acts of rational people. To be convicted, the person must have an evil mind and do a bad deed. *Mens rea* makes it possible to use abnormal mental states to absolve guilt.

The problem in court is that attorneys may confuse or abuse the notion of insanity, as with the designer defenses mentioned earlier (see page 82). Mental health professionals may be accomplices. Objections to the insanity defense include the fact that it's vague, the mental health research is always shifting, and psychiatric testimony on the issue is inconsistent. Mental health professionals must be ready for these attacks.

Rationale for the Insanity Defense

A legal defense of insanity presents the idea that someone has committed a crime but by reason of "disease or defect" is not responsible for his actions. That is, he could not understand what he was doing or could not control it. The thinking is that such a person should not be held criminally accountable for something he could not help. Grounds for punishment, retribution, and deterrence just don't apply.

To make some determination of the mental state at the time of the offense (MSO), the mental health professional must examine this person's actions leading up to the crime and coordinate all findings with police and medical examiner reports, including the defendant's behavior while incarcerated. Any mental health analysis must take into account what the laws and burden of proof requirements are in a given jurisdiction. It must be noted that some states have no insanity defense, so writers should always check their own state's rulings. There are also several types of insanity tests used.

This defense is unpopular with the public, who mistakenly believes that many criminals successfully use it to get away with crimes and that criminals are set free immediately after being acquitted. Generally the public only hears about some high profile case, like Sirhan Sirhan or Charles Manson, and they believe it must be typical of what goes on in the legal system. It isn't. Statistics differ from state to state, but in general, not guilty by reason of insanity is a high risk defense that succeeds only a fraction of the time. It is used in less than 3 percent of criminal cases, and it fails more often than it succeeds. Most of the successes (85 percent) result from plea bargains because a judge can often see that the case is clear-cut. Thus, few juries are "fooled," but juries have certainly convicted people who are genuinely psychotic as well. What they generally get are the borderline cases, which are the most difficult to decide.

Lawyers who opt for this defense know the risks—including the impossibility of going back to a plea of innocence. Those defendants found not guilty by reason of insanity have to undergo extensive psychiatric testing in a locked facility to determine if they are dangerous to the community. They do not just walk out of court smiling—they may even be detained longer than they would have been had they received prison sentences. (A prison sentence for a given crime is a set amount of time; someone being evaluated for a mental illness deemed a danger to society could remain indefinitely hospitalized. Thus, a defendant who might have gotten fifteen years for manslaughter if sane might be hospitalized for much longer if psychotic and unresponsive to therapy or drugs.)

Where did this defense get started?

The M'Naghten Rule

As early as the thirteenth century, English kings pardoned murderers because their actions seemed the result of madness. Criteria for this finding were vague, so in 1843, the notion was formalized and became an accepted standard for English law. It also affected the American court system. The House of Lords made a ruling in response to the controversy surrounding the insanity-related acquittal of Daniel M'Naghten, who killed Prime Minister Robert Peel's private secretary while gunning for Peel himself. The defense counsel argued that while M'Naghten knew what he was doing, he was unable to control himself because he suffered from paranoid delusions. He was acquitted, but the public did not accept this verdict. A royal commission was appointed to study the issue. In 1843, they established the M'Naghten Rule.

The House of Lords made it a requirement that to establish a defense on the ground of insanity, it had to be proved that "at the time of the committing of the act, the party accused was laboring under such a defect of reason, from disease of the mind, as not to know the nature and quality of the act he was doing; or if he did know it, that he did not know he was doing what was wrong." That is, such a defense had to prove more than just cognitive impairment; it had to go on to allow that the behavior was not under the subject's control. While United States courts have attempted to formulate more specific standards, many jurisdictions still rely on some form of the M'Naghten Rule.

The Durham Rule and the American Law Institute

By 1954, in the United States, when criticism against the M'Naghten Rule became pronounced, an alternative test was proposed for a form of diminished responsibility. One court proposed that the defendant is legally responsible if the mental duress from which he suffered robbed him of the power to freely choose between right and wrong, and the alleged act was so connected with the mental disease as to be the result only of that disease. Such people would not be deterred by criminal sanctions. This is also called the "irresistible impulse" test, and it, too, met with resistance.

Because of problems with these formulations, in 1954 a new ruling attempted to revise the idea of insanity. Also known as the "product test," the Durham rule stated that "an accused is not criminally responsible if his unlawful act was the product of a mental disease or defect." In other words, did the mental disease or defect exist at the time of the offense, and was the offense its direct result? While this test removed the legal strictures, it lacked defining guidelines.

With the M'Naghten Rule too narrow and the Durham rule too broad, the American Law Institute created a new standard in 1961 as part of its Model Penal Code, to which most states turned: "A person is not responsible for criminal conduct if at the time of such conduct as a result of mental disease or defect he lacks substantial capacity either to appreciate the criminality of his conduct or to conform his conduct to the requirements of the law." The key word was "substantial," which loosened some of the previous restrictions. A defendant needed to understand the nature of his offense and be able to conform it to the law. A second paragraph specifically excluded "psychopathic personality" from this formulation.

However, after John Hinckley was found not guilty by reason of insanity in 1982 after shooting President Reagan, the outcry meant a new reform:

the Insanity Defense Reform Act of 1984. It removed the volitional prong and returned to the more cognitive-centered test of the M'Naghten Rule.

In short, a mental disease is a mental illness, and a defect is any mental condition that cannot be improved. Legal definitions and procedures vary on this highly controversial defense, but most defendants acquitted by reason of insanity are actually diagnosed as psychotic or under some temporary form of mental breakdown.

Guilty but Mentally Ill

Michigan instituted this legal standard in 1975 in an attempt to decrease the number of insanity acquittals, and some thirteen states have followed suit. Juries are given choices among guilty, not guilty, not guilty by reason of insanity, and guilty but mentally ill. The latter means that the defendant committed the act, did not meet the standard to be declared insane, but nevertheless is mentally ill. The defendent gets the same sentence as if he was guilty, but he may be confined and treated in a different place. Generally, he must be incarcerated in a place where he can receive psychiatric treatment.

In such cases, the mental health professional must do a thorough insanity evaluation, including looking for evidence of other mental illnesses that would meet the guilty but mentally ill standard, according to the state's mental health codes.

> **Quick Definitions**
> - **Automatism:** committing a crime while unconscious
> - **Diminished capacity:** a mental disorder that diminishes control over behavior or impulses
> - **Affirmative defense:** having a defensible reason for the crime
> - **Intoxication:** committing a crime under the influence of a substance
> - **Infanticide/Neonaticide:** killing of one's child due to postpartum mental stress thought by some to be a form of temporary insanity

Other Mitigating States
Automatism

In 1955 a man inexplicably attacked his ten-year-old son. He called him to a window, struck him in the head with a mallet, tossed the boy out the window, and then drove away. He was seized with a feeling of dread that something had happened, so he drove home and was arrested. The defense at his trial was that a brain tumor had caused a state of automatism, and therefore he was not responsible for his actions. He lacked *mens rea*, so he was acquitted, but this was not an insanity acquittal (although there have been cases in which automatism caused by a mental disease were considered "insane automatism").

Some criminal acts may be committed involuntarily, such as while sleep-walking or as the result of a head injury. Such crimes get at the *actus reus* component of criminal responsibility. This defense does not work if it can be shown that the defendant had this condition on previous occasions and did not take steps to remedy it. It is a rare defense but was used not long ago in Arizona. Scott Falater stabbed his wife forty-four times and then drowned her in their swimming pool. He then went inside, washed off his hands, and stashed his bloody clothing into the trunk of his car. He claimed that he was sleepwalking and did not know what he was doing. In that case, he had no intent to do what he did. Apparently, he did have a history of sleepwalking but nevertheless, he was convicted of first-degree murder.

Yet in Canada, a man who drove to the home of his in-laws and killed one of them successfully used the same defense. In 1987 twenty-three-year-old Kenneth Parks savagely beat to death his mother-in-law and father-in-law with a tire iron and then stabbed them each with a knife. His father-in-law survived. Parks claimed he was asleep during the entire episode. He got into his car, drove to the police, and said that he had killed two people. Somehow, he got the medical experts to agree that he had not had voluntary control over his actions. He was acquitted.

Diminished Capacity

The American Law Institute Model Penal Code specifies the following four degrees of culpability in a crime:

1. purpose
2. knowledge
3. recklessness
4. negligence

Because of these different ways of mentally participating in a crime, a defendant can give evidence that focuses on *mens rea* without having to claim insanity. He can say he did not purposely or knowingly commit the crime or that he could not meaningfully premeditate it. It could win him a lesser verdict, such as manslaughter, instead of first- or second-degree murder.

This is not the same as the diminished responsibility doctrine, which is closer to a temporary insanity defense. This is a mental disorder that is not full-blown psychosis but which diminishes control over forming the *mens rea* for the offense. This is where designer defenses come into the picture. At times, diminished responsibility and diminished capacity are used interchangeably, which contributes to the general confusion on the subject, but writers can check with attorneys in their state to determine the proper legal wording.

Half of the states allow some clinical testimony on diminished capacity but generally with some restrictions. Perhaps the most famous trial involving this plea, which took place in 1978, was when Dan White shot and killed San Francisco Mayor George Moscone and supervisor Harvey Milk. White had resigned his supervisory position and when he could not get it back, he loaded a .38 revolver and went to the mayor's office. He emptied nine bullets into the two men. His attorneys argued in what has become known as the Twinkie defense that his diet of junk food had chemically altered his brain, making it impossible for him to form rational judgments. Thus he could not harbor malice or deliberate a crime. He was found guilty of voluntary manslaughter. He served less than five years in prison. In 1982 California voters abolished the diminished capacity defense.

Affirmative Defenses

These include self-defense, entrapment, acting under duress, and being provoked. These defenses acknowledge the crime but offer reason to acquit based on strong mitigating factors.

Intoxication

Voluntary intoxication is when a person inexperienced with the effects of substances consumes drugs or alcohol and then commits a crime. If that person can prove she did not know the risks, then she may be able to enter a diminished capacity plea. Involuntary intoxication occurs when someone was forced to consume a substance and thus had no choice in the matter. A third form of intoxication defense involves chronic use of psychoactive substances.

Infanticide/Neonaticide

Nearly half of all child murders occur in the first twenty-four hours of the child's birth. Women who kill their infant children have pleaded a form of postpartum insanity. Some also claim to be victims of battered woman syndrome, in which they develop a certain form of helplessness that disturbs their judgment. The idea behind such a defense is that the offender underwent a form of character change and committed an act that was not normal for her. England is more lenient about this defense than the United States, where inconsistencies from state to state make this issue something of a legal hot potato. Juries seem to take into consideration that birth can be traumatic, but some cases appear to be the result of kids who kill babies to hide their shame from parents or just to relinquish responsibility.

The 1998 case of Tanya Hudson in Florida (retried in 2000) got national attention. This twenty-four-year-old woman gave birth on a floor in her parents' home and then placed the child underneath some clothing in a closet. She said the baby girl was born dead, but an autopsy contradicted this. Hudson was charged with first-degree murder, although she was convicted only of manslaughter. Her attempt at using the battered woman syndrome failed (it was strongly challenged by the prosecution's psychologist), and she was sentenced to four years in prison—a light sentence for killing a human being.

Mental State at the Time of the Offense and Criminal Responsibility Evaluations

The burden of proof for insanity rests on the defense. With a preponderance of the evidence or beyond a reasonable doubt (depending on the state), the defense has to counter the assumption that the person is sane.

The job of a mental health expert witness in a violent crime is to determine the defendant's mental state at the time of the offense. This is different from a competency hearing, which centers on the defendant's present mental state. The results of a mental state at the time of the offense assessment determine the type of defense that can be supported with mental health records. The choices include insanity, automatism, diminished capacity, character defenses, affirmative defenses, and substance abuse. All require an assessment of the client's mental state when the crime was committed. That means an investigation must be launched to map the client's thought processes, sense of reality, cognitive skills, and behavior leading up to and during the alleged crime.

The Mental State at the Time of the Offense Screening Evaluation is an interview device that assists evaluators in making determinations about the psychological functioning of the defendant during the time the crime was committed, specifically to see if he had a significant mental abnormality. A negative evaluation would mean there are no further grounds for a defense of insanity.

There are three sections in this examination: The first collects historical information about the defendant, the second focuses on the offense, and the third involves assessing the defendant's present mental status. Each section lists the goals that need to be achieved rather than offering specific questions. Any information gained with the exam can be supplemented with other records. The interview takes about an hour.

Section one covers the person's history of the following:
- bizarre behavior and disturbance of affect
- convulsive disorders
- mental retardation
- episodic disorders
- neuropsychological conditions

Section two takes information from both the defendant and from other sources on what happened
- leading up to the offense
- during the offense
- after the offense

The third section involves any kind of mental status exam to get at the person's state of mind at the time of the interview itself.

After all the data is collected, the mental health professional makes a judgment as to whether the defendant has a mental abnormality that might have affected his behavior at the time of the offense. That does not mean it necessarily impaired the person's functioning. If there is no evidence of that, then insanity is not an option.

No psychological test has been sufficiently standardized to deliver a definite opinion, and behavior during an evaluation only goes so far. A more substantial approach involves getting the following information:

- events and observations about the crime, including all sworn witness reports
- the defendant's memory of the event, including transcripts of any statements or confessions and all observations during a clinical interview
- statements from witness about all occurrences preceding the event
- results from a full psychological evaluation, which may include a Forensics-Only Assessment Instrument, which we'll discuss in the following section

Rogers Criminal Responsibility Assessment Scale (R-CRAS)

The Rogers Criminal Responsibility Assessment Scale is a structured scale that attempts to assess and quantify key symptoms of organic impairment, major mental illness, evidence of low intellectual function, anxiety, impulsivity, and cognitive control at the time of the offense. Testing for thirty different variables, each of which is rated on a numerical scale from 0 to 5 or 6, it goes into such behaviors as evidence of planning the offense, awareness of criminality, reported self-control over the behavior, and evidence of loss of control due to psychosis. In other words, in a formal manner, it attempts to get at the mental state at the time of the offense and provide the best type of information for making legal decisions, particularly about diminished capacity or insanity. It is used more as a general template for insanity evaluations than as a specific measure; it provides a framework for organizing clinical data.

To use the R-CRAS effectively, the examiner first prepares background material on situational factors, police reports, and a case history, which includes all other assessments and a description of behavior prior to, during, and after the offense. The patient's self-reports are then rated on a progressive scale for numerous factors under the following classifications:

- reliability

- the possibility of malingering
- organicity (intoxication or brain damage)
- psychopathology (*DSM* disorders)
- cognitive control (specifically, loss of control)
- behavioral control (ability to choose)
- awareness of wrongfulness
- capacity for self-care

This assessment device leaves a lot of room for clinical judgment, including errors, so whether or not to use it depends on the mental health professional's preference.

Regardless of the devices used, one of the most important jobs of the mental health professional during an insanity evaluation is to gather third-party information. The police and attorney notes are important but so are developmental histories. People who have known the defendant will have some experience with aberrant mental disorders and may know something about his behavior before and after the offense. Other important factors include the following:

- early childhood illnesses
- school misconduct reports/probation reports
- grades throughout his school years
- family history of mental illness or criminal behavior
- marital history
- social relationships
- medical and psychiatric records
- psychosexual history

A great many clues about character and what the person is likely or unlikely to do can be found in his personal history. Whether he has had past episodes of what could be considered psychotic behavior will also be evident.

Only a fraction of defendants easily meet the insanity requirement. Similarly, only a small number who come in for evaluation are obviously sane. Most fall into an ambiguous range. Sometimes the mental health professional cannot state an opinion, even after extensive examination, and he must reveal this to whoever hired him.

Insanity Defenses

Someone found not guilty by reason of insanity or guilty but mentally incompetent will generally fall into one of the following categories.

• **Mental deficiency:** This is a profoundly retarded person who lacks the capacity to comprehend what he has done. IQ tests provide the support for this diagnosis.

• **Neuropsychological defect:** Brain lesions, tumors, and other types of organic disturbance may be influential in the commission of a crime. These dysfunctions play a part in impulsivity, disruption of judgment, and diminished awareness. Brain injuries are evident in many serial offenders.

• **Emotional disturbance:** The person must be shown to have had such a disturbance as to be unable to appreciate what he did or to be unable to refrain from it. Psychosis alone is not necessarily relevant in the legal proceedings. A schizophrenic who chooses not to take his medication and who subsequently pushes someone in front of a train hardly wins a jury's sympathy.

• **Extreme emotional disturbance:** This category is tantamount to temporary psychosis at the time of the offense. It must be so severe that the offender did not understand the nature of his crime or was unable to exert his will to refrain.

Conditions that can contribute to what's known as partial or temporary insanity include the following:
• personality disorders
• epilepsy
• dissociative states
• post-traumatic stress disorder
• battered woman syndrome/learned helplessness
• impulse disorders (the impulse to steal, for example)

Psychologists are generally called to testify about these conditions, both during the defense and rebuttal phases of a trial. Sometimes (but not often) the conditions acquire the status of insanity, depending on how serious the impairment. Such defenses are always challenged unless resolved in plea bargains.

Competency vs. Insanity

To reiterate, competency and insanity should not be confused. One focuses on present ability and knowledge of the court procedure, while the other focuses on the mental state specific to the time of the offense.

A woman who was arrested for making terrorist threats was judged competent to stand trial, although psychological tests made it clear that she was intellectually deficient, delusional, and paranoid. How is this possible?

She understood what went on in court, who the personnel were, and what might happen to her, but she did not appreciate that what she had done was wrong. She had told a reporter who had done a series of stories on mental patients on the television news that if he appeared again, she would have to kill him. She repeated this threat several times, so she was arrested. She admitted to making the statements, but did not understand why it was not okay to have done so. She persisted in her delusion that the reporter meant her harm and that she needed to eliminate him. It is not clear whether she would have acted on her delusion, but her thoughts and reality processing were disturbed to the point that she clearly was psychotic.

She was found not guilty by reason of insanity and sent to a state hospital for a year, where she received treatment.

Sample Insanity Cases

A woman murdered her husband in what she described as a manic episode—temporary insanity. After the incident, she was hospitalized in a disorganized state. Although they had been separated, she claimed that she loved him. There appeared to be no clear motive for such an assault.

The mental health professional for the defense was the woman's own treating psychiatrist, who had records of treating her manic episodes. However, the mental health professional for the prosecution collected records and third-party testimony that indicated something quite different. The clinical interview showed no evidence of mania, but reports showed that she was taking lithium to balance mood swings from past manic episodes that had put her in the hospital. If she had taken it conscientiously, this would be inconsistent with a manic burst of aggression. In therapy sessions leading up to the offense, there was no sign of manic symptoms. The defendant was successful and competent in her business, and any aberration would have been noticed. Colleagues reported none.

In therapy the defendant showed verbal hostility over the separation but did not make threats. One of her children admitted that the mother and the victim had argued moments before the shooting. She also had asked her son to load a gun that she kept in the closet, and her reasons for having it loaded (protection) were inconsistent with actual events that she claims made her nervous.

After collecting these statements, the mental health professional found no evidence of temporary insanity. The woman's assault appeared to be the result of anger at her husband.

Edmund Kemper III murdered his grandparents when he was sixteen and was sentenced to five years in a hospital for the criminally insane. After the treatment, he successfully petitioned to have his records sealed. Later he was examined by psychiatrists and found to be sane—even as he had parts of one of his victims in the trunk of his car. To pass the test, he had memorized responses to twenty-eight standardized psychological tests. Yet he went on to murder seven more people, including his mother, and to have sex with the decapitated heads. At his murder trial, his insanity plea failed to persuade a jury; he was found guilty.

Yet Wisconsin serial killer Ed Gein was acquitted by reason of insanity. In the 1950s, he mutilated, skinned, and murdered at least two women, and he also robbed graves. He made some of the skin into a garment he could wear and kept genitalia in boxes in his home. Abnormally attached to his deceased mother, he appeared to be trying to identify with her. He went to a state psychiatric institute, where he eventually died.

Although the insanity plea is used infrequently and fails more often than succeeds, it clearly shows inconsistency in its application. Some clever psychopaths have managed an early release via this route. It may be that insanity cannot be assessed in any reliable standardized manner. Because of this, some people who should be judged insane will go to prison, and some who are

Policemen Search the Littered Kitchen of Ed Gein

In this kitchen, authorities found human skulls and other parts of human bodies, all of which was used as evidence against Ed Gein. In the shed near Gein's house, police also found the butchered body of Mrs. Bernice Worden. Writers can use photographs like this one to help create a realistic setting in their fiction.

not insane will be treated as if they are. This is an unfortunate consequence of the ambiguity in mental health issues.

A Model for Fiction

One of the best trial scenarios for fiction writers to study is that of Erik and Lyle Menendez, the brothers who slaughtered their parents in 1989 in Los Angeles. They both went through two trials, since the first trials ended in hung juries. In both sets of trials, mental health professionals testified for the prosecution and defense. In an odd twist, one of the mental health professionals for the prosecution had been a therapist for one of the brothers! There were several ethics violations by mental health professionals and a real battle over a new defense: the battered person syndrome. However, several affirmative defenses were added, too, to try to negate malice aforethought, and it was very difficult to sort through it all. There was even a profiler on hand to describe a "disorganized" crime scene and the probability that the crime was not planned. (She was wrong.)

Briefly, the boys shot their parents one night, called 911 to report intruders, and suggested possible Mafia connections. They then went on a spending spree while investigators moved in on them. Soon they were arrested and tried individually.

A former therapist undermined the defense strategy of portraying the boys as victims of verbal and sexual abuse who feared for their lives by describing the account of the murders in the brothers' own words. He said Erik had confessed they had wanted to kill their parents and had been inspired by a method from a movie they had seen. They killed their mother because they did not think she could emotionally survive her husband's murder. The cross-examination of this testimony attempted to shred the therapist's credibility, yet his words still had weight.

The defense then used a professor to discuss the effects of psychological abuse and a clinician who interviewed Lyle in prison for sixty hours. The clinician based his belief in Lyle's story based on his "affect," which included shame and reluctance. The prosecution thought the defense experts were so poor that she failed to call her own in rebuttal. That was a mistake; she misjudged the jury's degree of sympathy. The defense then used another psychologist to discuss the notion of learned helplessness, but on cross-examination she was forced to admit that the anecdotes the brothers told about other abuse were uncorroborated. (In other words, this mental health professional did not do her homework, and there was no proof of what she claimed had happened.)

When after all this the juries hung, a second trial was ordered, which took place in 1995. This time the Menendezes were retried together in front of a single jury. The judge ordered the defense not to use the battered person syndrome theory, since he believed it was not supported by proof. The defense attorneys then used a theory of self-defense, which amounted to nearly the same as the original theory. Yet juries had a more difficult time accepting that two grown men purchased guns and planned a double murder as an act of self-defense. No one could adequately explain why they didn't just leave and go live elsewhere.

Forensic psychiatrist Park Dietz evaluated Erik for the prosecution. He found no evidence of post-traumatic stress disorder. After hearing the results, the judge ruled that the parents' alleged psychological abuse was irrelevant to what the two young men had done. The jury was to evaluate the crime without reference to it.

It's likely that the initial defense strategies, aimed more at winning sympathy than proving the facts, had worked on the jury emotionally. By the second trial, the proceedings were more sober and the judge less inclined to allow the testimony of mental health professionals who blamed abuse.

In the course of the legal proceedings, the defense used six mental health experts and several different types of diminished capacity and affirmative defenses, which probably made things too complicated for the juries. It also tended to make psychological assessment appear to be a matter more of opinion than of fact.

In the end, the brothers were convicted of two counts each of first-degree murder, which got them sentenced to life in prison.

This is an excellent example of how mental health professionals are used, cross-examined, and rebutted in court and of how judges rule on social science and mental health testimony.

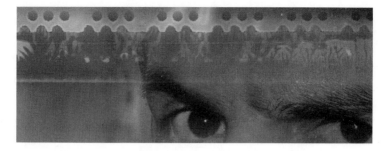

8

Crime Control

Purposes of Punishment

There are several goals associated with the idea of punishing crime, some of which involve or require the input of mental health professionals.

- **Deterrence:** The punishment given to an offender is assumed to be sufficient to discourage others from repeating this offense. It may also deter the person from repeating the same crime once released.
- **Retribution:** Offenders should get what they deserve in return for what they have done.
- **Rehabilitation:** The hope in delivering punishment is that it will have the effect of reforming offenders so they can change their ways and develop new values and skills toward making better lives.
- **Restitution:** Some sentences involve making offenders compensate victims for harms the offenders have caused.
- **Incapacitation:** Incarceration gets offenders off the streets and out of the community, and presumably they will age and mature past their criminal peak.

Most prisons end up being punitive, set up merely to keep offenders out of the community. The offenders are exposed more to criminal behavior and attitudes than to rehabilitative efforts.

Only the first goal, deterrence, does not involve clinical issues. How culpable an offender is can involve extensive examinations similar to the insanity defense, including how restitution might affect him. So can the issue of dangerousness, which may determine how long a sentence is. In addition, wherever rehabilitation still exists, mental health professionals may have recommendations. Mental health professionals may also be involved in researching the effects of certain prison systems on offenders and in making recommendations for change.

For example, social psychologists Craig Haney and Philip Zimbardo surveyed twenty-five years of prison reform. They documented evidence that society has developed a more hard-nosed and dehumanizing attitude toward criminals.

Other studies have focused on crime control in the juvenile population. One program involved allowing offenders to admit to wrongdoings without becoming outcasts. It appears to be cutting down on recidivism. Counseling itself seems to have little effect, as do the "Scared Straight" programs, where lifers tell kids what happens in prison. Mental health professionals are doing further work to learn more about appropriate socialization procedures.

Sentencing Recommendations

Determinate sentencing imposes a certain sentence for a certain crime. It focuses on the offense, limits judicial discretion, and provides a predictable schema. Indeterminate sentencing focuses more on the offender, taking into account mitigating factors and the need for extended treatment. The primary complaint about indeterminate sentencing is the great disparity among sentences for the same crime. States are varied on this practice, but in 1984 the federal government required determinate sentences for federal crimes.

If a court imposes a sentence, it expects a presentence report unless waived by the defendant. A parole officer prepares it, using information from the defendant's personal history and evaluations. It includes alternative sentencing plans and a recommendation. The mental health professional plays a role in this by providing information relevant to culpability and to predictions about future actions. For example, a psychologist prepared a report explaining why a jail sentence would work better for a certain individual than the boot camp the judge was considering.

Mental health professionals do play stronger roles where sentences are indeterminate (a minimum time is established at sentencing but the maximum time is to be determined later). Determinate sentences (a sentence whose length is established at the time of sentencing) de-emphasize risk assessment and rehabilitation.

Yet even in determinate sentencing, prison terms are decided according to certain factors, such as aggravating circumstances, routine crimes, and mitigating circumstances. Aggravating factors include the following:

- excessive use of force
- cruelty
- causing body harm
- threats
- multiple victims
- the defendant acted as leader in a crime

Mitigating circumstances include the following:

- being a passive participant
- having a mental impairment
- a victim who provoked the crime
- a crime motivated by necessity
- a defendant who protected someone or made restitution

Such statutes invite clinical participation, generally in the realm of proving information about mitigating circumstances for a reduced sentence. If the mental health professional can show evidence that the defendant lacked substantial capacity for judgment when the offense was carried out, or if there is evidence from circumstances such as growing up in a gang atmosphere, then the court may show some leniency.

Some criminal types get special sentencing provisions because they are thought to be different from the general criminal population. Repeat offenders and sexual offenders, for example, may get different treatments. The "three strikes and you're out" rulings involve enhanced sentencing after a third felony, and multiple sexual offenses can get treatment of indeterminate length. Mental health professionals are thought to be able to assess these types of offenders. This gets into issues of the prediction of dangerousness and risk assessment.

Assessment of Culpability

Mental health professionals can contribute to the legal process on the issue of sentencing in three ways.

1. Make the trier(s) of fact aware of situational factors involved in the commission of the crime that removed choice from the offender.
2. Provide facts about the offender's life history.
3. Prevent the trier(s) of fact from misunderstanding the victim's perception.

Sentencing in some crimes depends on the seriousness of the act. The mental health professional may remind the court about the offender's mental state at the time of the offense and may be allowed to offer further explanation. Factors such as family background, immaturity, neurological impairment, or stress may play a strong role. An offender's life story, if it contains difficulties that mitigate culpability, may be brought in more forcefully at this point. Juries having to dole out the most severe offenses are generally influenced by mitigating factors, as the jury was in the sentencing phase of the Menendez trial.

It may also be the case that a victim may have some say in what a "just" sentence would be. Victims may present a Victim Impact Statement. The way victims are interviewed for this may influence their responses, and a mental health professional can point out how victims can be affected. Mental health professionals can also describe how retributive thinking can influence victims to be more punitive than would ordinarily be the case for that type of crime.

Risk Assessment

Gary Gilmore had spent most of his youth in reform school and prison for numerous delinquent activities. It seemed that whenever he got out, he was arrested again. After being released in 1973 and then committing armed robbery, he was back in the courtroom. He asked permission to address the court, which was granted. Gilmore said that he had been locked up for the past nine and a half years, with only two years of freedom since he was fourteen. He argued that "you can keep a person locked up too long" and that "there is an appropriate time to release somebody or to give them a break. . . . I stagnated in prison a long time, and I have wasted most of my life. I want freedom, and I realize that the only way to get it is to quit breaking the law. . . . I've got problems, and if

Killer Gary Gilmore on His Way to Sentencing

After turning fourteen, Gary Gilmore only spent two years of his adult life outside prison. He claimed so much time in prison affected his ability to obey the law. Once set free, however, it was only a few months before he killed two men. This picture was taken right before the judge set the date for his execution.

© Bettmann/CORBIS

you sentence me to additional time, I'm going to compound them." It was both a plea for mercy and a threat.

The judge told Gilmore that he had already been convicted once for armed robbery, a serious charge, so there was no option but to sentence him to another nine years. Gilmore was hurt and angry. As promised, he became more violent while in prison and tried to kill himself several times. He was transferred to a maximum security penitentiary. Then, only three years into his sentence, a parole plan was worked out. Gilmore was released in April 1976, and by July he was back in prison for the cold-blooded murder of two men.

The question is, was Gilmore such a risk that even he did not know how dangerous he was, or might giving him a break at the time he asked have made a difference?

This is the question that a mental health professional faces—albeit not quite so dramatically—when asked to make an assessment of what could happen to a defendant if released. Underlying all sentencing structures is the implicit consideration of an offender's potential to do harm, so one key issue in risk assessment is community safety. The other is the hope to rehabilitate an offender who might then make a contribution to the community. Thus, indeterminate sentencing requires even more understanding of violence potential, because how many years a person may serve for a crime is directly related to these individual factors.

In fact, the Supreme Court has upheld the constitutionality of permitting the death sentence based on predictions of future violence. In a 1983 case known as *Barefoot v. Estelle,* clinical testimony on this issue was allowed. Thomas Barefoot had burned down a barn and then shot and killed a police officer. He was convicted and then subjected to a hearing for the death penalty. Part of the decision was to be based on whether the defendant posed a threat of future dangerousness. The state was supposed to prove this beyond a reasonable doubt. The prosecution relied on the testimony of two psychiatrists who were given hypothetical situations to consider that were similar to what had happened. The psychiatrists were asked if the individual in the situation would probably commit future violent acts. Both said yes. When witnesses came forward to say that Barefoot's reputation in the community was bad, the judge sentenced him to death.

Although the American Psychiatric Association protested the unreliability of this kind of mental health testimony, the Court cited precedents. Fortunately, risk assessment is improving with further research, and the predictions now utilize both clinical judgment and statistical data. The best predictions, however, are for short-term rather than long-term risk.

It was once the case that a mental health expert used her best clinical judgment to try to determine whether someone was going to repeat his violent behavior if let out into the community. Those people would be committed involuntarily for their own good. However, the psychiatrists were right in only one out of three cases. That means that there were many "false positives"—people were committed who would not be violent—and "false negatives"—people allowed to go free who then committed violence. The error rate was unacceptable.

In the eighties, a number of studies were undertaken to develop instruments that would improve the percentage of correct assessments of dangerousness. Instead of focusing on dangerousness itself, the studies emphasized what they called risk factors.

Interviews and inventories were developed to determine whether a defendant was a psychopath (which had a high correlation for recidivism), whether he was sexually deviant (another good predictor), how impulsive he was, whether he had a character disorder or mental illness, whether he had paranoid delusions, what his school record was, whether he had committed crimes as a juvenile, and what his past history of violence was. Out of these studies came guidelines for making predictions based on facts and logic rather than on intuition or psychoanalytic assumptions.

Risk management, i.e., devising programs that might help a person avoid repeating his crimes, focuses on those factors that yield to intervention, such as substance abuse or delusions. What becomes important in risk assessment is the individual's social support, living arrangements, and access to treatment.

After looking at the issues, we'll get back to the Gilmore case.

Dangerousness

Dangerousness has been a central issue in the legal/mental health arena for many years, yet establishing an empirical body of data from which to make accurate predictions has been difficult. Let's look at the four problems of dealing with dangerousness.

1. The Legal Definition

The definition of dangerousness varies from one context to another. It might be about emotional harm or physical harm; it could be about harm to property. The prediction may rely on items that range from various statements the offender has made to the results of psychological tests to actual past aggression. Some jurisdictions require proof of dangerousness, while others don't. There are no clear or consistent guidelines for a mental health professional to follow.

2. Confusing Research Literature

Research ranges from anecdotal or highly theoretical to experimental or statistical. Many of the studies suffer from limitations in method and interpretation, and there is little consensus on what produces the most valid results—especially for use in the courtroom.

3. Personal Biases

Mental health professionals who follow certain theories may make dangerousness part of their framework. For example, dangerousness may be viewed as a personality trait or a manifestation of a certain physiological or psychological pathology. Situational variables have received less attention but cannot be ruled out as influential. Sometimes dangerousness is linked exclusively to the crime with which the person has been charged. Racial, gender, and cultural biases may also influence a mental health professional's judgment, as does morality and even the likeableness of the defendant.

4. Fear of Responsibility

If an offender is released on the basis of a clinical opinion and that opinion turns out to be erroneous because the offender harmed someone, then the mental health professional may suffer consequences ranging from bad publicity to lawsuits. There is incentive, then, to be conservative, which means a potentially longer sentence for someone who may not actually pose a threat.

Another death penalty case in Texas, *Estelle v. Smith* in 1981, indicated a real need for standards. On the basis of a brief mental status examination, the state's psychiatrist testified that the defendant, Smith, was a "severe sociopath." Based more or less on an intuitive sense of the man's apparent lack of remorse for being an accomplice (not the killer) in a murder, the doctor stated that Smith would certainly commit other crimes. The psychiatric assessment was poorly rendered. The mental health community protested that it was unethical and not representative of responsible assessment, and both the courts and the psychological community made risk assessment procedures more rigorous.

The three basic approaches to dangerousness are as follows:

1. clinical
2. actuarial
3. anamnestic

The first approach relies on personal judgment and experience, which is unsystematic and has been shown to be fairly unreliable. Actuarial prediction identifies the specific criteria used—age, gender, race, IQ—and assigns weights to each based on significance. It does not consider case-specific information, and the statistical analysis may be too complicated for a jury. The third approach depends on factors that appear to have influenced a particular individual's show of aggression or destruction of property—such as a past record of criminal activity that shows patterns.

According to those researchers who have devoted considerable time to the subject, risk assessment research upon which judgments are to be made should meet seven criteria.

1. Dangerousness must be segregated into component parts: risk factors, harm, and likelihood of occurrence.
2. A rich array of risk factors must be assessed from multiple domains in the offender's life.
3. Harm must be scaled in terms of seriousness and must be assessed with multiple measures.
4. The probability estimate of risk must be acknowledged to change over time and context.
5. Priority must be given to actuarial research.
6. Research must be done in large and broadly representative samples.
7. The goal must be management as well as assessment.

All of these criteria are met in a study done in the 1990s by the MacArthur Research Network on Mental Health and the Law. The MacArthur Risk Assessment Study devised a comprehensive list of risk factors across the following four domains:

1. dispositional (demographics, personality, cognitive)
2. historical (various histories and records)
3. contextual (social support, stressors, means for violence)
4. clinical (*DSM* diagnosis, present functioning, substance abuse)

The relevant factors within these domains (1) have been associated with violence in prior research, (2) are believed by experienced clinicians to be associated with violence, and (3) are hypothesized to be associated with violence by existing theories of violence or mental disorder. This listing included factors not previously studied, such as social support, impulsiveness, anger control, psychopathy, and delusions.

Experts in these fields developed risk assessment instruments, such as Robert Hare's twenty-item Psychopathy Checklist-Revised (PCL-R), to assist with measurement and prediction. Of the four domains, only contextual and clinical were deemed relevant to risk management (as opposed to assessment), because these factors could be changed. All of the factors were field-tested and then submitted to a full-scale study, measuring the criterion variables by using official arrest and hospital records, regular self-reports over a one-year period, and collateral reports from knowledgeable informants.

It should be noted that there is no standard calculus for deciding how best to assess the factors in a given case, because there's an issue of individuality. In general, it is better when testifying in court to focus on a limited number of factors that seem most relevant to the case than to try to do a comprehensive analysis that will overwhelm the triers of fact.

Relevant Factors

In the general population, males are at a higher risk of becoming dangerous than females—particularly in adolescence and early adulthood.

The availability of weapons and certain attitudes toward guns also increases risk. Where the social support network for pro-social behavior is lacking, it is unlikely a mental health professional would suggest that the offender be returned to the community. Also, if the offender has shown aggression toward a range of victims or had a history of multiple assaults, that increases the risk of repeat offenses.

Despite protests by mental health groups over the years at the stereotype of the schizophrenic offender, there is a moderate association between current diagnosis of active symptoms of a major psychosis—especially one with paranoid delusions or thought control—and violence in the community. This risk increases with substance abuse and with the refusal to take medication. Although the violence may be aimed more often at someone in the home than at a stranger, the psychosis must still be taken into consideration in risk assessment. Several serial killers have had obvious psychotic disorders with persecutory delusions that seem to have influenced their violent acts. The Unabomber is a good example.

Another factor involved with increased dangerousness is substance abuse. Alcohol and drugs have been found to significantly contribute to violence, especially when the weather is hot.

Past offenses and a psychopathic personality are the two most relevant factors in risk prediction. In particular, someone who has been diagnosed with conduct disorder during childhood or adolescence and who shows repeated antisocial behavior is at high risk to become a repeated adult offender. (The different types of conduct disorders are examined in detail in chapter ten.) Association with delinquent peer groups is an added problem, since this becomes part of the social support group and the peer groups tend to defy authority.

Psychopaths are more likely to commit violence, use a weapon, and be aggressive in prison than other types of criminals. Following their release, they are more likely to commit other crimes, and they show more variety in the types of crimes they commit. They are more likely to prefer sadistic techniques and to be motivated by gain rather than arousal. They need stimulation, use massive denial, and relate to the world on the basis of power. On the Rorschach, psychopaths tend to create predatory symbolism, such as a clawed butterfly, out of otherwise benign stimuli. They seem alert to aggressors and to prey.

An impressive portrayal of a narcissistic psychopath was a character played by John Larroquette on several linked episodes of *The Practice*—and he *did* recidivate! His defense team got him off on murder, and he then killed again. Hannibal Lecter did, too.

Sexual sadists who are also psychopaths often coerce an accomplice, plan their crime carefully, and are motivated by grandiose rehearsal fantasies in which they "see" the crime performed over and over. Their relationships are generally defined in terms of threat and counterthreat, and they are less anxious about punishment. Sadism is found to be positively correlated with recidivism, as is the inappropriate age choice of a victim. According to the National Center for the Analysis of Violent Crime, rapists can be classified according to types that include the following:

- power-reassurance, who wants a consensual encounter
- power-assertive, who feels entitled

- anger-retaliatory, who is getting even with women
- anger-excitation, who is diminishing women's power

The last type will be most likely to recidivate, in part because their fantasies are complex, well entrenched, and resistant to treatments. They are sexually stimulated by the infliction of pain and resistant to the idea that they will be caught and punished.

Assessment Approaches

Several different types of studies exist that are developing risk assessment instruments. Some prominent examples follow.

One risk assessment instrument is the Self-Assessment of Reported Violence Inventory, which is based on the idea that it is important to observe a criminal's level of insight regarding his thoughts and feelings before, during, and after a violent act. His unwillingness or inability to evoke memories of what he was experiencing and thinking about during an act of violence suggests a poor prognosis. This kind of instrument depends for analysis on clinical observation and interpretation. One useful item unique to this inventory is a questionnaire for assessing attitudes about weapons, which can bring out responses that no other survey gets.

The Violence Risk Assessment Guide (VRAG) was developed in a program that began twenty-five years ago at the Oak Ridge maximum security psychiatric hospital in Ontario, Canada. Its developers claim that the VRAG is the most accurate risk assessment instrument available, far superior to clinical judgment. It's an actuarial instrument for the prediction of violent recidivism, which means it has tested variables relevant to prediction in relationship to an outcome variable (any new criminal charge for a violent offense). The researchers examined records of institutionalized offenders, including any violent conduct in the institution for which they would have been criminally charged had they done it in the community. Predictor variables numbered around fifty and reflected all those for which there was any empirical support for associations with violence. It also included variables without empirical support but to which clinicians attached significance, such as expressions of remorse.

After extensive testing and correlation analysis, the researchers came up with an assessment instrument that included twelve key variables, such as elementary school maladjustment, victim injury, *DSM* categories, and Psychopathy Checklist-Revised score, with a nine-point risk scale for scoring each item. Individuals at the upper end were almost certain to recidivate.

They then extended the use of the VRAG to sex offenders, which is the SORAG (Sex Offender Risk Assessment Guide). The SORAG has fourteen variables and is also scored on a nine-point scale.

An anamnestic approach would involve a thorough reconstruction of the offender's past history of violence, similar to the way an insanity evaluation might be done. A clinical interview is important to this, as is third-party data and archival information. The mental health professional making this evaluation will be looking for specific themes or repeated patterns that indicate how the violence gets instigated, how it is supported, and whether there are factors that could be changed for a more positive influence. Getting specific information provides a more valid recommendation for prediction and management.

To Let Him Go or Not Let Him Go

The question, then, is which of these approaches or instruments would be most helpful in making the decision in a case like Gary Gilmore?

There are limitations to any studies that rely on official records or self-reports, because both can be faulty, although self-report has been found to correct gaps in official data. Even so, it is not altogether reliable, either. Those studies that sacrifice depth (individual history) to breadth (statistics on a wide variety of factors) may also be missing something significant, although the same can be said of the reverse. It's important to note that risk factors in any individual's life fluctuate over time, so any study that fails to take this into account will have some reliability issues. Additionally, studies that utilize *DSM* categories incorporate the problems that the *DSM* has with empirical validation, prediction, and politics.

The insight-based assessment erroneously implies that insight translates into change, and a lack of insight might be attributable to other causal factors than a personality disorder. A case could be made for Gary Gilmore having "attachment issues" and possibly a character disorder. However, an insight-based inventory of his case misses the benefits of actuarial data, which would rely on his membership in a statistically significant population, e.g., juveniles who commit crimes, people who abuse alcohol, boys with violent fathers.

In contrast, the VRAG and SORAG developers are so set on having their actuarial data replace clinical judgment that they miss the benefits of case-specific information and of changes over time. While this kind of data gives more weight to situational variables than does clinical judgment, it does not account for variability within the data. It also fails to clearly distinguish between clinical and historical factors, and it is so attuned to past factors that it may disallow future changes such as one's living situation, employment, access to weapons, or social support system. An additional problem is that there is no true data for recidivism for the most violent offenders, because they are lifers and have never been released from confinement. In addition, the samples used to develop and cross-validate these instruments came from a particular psychiatric facility, so the value of many of the variables may be specific to that population. Also, the predictor variables were scored from file information that was old and based on categories from the *DSM-III*, which is outdated.

The best choice appears to be the MacArthur Foundation's list of factors, in part because it makes use of the Robert Hare's Psychopathy Checklist-Revised. The criteria are identified and weighted, the data categories are driven by empirical research that demonstrates risk, and the individual is assessed clinically for prior displays of aggressive behavior. This approach recognizes the most significant factors.

Given what we know of Gilmore's history and matching it against the risk factors listed on the MacArthur study, it appears that giving Gilmore his freedom would have only ensured repeated offenses—which tragically turned out to be the case. He

- showed numerous incidences of delinquency
- had poor anger management skills
- was twenty-seven years old
- was male
- came from a deprived social class
- had mental illness in both parents
- was highly impulsive
- was abused as a child

- had a poor record of school attendance
- showed a history of violence toward himself and others
- abused alcohol and drugs
- had access to guns

His social networks were mostly other criminals, and his family structure was unstable and far from law-abiding. Despite his plea, there appears to be little reason for optimism.

The fact is, Gilmore's armed robbery offense had occurred while he was already on a qualified probation plan, which allowed him to go to art school to see if he could live responsibly. He believed he would do something with this opportunity, but instead of registering for school his first day out, he got drunk, located a gun, and held up a convenience store. Thus, the very chance he was requesting had already been granted once. For reasons that seem to have been beyond his own comprehension, he had not taken advantage of it.

A risk assessment on Gilmore would have determined that even with support on a parole plan, it was unlikely he would have improved his behavior. No mental health professional educated in the risk assessment research today would have supported this plan.

Even so, at this stage in the research, dangerousness predictions have not been proven to be highly accurate, particularly within an ambiguous legal context. At best, a mental health professional ought to make recommendations about relative risk, with comprehensive information about the risk factors upon which she focuses in a given case. A mental health professional can also suggest ways for reducing the risk relevant to the individual's situation (e.g., social support networks, a community program, substance abuse programs, better living arrangements, supervision).

Capital Sentences

The stakes are high in capital cases, so mental health issues become all the more relevant—including competency to be executed.

Almost every state provides for the possibility that some offenders are incompetent to serve their sentences, specifically to be executed. This involves determining whether they are severely mentally disturbed. There are times, as in the case of *Perry v. Louisiana,* when a prisoner who seems perfectly placid while on medication chooses to go off and thus becomes too mentally ill to be executed. The question, then, becomes a matter of forcing the person back onto his medication so he can be killed or allowing him to remain unmedicated. No state allows the execution of someone deemed incompetent. It is a violation of the Eighth Amendment. The person must show an understanding of the nature and effect of the death penalty. In Perry's case, the trial and appellate courts ordered him to be forcibly medicated, but the United States Supreme Court vacated these orders, allowing medication only when a prisoner is considered dangerous to others. The Louisiana Supreme Court decided it was impermissible to forcibly medicate someone to render them competent merely for the purpose of execution.

In capital sentencing, the prosecution must prove at least one aggravating factor on a specific list. The defense may present any amount of mitigating information about character, treatability, and risk factors.

Some of the mitigating factors include the following.
- the defendant was under extreme emotional duress
- the defendant's capacity to appreciate what he did was impaired
- there were extenuating circumstances at the time of the offense
- the defendant suffers from a mental illness
- the defendant is no longer dangerous

When dangerousness is an issue, the Supreme Court has held that the defendant is entitled to psychiatric assistance.

A mental health professional who is called in but who was not a contributor to the presentence report should get access to it, as it may contain important information.

Risk Assessment in Fiction

A fairly exhaustive risk assessment analysis was made for Ted Kaczynski as part of his competency hearing. This involved citing his history of violence, paranoid delusions, suicide attempts, and reactive personality in an attempt to argue that Kaczynski be confined to a maximum security prison for life, segregated from other prisoners. (A plea bargain had saved him from the death penalty.) The defense had argued that it was too harsh. Thus, a mental health professional for the defense in a case like this might be pressured to underplay certain factors.

The most obvious role of a mental health professional for a tense fictional scenario is to make an unethical or mistaken prediction that frees a violent offender. Imagine if Kaczynski had been released because of some mental health professional's report!

Another important role for mental health professionals in the sentencing process is intervention and treatment. These are taken up in the next chapter.

9

Treatment and Rehabilitation

Assessment of Needs

Suggesting and providing treatment are the forensic roles most suited to mental health clinicians in terms of their orientation. They can use their training and education specifically to assist offenders in a therapeutic manner. For example, on the television show *Oz*, which features characters on an experimental floor in a maximum security prison called Emerald City, Sister Pete is a nun who runs the social work and counseling program. One man came in to talk about his difficulty in coming to terms with the fact that he had murdered someone, and he asked to see the crime scene photos. She arranged it and then did the necessary counseling when he was overcome. Another convict was having terrible nightmares, and a third was obsessed with a nurse.

Sister Pete decided to start a victim/offender program that brought together families of the victims with the offender himself, in an attempt to get closure and to force the offender to assess the human elements of his crime. In some cases, it worked; in other cases, it didn't. Yet her character showed what some mental health professionals end up doing in prison environments.

Aside from case management in prisons, mental health professionals may work in forensic hospitals or consult only in specific cases.

The types of offenders involved in regular supervised treatment generally suffer from mental disorders. They have been judged incompetent to proceed with a trial or have been acquitted for some form of diminished capacity or insanity. Referrals for mental health treatment come from attorneys or judges who sense something is amiss.

Youthful offenders who may change with positive intervention can also be referred for treatment. If intervention occurs before a serious offense, it can make the difference between a pro-social and an antisocial adult. For example, in the case of Roderick Ferrell mentioned in chapter two (see page 25), had he gotten some treatment in a juvenile facility for some of his earlier problems with animal cruelty and substance abuse, it is unlikely he would have felt so immune to arrest as to go kill an elderly couple.

Some offenses, such as serial arson, kleptomania, and substance abuse, signal psychological problems from the start. There are specific programs for many of these offenders.

Someone who has no criminal history but who suddenly commits a serious crime may have succumbed to a psychological problem due to stress, adult-onset illnesses, or some other treatable condition. If it is identified, a mental health professional can be helpful in correcting the situation and even in getting a transfer or early parole.

Treatment Evaluations

The treatment evaluation generally occurs at the time of sentencing. The offender's status is grouped into one of the following specific types of classification:

- need for substance abuse/addiction counseling
- need for attention to intelligence deficits
- need for education on a specific issue
- need for vocational training
- need for better social skills
- need for psychiatric drugs

How an offender gets classified is directly related to the results of psychological assessment tests, clinical interviews, structured questionnaires, and information about how well any given treatment works.

The National Institute of Corrections offers a manual for mental health professionals working within correctional institutions. The manual helps them decide which tests and treatment procedures to use with each classification area.

The mental health professional should aim for reducing risk in high risk individuals, identifying factors that are criminogenic, and focusing on skills development that may offer a different type of life for the offender. This approach has been shown to reduce the recidivism rate more effectively than focusing strictly on punishment and supervision—especially with juveniles.

For treatment suggestions regarding those offenders who may merit a more lenient sentence and actual release, the court wants to know the following information:

- the offender's motivation for treatment
- evidence of remorse
- the family and social situation
- history of past treatment and its outcomes
- past offense record
- evidence of mental disturbance or psychopathy
- the efficacy of the type of treatment suggested in a nonprison environment
- potential consequences to a community in the event the treatment does not work

In other words, the mental health professional hired to offer a consultation is providing risk management specifications. Some of the issues for an inexperienced mental health professional (who seems to pop up a lot in fiction) include the following:

- the tendency to view problem behavior as a manifestation of personal pathology rather than as the possible result of situational factors (so they overdiagnose)
- the failure to understand the limits of the prison system in terms of what can actually be done for an offender
- the mistake of linking an offender's participation in therapy with the criteria for termination of his sentence
- the attempt to make the ultimate legal decision rather than provide information toward that end

Violence Management

Offenders with impulsivity issues and tendencies toward violence have to be handled carefully, especially during violent episodes. An examining mental health professional needs to adopt certain types of management skills.

- know where the security personnel are
- remove anything that could be used as a weapon
- use calming influences, such as a quiet environment
- control the mood by pacing things slowly
- assess the need for antipsychotic drugs
- assess the need to transfer the offender to a more secure prison or just away from certain influences such as gangs
- assess for suicide risk (determine the presence of sadness, a suicide plan, or suicidal ideation)
- teach alternatives to violence (toward self or others)

Substance Abuse Screening

It once was the case that the top three crimes for which people were incarcerated were robbery, burglary, and murder. Now the prison population is predominantly comprised of people who have violated drug laws and committed theft. One-third of the prison population satisfies the American Psychiatric Association's criteria for substance dependency. Rehab programs for substance abuse involve mental health professionals. Accompanying substance abuse treatment are programs for anger management, conflict resolution, and dealing with anxiety.

Several screening devices and simple screening interviews exist for assessing substance abuse. The basic questions for alcoholism are:

- Do you drink?
- Have you ever had a problem with alcohol?
- Have you ever blacked out from drinking?
- Has drinking ever caused problems for you on the job or at home?

For any substance dependency, the basic questions are:

- What kinds of substance(s) do you use?
- Are you using it more often than you used to?
- Are you using more of it than you used to?

- Are you craving it more than you used to?
- Has the use of this substance impaired you in any way?
- Have there been any adverse consequences from using this substance?
- Do you tell people you use it less than you really do?
- Have you had trouble cutting back?
- Are you preoccupied with using it?
- Do you plan social occasions as a reason to use it?
- Do you have trouble seeing the consequences of your use of this substance?
- Do others cover for you?
- How old were you when you began to use it?
- Is there a family history of using this substance (or any other)?

Treatment in a correction setting focuses not only on the substance abuse issues but on potential problems with transition back into a community. Many offenders are unprepared for dealing with their former peers and neighborhoods, which tend to support their illegal activities. Relapse then becomes inevitable, unless the mental health professional in the correctional setting can follow through with a long-term plan.

Those programs with the most promise are behavioral and cognitive.

- **Controlled drinking approach:** This approach focuses on decreased use rather than total abstinence.
- **Community reinforcement:** Community reinforcement relies on positive and negative reinforcement to reshape behavior into a better form of coping. The offender identifies those people or situations that trigger addictive behavior and attempts to minimize contact with them. He also works on controlling urges and getting his support group involved in keeping him clean.
- **Supplementary services:** These services include counseling, educational support, parenting skills, stress-reduction training, vocational counseling, nutrition, and recreational opportunities.

Such programs, while somewhat effective, are scarce or poorly funded. Thus, it is up to mental health professionals to do more research and community education to assist in controlling crime and recidivism.

A great place to start would be the Supermax prisons, such as Oak Park Heights in Illinois. Supermax prisons are where the most violent prisoners are sent but where they can also get involved in pro-social programs. Generally in a Supermax, prisoners are locked in their cells twenty-three hours a day with only an hour for supervised exercise. At Oak Park Heights, however, they are allowed much more freedom if they agree to go through rehab programs. They can take classes, get counseling, learn vocational skills, and get degrees that will prepare them to change their lives for the better. They do all of this without guards, and in thirteen years of running the program, there have been no incidents. The inmates who have succeeded claim that the trust factor was a significant motivator.

Psychopharmacology

Treating people in a correctional setting who have mental illnesses, mood disorders, or personality disorders inevitably involves drug treatment. This tends to be a complicated area, in part because new drugs are being discovered all the time, so writers need to do their research. Drugs have trade names, generic names, and pharmacologic classes. For example, Prozac is a trade name, fluoxetine is its generic name, and it is known as an antidepressant that operates as a selective serotonin re-uptake inhibitor (SSRI), meaning it has a direct effect on increasing the body's calming serotonin effect. And that's one of the easy ones!

Briefly, the types of drugs typically used fall into the following categories.

- **Neuroletics/antipsychotics:** These drugs are used to treat psychotic episodes and come in different potencies with varying side effects. The most common are Thorazine, Haldol, Clozaril, and Resperidol.

- **Antidepressants:** Antidepressants are either tricyclic antidepressants (TCAs) or monoamine oxidase inhibitors (MAOIs). Most typical are lithium for bipolar disorders and the selective serotonin re-uptake inhibitors (SSRIs), notably Prozac and Zoloft, for depression. Bupropion is a novel class of antidepressant that has no action on the serotonin system.

- **Benzodiazepines/anxiolytic drugs:** These drugs inhibit anxiety found in post-traumatic stress disorder episodes, obsessive-compulsive disorders, social phobias, and panic disorders. Valium and Xanax are the most common, but some types of antidepressants or antipsychotics may also be used.

A fairly simple reference guide for matching drugs to disorders is *A Pocket Reference for Psychiatrists.*

The goals of drug therapy are to diminish acute episodes or prevent a relapse through maintenance. Careful supervision is often needed to prevent inmates from hoarding pills or selling them to other inmates.

Psychotherapy With Offenders

Although criminal behavior tends to burn out by middle age (except with psychopaths), many people are released from prison before that, and they need to have some coping skills if they are to avoid moving toward criminal lifestyles. To this point, recidivism rates hover around the one-third mark; since there are many more prisoners than there used to be, this number looks pretty grim.

Prison itself will not correct the behavior. In fact, studies have shown that prisons tend to be criminogenic. Rehab programs tend to affect only a small population, but they show what can work. Although psychiatric treatment tends to focus on the mentally ill, anyone can benefit. Many criminals show a certain amount of thought distortion and disinhibited impulse management. Many suffer from character disorders. The types of treatments that are likely to be found in a correctional setting are the following.

- **Crisis intervention:** Crisis intervention is used in such cases as self-mutilation, suicide attempts, inability to adjust, and severe anxiety disorders.
- **Management of self-destructive behavior:** Suicide, drug abuse.
- **Victim/offender interaction:** This attempts to confront offenders with what they have done to other people's lives.
- **Long-term stress management:** These skills help offenders avoid or minimize the effects of provocative situations.
- **Frustration tolerance**
- **Identity restructuring:** This uses education and skills training to help offenders grow more empowered with pro-social roles.
- **Addictions:** Substance dependence, sex offenders, and other types of

compulsive behaviors have structured programs for management.

- **Malingering:** Anything can be faked as a way of trying to get out of the prison population.
- **Outpatient follow-up and community programs**
- **Group therapy**

Unfortunately, mental health professionals are viewed as part of the correctional system and may be treated with indifference or hostility. Many prisoners also feel the need to appear tough, so they resist counseling. They don't want to be victimized.

In addition, therapists may encounter some personal difficulties. If they sympathize too much with prisoners, they may fall into believing that prisoners are mistreated. Therapists who work with offenders need to be empathetic without buying in to the offenders' stories. They have to confront and be firm without being demeaning or controlling. Therapists should understand the various coping strategies that develop in prison without taking those things personally, and they should care without taking the problems home. They also need to find small satisfactions in limited steps toward progress.

Female mental health professionals working in prisons can be subjected to sexual name-calling, attempts to touch them, or verbal abuse. They're often viewed as vulnerable, and if the guards fail to warn or take measures to protect them, they can be quickly overwhelmed. In 2001 convicted murderer Kenneth Kimes used a pen to grab reporter Maria Zone and threaten her life. He held her hostage for over four hours while he demanded that a vehicle be prepared to take him and her to Canada. It was a dramatic situation—one that would be interesting to explore through the plot of a novel.

A good example of conflicts that can develop for fictional treatment is found in the movie *Instinct*. A young psychiatrist must examine the competency of an inmate who refuses to talk, and he finds himself in a strained relationship with the prison counselor and guards, not to mention his client. He dislikes the system as he finds it and tries to make changes that could improve the lives of the prisoners. The warden is unhappy with this, having established a status quo. The psychiatrist finds out that forensic hospitals do not necessarily accommodate a therapeutic program, but he also begins to understand why.

Treatment for Sex Offenders

Sex offenders are generally grouped by the type of offense they commit, which includes the following:

- pedophiles (child molesters)
- rapists (according to subtypes listed on pages 161-162, with special emphasis on violent sexual sadists)
- exhibitionists

A thorough assessment needs to be made to determine immediate treatment needs, future risk, and outcome results of any previous treatments. Some of the issues involve

- accepting responsibility
- dealing with cognitive distortions, especially certain forms of self-deception that are unique to sex offenders
- development of empathy for the victim(s)
- reshaping sexual motivations
- enhancing social skills
- developing a plan to prevent re-offending

What counts for keeping any type of therapeutic program in force in a correctional setting is its effect on the recidivism rate. If a form of therapy cannot prevent an offender from repeating his crimes, then it is viewed as gratuitous. Seventy-five percent of violent offenders released from prison who have no family support, stable employment, or positive peer group will re-offend. Mental health professionals work to find ways to make a difference in this outcome.

10

Juveniles and Crime

A Groundbreaking Case

By the time he was fifteen, Willie Bosket had committed over two thousand crimes in New York, including stabbing several people. The son of a convicted murderer, he never knew his father but revered him for his "manly" crime. Just as he was turning sixteen, his crimes became more serious. Killing another boy in a fight, he then embarked upon a series of subway crimes, which ended up in the deaths of two men. He shot them, he later said, just to see what it was like.

He knew the juvenile laws well enough to realize that he could continue to do what he was doing and still get released when he was twenty-one. So he had no reason to stop.

Yet it was his spree and his arrogance that brought about a dramatic change in the juvenile justice system, starting in New York. The "Willie Bosket law," which allowed dangerous juveniles as young as thirteen to be tried in adult courts, was passed and signed in six days.

Family Court

The number of juveniles committing violent crimes as serious as murder rose dramatically in the 1990s. Some criminologists predict this will only get worse—especially as incarceration comes to represent a rite of passage for some big-city gangs.

The court into which juveniles have traditionally been brought has evolved through several stages. Family court owed its existence and philosophy to the medieval English doctrine of *parens patriae*—meaning the court could step in and operate as a parent. For several centuries children younger than seven were offered the presumption of infancy—that they lacked criminal intent. From age seven to fourteen, the asssumption of the capacity to form criminal intent was rebuttable with proof of immaturity.

American reformers built prisons for the purposes of rehabilitation, meaning they were appropriate for younger offenders as well, and children were eventually included into the mix of adult criminals. In the 1820s, other reformers established places specifically for "juvenile delinquents." The first such place opened in New York City in 1825. Punitive measures and strict discipline were used to reform youthful offenders.

A generation later, "child savers" decided that such institutions should be more like family settings than prisons. Thus, reform schools were born. However, these institutions soon fell into using some of the same brutal conditions, and even then some cases still called for harsher criminal treatment. For example, in 1874 fourteen-year-old Jesse Pomeroy was arrested in Boston for murder. He had sadistically tortured seven young boys and murdered a ten-year-old girl and a four-year-old boy. The latter he viciously mutilated. In an unprecedented trial, Jesse was sentenced to be executed. This was later commuted to life in solitary. At no point did he show remorse or any inclination to be reformed. He was a born psychopath, and the courts in those days had little recourse for dealing with such an offender.

Nevertheless, the majority of juvenile crimes were minor. Because of that a social worker in Chicago advocated for a separate branch of the court to deal with juvenile offenders, which would be civil rather than criminal. This represented a return to paternalism. The court would try to understand and treat the child, working with his youth to lead him back on the right path, and he would not be stigmatized with a criminal record. Thus, the Illinois legislature created the first juvenile court in 1899. The idea soon spread across the country. The age of immaturity was raised to seventeen.

The juvenile court functioned as a wise parent, aimed at protecting children's welfare. Their developmental needs, not what they had done, were the focus of treatment. Three different youths could initiate three different offenses and get the same treatment. Courts became more like social service agencies. Punishment was lenient, and court personnel were less formal. The courtroom involved the setting of a family conference around a table. The press was excluded from these proceedings, and the records were sealed. The first crime was generally dismissed, and probation officers were assigned to give judges progress reports, with a maximum sentence of eighteen months.

Even the terminology changed. The accused was a "respondent," not a defendant, and he was brought in through an "intake" procedure, not an arraignment. A label was attached along the lines of CHINS or PINS—Child or Person In Need of Supervision. Then, a petition was drawn against him, so he was not indicted, and he went through a hearing, not a trial. The verdict was a "disposition."

Some of this changed in the 1960s when it became clear that this approach to juvenile offenders was failing. To many kids, it was a joke. A "slap on the hand," no matter what the child did, was hardly deterring or reforming.

Another more serious problem that arose was the lack of due process afforded to children. There were no legal safeguards as adult courts ensured. Young people had no lawyers and no rights. The proceedings were criticized by legal personnel as tantamount to a kangaroo court. Children were interrogated without their parents being present, as occurred in *In Re Gault*, and could be subjected to long periods of intimidation. They could be accused without the right to face their accusers. The judge could make placement decisions even in the absence of evidence, and the accused could be sent to a juvenile facility without the right to appeal.

New York revised its laws in 1962 to offer all children the right to an attorney and assure them other aspects of due process. In several precedent-setting cases, children were awarded most of the rest of the rights possessed by adults: to counsel, to confront and cross-examine witnesses, and the privilege against self-incrimination. They also had to be read their Miranda rights before any interrogations. Lawyers entered the scene and changed how youth cases were settled, which made family court more adversarial.

In terms of basic proceedings, if an offense does not seem serious, the arresting officer might issue a citation to appear before a probation officer, or the probation officer may contact the child. If detained, the officer must notify the child's parents and allow the child one phone call. If detained at a juvenile facility, the various options include counseling and release, referral to a community program, informal supervision, or referral to a prosecutor. The child may then be further detained or released into parental custody.

If an attorney is requested, she represents the minor, not the minor's parents. She may be a public defender or a counselor experienced in juvenile cases. She may also use expert witnesses to assist her, if necessary. Reports are submitted in court, and the attorney can cross-examine anyone who prepared them, along with any witnesses to the incident. She can also make a plea bargain if her client so chooses. The juvenile has no right to bail, trial by jury, or a preliminary hearing.

Even with these formalized changes, the court did not abandon its parental function. For the next twenty years, a youthful offender went through a hearing to establish his delinquency status, and the court then used its discretion to decide on the rehabilitative disposition.

An increase in violent juvenile crime in the 1980s precipitated another reform. This time the emphasis was punitive. Certain statutes made it easier to waive youthful offenders into adult courts at increasingly lower ages, although the offenders still had to be found incapable of being rehabilitated. Sentences were also extended, so from the offender's point of view, due process issues became more significant.

An episode of *Law and Order* effectively exploited this issue. A twelve-year-old boy was ordered by a drug dealer to shoot his friend, who was being uncooperative. The boy shot past the friend and killed a woman in her bed. He was waived into adult court and charged with second-degree murder. His lawyer believed she could prove he was amenable to rehabilitation, which meant he could be remanded to family court. The court ordered a psychological evaluation, which indicated that rehab was possible but iffy in light of the kid's damaging home life. That meant a case could be made to keep him in criminal court, so the district attorney cut a deal: If the kid rolled over on the drug dealer, he would be remanded.

The obvious role of the mental health professional in juvenile proceedings is to offer evaluation and treatment.

- When courts are in a phase where the emphasis is on rehab, a clinician plays a stronger role because clinical assessment has a more significant function in the disposition.
- Mental health professionals may contribute to the intake procedures for probation evaluations.
- Reports are required for waiver to criminal court, often including risk assessment predictions.

- Adjudication in juvenile court may involve competency issues.
- Rehabilitation evaluations are used to determine a placement in the child's best interests, including changes and extensions.
- Emergency needs may have to be assessed during pretrial detention, e.g., suicide risk.

Those who evaluate juveniles must possess knowledge about the following issues:

- the juvenile psychopath
- latest research in developmental theory
- adolescent psychopathology
- delinquency and conduct disorders
- assessment instruments for adolescents
- ambiguities in court procedures relevant to juveniles

Types of Evaluations
1. Waiver (Bind Over or Certification) Evaluations
A prosecutor requests a way to waive jurisdiction so the offender can be sent to adult criminal court. This is generally done when it is determined at a special hearing that the youth is not amenable to rehabilitation. A mental health professional is generally present to talk about the potential for rehab success and risk factors. Sometimes youths of a certain age who commit serious crimes like murder are already sent to the criminal court through statutory exclusion, although there is some discretion for transferring them back to juvenile court, as in the *Law and Order* case mentioned on page 180.

2. Disposition Evaluations
A disposition evaluation helps decide the outcome of determining that a youth is delinquent. A community service program or commitment to a residential facility requires some idea of how well the youth will do. A mental health professional may determine, for example, that it is better to keep a youth in detention closer to his family than to send him to a boot camp far away. Youths who need mental health care especially need to be properly evaluated by mental health professionals.

3. Progress and Outcome Evaluations

During a rehab effort, there may be certain points when an evaluation is called for, especially if there is any consideration for possible transfer to another facility. It may also be the case that court custody will be extended past the usual maximum age, and that needs an evaluation report. Mental health professionals also collect outcome data for research.

Mental Health Professionals in Court

In a 1999 case in Michigan, eleven-year-old Nathaniel Abraham was on trial for murder. He was the youngest defendant in a murder trial in that state. That such a young boy could do this rattled the community, and the case became an international sensation. In Michigan law, there is no age limit for when a child can be waived to adult court. To the surprise of people around the country, Abraham was so waived, and the case became an issue for Amnesty International on the rights of children. It was not in Abraham's best interests, the organization insisted, that he be charged as an adult. However, the people of Michigan wanted their communities protected from someone like him.

Abraham was charged with shooting a stranger, eighteen-year-old Ronnie Greene, outside a store in Pontiac, Michigan. Abraham had a stolen rifle and allegedly had bragged about planning to shoot someone. He practiced on targets and boasted about the shooting afterward. After his arrest, Abraham claimed the shooting was accidental.

The primary question about this case that concerned mental health professionals was whether he was competent to understand his rights and whether he could form criminal intent. Supposedly Abraham offered a "confession" in which he said he was aiming at trees, and once he had an attorney, his competency to waive his rights became the primary focus. That is, if he did not understand that he had the right to make no statement at all, then this confession should not have been allowed.

Appellate cases involving children ages twelve and younger have usually resulted in the opinion that they lack the requisite understanding of their rights. Especially at risk are those with poor cognitive development (which was true of Abraham). A study done with resources from the National Institute of Mental Health showed that youths younger than fourteen performed significantly more poorly than older adolescents on comprehension of their Miranda rights. Just because those rights are stated or read to them does not mean they know what the rights mean. They've heard them on crime shows on television, so they might say they understand, but their actual comprehension level needs to be tested.

In *Kent v. U.S.*, a 1966 case involving a juvenile, the conditions for waiver to adult court included the following:

- weighing the seriousness of the alleged offense against community protection
- judging whether the offense was committed in an aggressive or violent manner
- judging whether the offense was against persons or property
- evaluating the sophistication and maturity of the child
- weighing the likelihood of reasonable rehabilitation

In Abraham's case, where the intent behind the shooting was ambiguous and where he was clearly an unsophisticated boy, the factors involved in sending him into an adult court seem weighted heavily in terms of community protection.

A key issue was whether he got the mental health treatment he needed while in prison. He was not granted this until almost a year after his arrest, despite the fact that tests given to him at that time indicated mental impairment. The prosecutor opposed moving him to a better facility and ignored the request that he receive counseling. The only treatment discussed with him was drug therapy, which frightened him. He was offered this without his mother or attorney present, and he did not understand what would happen to him. These items were all presented in court by the psychologist on his defense team.

Three mental health experts—a psychiatrist, a psychologist, and a child psychologist—examined Abraham. They stated that he was mentally younger than his chronological age and that his IQ was borderline retarded at 75. In fact, his mental age was closer to eight, which meant he did not possess the ability to form criminal intent. In addition, he did not understand his rights, did not have the ability to plan long-range, was impulsive, and had no judgment skills. He was a "lost puppy" who should not have been deemed competent to stand trial. The boy admitted that he did not really know what his rights were or what a Miranda warning was. He did not seem to know what went on in court or what he faced.

In rebuttal the prosecution hired a child psychologist who said that Abraham certainly understood the harmful nature of guns and that there was no evidence of diminished capacity (although on cross-examination, it was made clear that there was no procedure for assessing diminished capacity in an eleven-year-old).

Since it is the court and not a mental health professional that ultimately decides competency, and since the case was a politically high profile venture, Abraham's trial went forward.

Juvenile Crime

In a groundbreaking study in 1999, *The New York Times* collected one hundred cases over the past fifty years of "rampage killers" in America. They separated out the nineteen teenaged killers and found that while adults tended to act alone, kids often acted with the support of their peers. In some instances, those kids were helped by other kids who drove them to school, showed them how to use guns, helped them get firearms, or simply came to watch. There were times when these students were actually goaded into doing it. Quite often the killers boasted about what they were planning and even encouraged friends to be witnesses.

In forty cases of school violence in the past twenty years, the Secret Service's National Threat Assessment Center found that teenagers often told someone before they did the deeds. Most of these kids were white, and they preferred (and somehow acquired) semiautomatic weapons. Almost half had shown some evidence of mental disturbances, including delusions and hallucinations.

There are many overlapping conduct disorders that specifically play into juvenile crime. A mental health professional must know the differences if she has to evaluate a juvenile for waiver, sentencing, or treatment. Given a child's developing and changing personality, it is difficult to diagnose mental disorders among adolescents. Additionally, some common behavioral manifestations of youth, such as anger, mood instability, and defiance, match symptoms of disorders. It is difficult to know when this behavior in a specific individual is a phase or a serious problem, even among developmental experts.

A general conduct disorder is a persistent pattern of antisocial behavior during childhood and adolescence that includes the following actions:

- violating social rules
- aggression toward animals or other children
- destruction of property
- deceitfulness
- theft
- serious rule violations

Six different diagnoses are used in the *DSM-IV*.

1. **Conduct disorder (CD):** This is a behavioral problem involving persistent violations of the rights of others or violation of age-appropriate social rules.

2. **Oppositional defiant disorder (ODD):** Such youths usually exhibit a pattern of defiant and disobedient behavior, including resistance to authority figures, albeit not as severe as conduct disorder. Oppositional defiant disorder includes recurrent temper problems, frequent arguments with adults, and evidence of anger and resentment. Additionally, the defiant child/adolescent will often try to annoy others and will become easily annoyed. She will usually blame others, avoid taking responsibility for mistakes, and may also display vindictive behavior. If left untreated, these children will develop conduct disorder.

3. **Disruptive behavior disorder—not otherwise specific (DBD-NOS):** This is a category for those who show ongoing conduct disorder and oppositional defiant disorder but who fail to meet the criteria for either diagnosis.

4. **Adjustment disorder—with mixed disturbance of emotions and conduct:** This is an array of antisocial behaviors and emotional symptoms that set in within three months of a stressor and fail to meet the full criteria of the previously mentioned disorders.

5. **Adjustment disorder—with disturbance of conduct:** This is similar to the other adjustment disorder but with antisocial behaviors only.

6. **Child or adolescent antisocial behavior:** This is a category for isolated antisocial behaviors not indicative of a mental disorder.

The *DSM-IV* also added disruptive behavior disorder—not otherwise specified (DBD-NOS), which allows clinicians to diagnose behavior problems that fail to meet criteria for conduct disorder or oppositional defiant disorder.

If that is not sufficiently complicated, childhood antisocial behavior has also been linked with attention deficit hyperactive disorder (ADHD or ADD). This diagnosis has changed somewhat over the years, and new research is continuing to refine it. In many respects, it represents two separate problems, although they appear to be linked. Children may have attention deficit disorder (primarily inattention), attention deficit hyperactive disorder (primarily impulsive/hyperactive), or a mixed type incorporating attributes of both disorders. Inattention is usually identified in school when certain children are distracted by almost anything. Disorganization is common, and the child may lose personal items regularly. Even when spoken to directly, the child may not pay attention and will be unable to provide feedback when asked. Hyperactive children frequently get into minor difficulties.

It is not the case, as many people believe, that a child diagnosed as conduct disordered will inevitably grow into an adult with antisocial personality disorder or the propensity to commit antisocial acts. The relationship between these two conditions is more complicated. As many as two-thirds of children with conduct disorder stop their destructive behaviors by the time they reach adulthood. Conduct disorder may be a precondition for antisocial personality disorder but does not predict it. Risk factors that a child displaying a conduct disorder will continue to act out in antisocial ways appear to be linked to (1) hyperactive and impulsive behaviors, (2) an early onset of minor crimes, (3) committing different types of aggressive behaviors, and (4) displaying disruptive behaviors in different settings. Age of onset seems to be paramount. In short, the relationship between adult antisocial disorders and childhood conduct disorders rests on an array of complicating factors, frustrating both research and intervention specialists. Yet some researchers have taken a different tack, identifying many of these complicating factors as manifestations of a single construct: childhood psychopathy.

Children Without a Conscience

Psychopathy is an important clinical construct in the evaluation of adolescent offenders. In a study of eighty-one boys in a residential treatment program, aggressive conduct disorder symptoms and deceit/theft symptoms were shown to be predictive of adolescent psychopathy in those aged fourteen to seventeen.

In another study, the two factors in young offenders indicative of psychopathy were impulsive/conduct problems and callous/unemotional attitudes. They assessed ninety-five clinic-referred children and found that psychopathy and conduct problems were interacting constructs in children, similar to the way criminal behavior and psychopathic traits interact in adults. The salient traits were grandiosity, irresponsibility, and susceptibility to boredom; these were associated in children with conduct problems and in adults with antisocial behavior.

Psychopathy appears to be associated with oppositional defiant disorder, conduct disorder, and hyperactivity. There may be a neurological deficit that manifests as a lack of behavioral restraint, such as with hyperactive and impulsive children. In adulthood these become irresponsible and impulsive behaviors. Psychopathy was assessed in 430 boys, ages twelve and thirteen, by using reports from caretakers and translating them from Robert Hare's Psychopathy Checklist to the childhood level, as the Childhood Psychopathy Scale (CPS). It turned out that childhood psychopathy fit the general framework of adult psychopathy as assessed by the Psychopathy Checklist. Children with psychopathic personalities were shown to be stable offenders (more repeat offenses), more impulsive, and prone to the most serious offenses. Childhood psychopathy has proven to be the best predictor of antisocial behavior in adolescence, especially in boys who are hyperactive and impulsive and who suffer from attention deficits.

Common traits in the background of psychopathic children include the following:
- a mother exposed to deprivation or abuse as a child
- a mother who shows a tendency toward isolation
- a transient father or a family that migrates frequently
- a mother who cannot maintain stable emotional connection with the child

- low birth weight or birth complications
- hypersensitivity or hyposensitivity to pain
- hyperactivity
- lack of attachment to adults
- failure to make eye contact when touched
- absence of fear of strangers
- low frustration tolerance
- transient psychotic episodes
- sense of omnipotence
- easily distracted
- transient relationships
- cruelty toward others

Juvenile Assessment

When the court orders an evaluation, judges are looking for a diagnosis and very clear recommendations. If there is evidence of an antisocial character, a detention facility is generally the answer, including wilderness camps, boot camps, rehab units for substance abuse, psychiatric treatment centers, training schools, and offender programs. Other types of programs may be run in foster homes or the community.

Evaluations usually must be done within days of the hearing, and a mental health professional should have a flexible test battery for the assessment of different traits and abilities. These tests should not take more than about four hours to administer. A typical battery may include several of the following tests.

- Wechsler Intelligence Scale for Children—Third Edition (WISC-III) measures IQ for juveniles under sixteen, while the Wechsler Adult Intelligence Scale-Revised works better if they are sixteen or older.
- Wide Range Achievement Test (WRAT) measures school achievement and academic ability.
- Minnesota Multiphasic Personality Inventory for Adolescents (MMPI-A) for personality factors, especially elevations on the psychopathic deviate scale.
- Projective drawings that tap unconscious material.
- Beck Depression Inventory (see page 99).

- Jesness Inventory for the classification of delinquents. Its eleven scales include Social Maladjustment, Values Orientation, Immaturity, Alienation, and Manifest Aggression. A delinquent may be undersocialized, conformist, group oriented, independent, introspective, pragmatic, inhibited, or adaptive.

- Carlson Psychological Survey (CPS) was also designed specifically for forensic assessment. This test has five scales for Chemical Abuse, Thought Disturbance, Antisocial Tendencies, Self-Depreciation, and Validity. From this, one can come up with eighteen personality types and match them against predictions for such things as their adjustment to institutionalization, their behavior on parole, and post-release adjustment.

- Quay Typology is a system that classifies youths in terms of Conduct Disorder, Socialized Aggression, Attention Problems, Anxiety-Withdrawal, Psychotic Behavior, and Motor Tension Excess. This is often paired with the Revised Behavior Problem Checklist, which is given to an adult who knows the child well enough to give an evaluation.

Mental health professionals need to recognize that truly criminal types, no matter what their ages, often fall into errors of thinking that direct their behaviors. They have notable character disorders that are likely deeply entrenched. They may need a longer-term program than most offenders committing the same types of crimes, and they may also need a different type of assessment test.

Of the psychopathy assessment devices, Robert Hare's PCL-R (the Psychopathy Checklist revised to include fewer items) appears to be highly reliable. That is, individuals at high risk to commit crimes can be reliably diagnosed with the PCL-R. Hare and some of his colleagues went on to develop the Psychopathy Screening Device (PSD) for children as a twenty-item, 0 to 2 rating scale similar to the PCL-R. It has a similar two-factor structure (Callous/Unemotional and Impulsive/Conduct problems). Researchers used the Psychopathy Screening Device in the context of reinforcement sensitivity with thirty-nine children aged nine to sixteen. They found that those children who played cards badly and also made little distinction between moral and conventional transgressions (like cheating) had higher ratings on the Psychopathy Screening Device. Since adult psychopaths had similar results, this indicates that the Psychopathy Screening Device may be a reliable prediction of adult psychopathy.

A similar instrument used on children is the Kiddie-Mach scale, based on the Mach IV scale. "Mach" is a psychological concept that derives from the sixteenth-century writings of Niccolo Machiavelli, *The Prince* and *The Discourses*. It was worked into a quantifiable personality construct that appeared to be involved in strategies that people used to gain and maintain interpersonal power. The successful manipulator would have the following traits: lack of interpersonal affect, lack of concern with conventional morality, lack of gross psychopathology, and low ideological commitments. These characteristics are central to the definition of psychopathy. The Mach IV contained twenty statements rated on a scale. It integrates the psychopathy constructs found on the Psychopathy Checklist-Revised with Machiavellianism.

More work must be done to determine which of the childhood psychopathy assessment devices is most effective, and this will probably require extensive longitudinal studies. Yet the fact that researchers with specialized knowledge in psychopathy are moving away from the multiple conduct disorder diagnoses toward a more cohesive predictive construct should facilitate better agreement on the findings. It should be clear that the limited intervention resources available ought to be directed toward children who exhibit traits common to a constellation of disorders—hyperactive, impulsive, attention-deficit and conduct problems—because children who manifest all of these seem the most strongly correlated with adult manifestations of psychopathy. Classifications that focus primarily on behavior to the exclusion of personality characteristics will continue to fall short of the predictive value needed for locating the "fledgling psychopath"—the person most likely to become a serious and chronic antisocial adult.

Risk Assessment, Treatment, and Prevention

There is a consistent relationship between certain factors and the risk of future recidivism in adolescents, especially in terms of violence. These factors include the following:

- past behavior (frequency, severity, and recency)
- substance use and abuse

- peers (especially organized aggressive peers)
- family aggression (especially antisocial)
- social stress (relationships, grades, failures)
- character disorders (angry, impulsive, nonempathic)
- mental disorders (depression, attention deficit hyperactive disorder, paranoia, post-traumatic stress disorder)
- opportunity (access to weapons, anger at a particular person)
- degree of resilience (ability to overcome negative factors)
- ability to connect

During the first three to nine months of life, an infant develops bonds with the parent. Some infants are easy, some difficult. Parents have to deepen this bond, because a strong factor in the development of psychopathy is the child's lack of connection with others. The ability to connect is crucial during these early months. One two-month-old baby who had been placed in several foster situations showed signs of being unattached: She would not make eye contact and reacted violently when picked up. The foster mother who decided to try to change this used behavior modification to get the baby to make eye contact while she was feeding. It took almost seven months, but eventually the child responded with less rigidity.

Attachment at an early age helps children:
- develop intellectually
- develop a conscience
- cope with frustration
- become self-reliant and self-valuing
- develop empathic relationships

Self-worth, resilience, hope, intelligence, and empathy are essential to building character for effective impulse control, anger management, and conflict resolution. Without these skills, children cannot establish rewarding relationships with community systems, which puts the entire social structure at risk.

While a born psychopath may have neurological disorders that defy every treatment, it still seems that many criminals with certain psychopathic traits may be turned toward something pro-social with the right nurturing.

A Case for Fictional Development

When children are not afforded due process, they can become victims of the legal system, as was the case in the following story. In Ohio a little girl was murdered. Her neighbor, a twelve-year-old boy, was brought in for questioning because at one time he had threatened to kill her. Eventually, he confessed and was convicted.

However, there was no physical evidence, and yet he was grilled for nearly two hours without his mother knowing and without an attorney present. He had no idea what his Miranda rights were. To get the confession, the police had used an interrogation technique that involved sitting close, using trickery and deceit, offering motives and an excuse, telling him exactly how he committed the crime, offering him two options (a good and a bad reason for it), and offering to "help him" by getting him counseling.

Over a dozen times he denied any involvement, but his interrogators ignored him. They asked him questions that contained the information they wanted to know, so finally the boy just parroted that information back to them. He believed it was the only way to get them to stop. He just wanted to go home.

A sociologist with expertise on interrogation methods intervened and demonstrated how this boy might have confessed to something he did not do. It was a clear case of forced confession, and eventually the conviction was overturned. However, the boy had been badly shaken by the experience—especially when it came out that tracking dogs had followed a scent right after the murder to the home of a convicted child molester.

The handling of children after they commit crimes can become muddled between the way they were dealt with in the past as children in need of rehab and the more adult-oriented (and punitive) way the juvenile system has evolved. This muddle has been handled on television shows like *C.S.I.* and *Law and Order*. On an episode of *C.S.I.*, for example, a juvenile who raped and shot a woman was tracked to his home. He shrugged off the crimes, knowing that in "juvie" he wouldn't get much time. The crime investigation unit knew this, too, and their frustration over the legal inequity showed.

It's important for writers to check with their state laws and procedures but also to research how some cases like this can fall through the cracks.

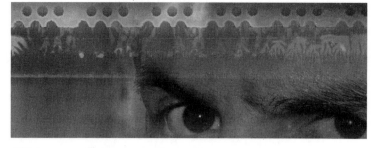

11

The Psychologist as Consultant/ Investigator

Profiling

"I use a formula," says John Douglas, former FBI profiler and author of *Mindhunter.* "How plus Why equals Who. If we can answer the hows and whys in a crime, we generally can come up with the solution."

In the past two decades, there has been an increased use of profiling in criminal investigations, although it remains a controversial tool. Not everyone believes that devising hypothetical portraits of suspects contributes to solving crimes, but some profiles have been surprisingly accurate. The problem is that it's difficult to know when you're working with a good one until the suspect is caught and compared against it. There have even been cases in which a suspect seemed a perfect match, but not only was he not the offender, but the person eventually arrested wasn't even close to a match. Nevertheless, profiles are here to stay.

Hitler was profiled to try to determine his vulnerability and plan of action, and profiling was used (ineffectively) with the Boston Strangler. Thomas Harris includes this device in *The Silence of the Lambs* and *Red Dragon,* and Faye Sultan offers female profiler Portia McTeague in *Help Line.* Even the early fictional detectives like Sherlock Holmes and Edgar Allan Poe's C. Auguste Dupin describe some of what's involved in the process in that the finest details of a crime scene must be noted and perhaps examined in ways no one expects. Intuitive thinking is essential, coupled with logic.

Outside fiction, profiling has been developed in the FBI's Behavioral Science Unit (a.k.a., Investigative Support Unit) by such people as John Douglas (*Mindhunter*), Robert Ressler (*Whoever Fights Monsters*), and Roy Hazelwood (*The Evil That Men Do*). However, police departments all over the country also use profiling in their crime-fighting arsenals—and they often call on forensic mental health professionals to assist in consultations.

It must be noted that profiling is an art, not a science. While based on patterns derived from past cases, it can go wrong and sometimes is no help at all. The idea is to use it as just one tool among many in police work. It can be a guide but should not be taken as gospel.

Probing for an experiential assessment of a criminal prior to actually questioning a suspect involves looking at such data as the following:

- the weapon used
- the killing site (and dump site, if different)
- the position of the body and whether it was moved
- the type of wounds inflicted
- minute details about the victim
- offender risk factors
- the method of controlling the victim
- evidence of staging (faking a specific type of crime scene) or signature (behavior done for emotional satisfaction)

The basic idea is to get a body of data yielding common patterns so one can give a general description of an UNSUB (unknown suspect) in terms of habit, possible employment, marital status, and personality traits. According to John Douglas, the "signature" is key: "I've found that signature is a more reliable guide to the behavior of serial offenders than an MO [modus operandi]. That's because the MO evolves, while the emotional reasoning that triggers the signature doesn't." By that he means the method used to commit a crime is practical—doing what needs to be done to achieve an end—while the signature satisfies a need that may be unique to the offender.

Information for developing common denominators was compiled from interviews with known killers like John Wayne Gacy, Sirhan Sirhan, David Berkowitz (a.k.a., Son of Sam), and Richard Speck. Profiling involves mental

Note Found in Son of Sam's Car

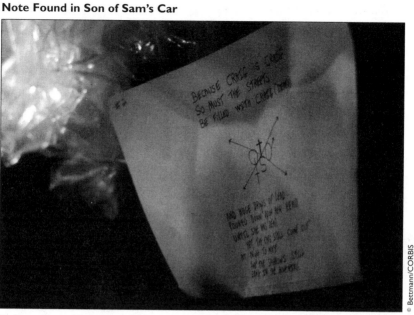

Profilers often use letters to help track criminals. David Berkowitz, who called himself Son of Sam, mailed several notes to police and newspaper reporters throughout his killing spree. By comparing those letters with this note found in Berkowitz's car, the police had more proof that he was the killer.

health professionals using their expertise in human behavior, motivation, and patterns of pathology.

Contrary to popular belief, it's not necessary that the offender be a serial criminal. Profiling can be done from a single crime scene, and since 70 to 75 percent of murders are situational, developing a way to profile without reference to repeated patterns is useful.

For example, FBI profilers were asked to provide information about the rape/murder of a young woman who lived alone in Texas. They had no crime scene photos and were not even allowed very far into the crime scene area, so they did their analysis from written reports and from an examination of the body. The killer had entered through an open window. There was facial battering, and the victim had shed a lot of blood. She had been accosted in her kitchen and dragged to the middle of her living room floor. It appeared to be a spontaneous, disorganized killing using a weapon found inside the apartment. There was no planning. The UNSUB had no shoes on, so he'd come on foot. That meant he lived in the area and probably did not own a car. Not bringing a weapon with him negated a plan to kill. There was no apparent ritual involved.

The profilers believed the killer was young, single, black, and unsophisticated. He was probably volatile and uneducated. He likely had a record of breaking and entering and may have committed past rapes. He did not know the victim but knew her habits. Checking on reported rapes within a mile of this apartment turned up a suspect who proved to be the guy they were after. The profile turned out to be highly accurate.

Having said that, it must be noted how much information the profilers tried to gather before making this assessment. Trying to devise a profile the way a criminal behavior expert did in the Joe Eszterhas script *Basic Instinct* is ludicrous. The man was called in as a consultant by the police psychologist. He had not even discussed the details with the detectives but had based his entire, overly dramatic, jargon-laden assessment on the fact that the crime had many similarities to the plot of a suspense novel that had been authored by the prime suspect. Presenting mental health professionals in such situations makes their part in profiling a joke.

Before providing analyses, responsible mental health professionals gather as much information as they can, looking at crime scene photos, autopsy reports, witness statements, police reports, and sometimes even going to the crime scene itself. And they will always caution investigators about profiling's limitations.

A good profile is an educated attempt to provide parameters about the type of person who committed a certain crime, based on the idea that people tend to be slaves to their psychology and will inevitably leave clues. The kinds of information sought include the following:

- offender's gender
- modus operandi (MO), or method of operating
- evidence of an organized or disorganized personality
- geographic stability vs. transient
- evidence of being impulsive or compulsive
- the type of personation or signature at the scene
- the type of fantasy that seems to be involved
- evidence of ritual
- whether a trophy, or souvenir of the crime, was taken

A profile is most easily developed if the offender displays some evidence of psychopathology, such as sadistic torture, postmortem mutilation, or pedophilia. Some killers leave a signature, such as staging the corpse for the most humiliating exposure or tying ligatures with a complicated bow. A signature helps link crime scenes and alert law enforcement officers to the presence of a serial rapist or killer. If a pattern is detected, it may also help predict future possible attacks, the most probable pickup or dump sites, and victim types.

Patricia Cornwell's *The Body Farm* includes an excellent example of how profilers look at a crime scene and go through the life and movements of a victim to figure out who might have killed her. Medical examiner Kay Scarpetta meets with nine law enforcement officers and FBI profilers on a case involving the murder of an eleven-year-old girl. They look through her diary, talk to her mother, and question several friends and witnesses to get a full description of her actions prior to her death. They also examine autopsy findings in minute detail.

The best profilers have gained their knowledge from experience with criminals and have developed an intuitive sense about certain types of crime. Their base of information derives from both physical and nonphysical evidence. Generally, profilers employ psychological theories that provide ways to analyze mental deficiencies such as delusions, personality characteristics like hostility, criminal thought patterns, and character defects. They also need to know about actuarial data such as the age range into which offenders generally fall and how important an unstable family history is to criminality.

Profiling is not just a personality assessment of the UNSUB. Noting an UNSUB's age, race, sex, occupation, educational level, social support system, type of employment, and other sociological factors are just as important as evidence of a character disorder. It's also important to include an analysis of the place a killer chooses as a body dump site, such as Ted Bundy's preference for the heavily wooded mountains outside Seattle.

A relatively recent development is the analysis of a suspect's geographic patterns: where a victim is selected, where the crime is committed, the travel route used for body disposal, where and how the bodies are dumped, and the relative isolation of the dump site. This information tells about the suspect's mobility, method of transportation, potential area of residence, and ability to traverse barriers (such as crossing state lines or going over a bridge).

Familiarity is part of one's comfort zone, and many murderers begin a crime spree in areas where they live, with victims with whom they feel relatively safe. Some profilers think killers have mental maps, based on their habits and centers of activity, that will influence, if not altogether dictate, their behaviors.

One killer who was believed to have murdered at least seven young women lived near where he abducted them. There were many geographic similarities among his crimes. Six of the bodies were found in rural areas, and five of the body dump sites formed a tight circle within a few miles' radius. This indicated that the UNSUB traveled this way back and forth and knew the area well. Two girls were actually killed in the same place and transported elsewhere. It was clear that he tended to stick to an area he knew well.

Geographical profiling is applicable even to single cases in terms of learning things about a perpetrator. In the famous 1947 case of the Black Dahlia in Los Angeles, this young woman's naked body, severed in two and drained of blood, was left in an abandoned lot of a residential area just steps from the sidewalk. It was placed there after the dew had settled. That indicated a bold or deranged killer because he could easily have been seen.

The crime sites most valuable for this kind of analysis are those in which the killer has exercised spatial intentionality—predatory acts and body disposal planning. In a localized rampage, one can tell nearly as much from the paths connecting sites of offense as by the sites themselves. When a killer travels, such as in the recent string of murders along railroads, much can be learned from the types of places in which the perpetrator chooses to kill— and people can be alerted.

Examples of Accurate Profiles

One of the most astounding profiles ever developed was done in 1957 by psychiatrist James Brussel in the case of New York's "Mad Bomber," George Metesky. Brussel studied photos of the bomb scenes, analyzed letters written to the newspapers, and concluded that the bomber was paranoid, hated his father, was obsessed with his mother, worked at Consolidated Edison, had a heart condition, lived in Connecticut, was heavyset, middle-aged, single, Catholic, lived with a brother or sister, and would be wearing a double-

Taking Fingerprints at the Crime Scene

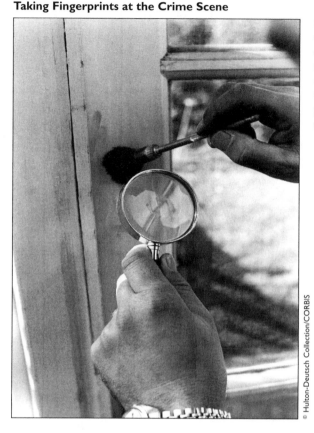

Fingerprints taken at the scene of a crime can not only help police verify a criminal's identity, but the way in which they were left can tell a profiler a lot about that criminal's personality.

© Hulton-Deutsch Collection/CORBIS

breasted suit, buttoned. Although investigators found Metesky in his pajamas (at the Connecticut home of his two sisters), when they requested that he get dressed, he came out wearing a double-breasted suit, buttoned.

Richard Trenton Chase, the "Vampire of Sacramento," was also quickly identified and apprehended with the help of a psychological profile in 1978. Chase had murdered a woman, eviscerating her and drinking her blood. It was so brutal that the FBI was called in. Agents Robert Ressler and Russ Vorpagel developed a profile.

They figured the UNSUB for a disorganized killer as opposed to an organized one, with clues pointing toward the possibility of paranoid psychosis. He clearly had not planned the crime and did little to hide or destroy evidence. He left footprints and fingerprints and had probably walked around in daylight with blood on his clothing. In other words, he gave little thought to the consequences. At the very least, his residence would be as sloppy as the place he ransacked, and he probably had no car. That meant it was likely that he lived in the vicinity of the crimes. He was white, aged twenty-five to twenty-seven, thin, undernourished, lived alone, and probably had crime evidence in his home. He was likely unemployed and the recipient of disability money. All of this was derived from their experiences with violent sexual assault—that it tended to be intraracial and done by men in their twenties. Crime scene photos showed the disarray that probably mirrored the UNSUB's personal habits. From what they knew, it was also likely that he would kill again and keep on killing until he was caught. They had to work fast.

Three days after the first murder, the killer struck again, this time slaughtering three people in their home. He grabbed a baby and stole the family car but then abandoned it in broad daylight. This suggested an oblivious, unhinged mind. They figured he lived close by. Within two days they found Chase living less than a block from the abandoned car. His appearance was just as anticipated, and he suffered from paranoid delusions. Body parts and a bloodstained food blender were found in his apartment. He lived alone, was unemployed, and had a history of psychiatric incarceration. He had been released just a few months before he began to kill. Chase's arrest stopped a string of murders that apparently was to include some forty-four more victims that same year.

A dramatic example of how profiling can be used even after the criminal is caught is shown in *Citizen X*, the film based on the story of prolific Russian serial killer Andrei Chikatilo. From 1978–1990, Chikatilo raped, brutalized, and murdered at least fifty-two children.

Trying to narrow possibilities, the chief investigator asked several mental health experts to draw up a profile. Most refused, due to insufficient detail. One psychiatrist, Alexandr Bukhanovsky, agreed to study the few known details and the crime scene patterns to come up with a profile. The killer, he said, was a sexual deviate, twenty-five to fifty years old, around 5'10" tall. He thought the man suffered from some form of sexual inadequacy, and he blinded his victims to prevent them from looking at him. He also brutalized their corpses, partially out of frustration and partially to enhance his arousal. He had difficulty getting relief.

It took the police many years to catch Chikatilo and nine days to get his confession. For the first eight days, the state interrogator unsuccessfully used typical methods of domination and coercion. Finally, when no confession was forthcoming and the probability loomed large that the man would be released, they brought in Dr. Bukhanovksy. Painstakingly, he read the profile to Chikatilo, admitting that he might have gotten some of it wrong. His description went into the nature of Chikatilo's mental illness and some possible reasons for it. As Chikatilo listened, he heard his secret life described so clearly that he began to tremble. Finally he broke down and said that it was all true. He had done those horrible things, and he began to confess in detail to the police interrogator.

As exciting as profiling is, crime writers should realize that it is not universally respected nor is its success rate analyzed or documented. (One famous example of an inaccurate profile is Ann Burgess's analysis of the Menendez double murder as being disorganized, when in fact it was carefully planned.)

Profiling and the Victim

Complete background on victims is vitally important to devising profiles. Risk factors must be identified as well as any potential relationships with the offenders. Where the victim was assaulted, abducted and/or killed determines the degree of risk, as does the victim's age and occupation. Among low risk victims are those who live fairly normal lives and are assaulted in daylight or in their homes. High risk victims include prostitutes, women who travel alone, substance abusers, and people who work at night. Medium risk is somewhere in between, such as a normally low risk person who decides to visit an ATM machine at night.

If the victim is still alive, he or she can provide some details. Profilers lay out a time line of the victim's known movements up until the point of the crime, relying on diaries, witness statements, phone messages, purchases made, and what acquaintances may know. Any communications that establish the victim's frame of mind are significant, especially if there was any anxiety about another person. Whether there was any degree of compliance is noted, because it may imply acquaintance. Another source is the victim's mental health history, criminal history, and any record of substance abuse.

It is important to try to determine why a particular person was targeted— whether it was opportunity or involved some relationship or fantasy that implies preselection. Then, the profiler determines how the victim was approached and whether there was resistance. It is also important to note the time of day the offense took place. That may indicate something about how the victim might have known the offender—possibly via employment. If there was transportation involved, it can mean the possibility of a broader geographic area involved than just the victim's neighborhood. In other words, the victim may have been randomly selected because he or she was at a certain place at a certain time that happened to cross the rapist's or killer's path.

Multiple victims, such as in mass, spree, or serial killings or serial rapes, means collecting much more data, but it also means the potential for finding more clues and seeing patterns. It also means the offender was willing to take more risk.

Profiling and the Profiler

A profile, while helpful, should not be the most significant tool in the investigation but just one of many. It is based in fact, but it is speculative and can be inaccurate. If used improperly, it can narrow down suspects in ways that mislead. A profile is as good as the profiler.

A profiler should possess the following traits:

- creative thinking abilities
- persistence
- the ability to think under pressure
- the capacity to self-correct
- an eye for patterns
- an ability to synthesize disparate information

According to former FBI special agent and profiler Roy Hazelwood, the first thing that profilers need is common sense. "Another term for that," he says, "is practical intelligence. Number two is an open mind—you have to be able to accept other people's suggestions. Number three is life experience. Number four is an ability to isolate your personal feelings about the crime, the criminal, and the victim. Number five would be an ability to think like the offender thinks."

Profilers have behavioral science backgrounds and experience with the many facets of a profile, such as the following:

- how to analyze an offender's self-report
- how to collect and analyze information about pre- and post-offense behavior
- how to interview suspects
- how to get an offender to inadvertently reveal his part in a crime
- how to determine when a profile is being used incorrectly

A fictional character that embodies these traits is Jake Donovan in the novel *Broken Wings* by John Douglas and Mark Olshaker. Donovan is a former FBI profiler who investigates an FBI director's equivocal death—one in which the circumstances are ambiguous. It looks like suicide, but a good profiler pays attention to every detail and accepts nothing at face value. Donovan tries to imagine the final moments of the man's life from the victim's perspective and then determines whether everything at the scene is consistent with that. When it appears that there are key problems, the potential that the crime is a homicide changes the scope of the investigation. Many of Donovan's methods and ideas come from Douglas's own career as a profiler.

Profilers may end up testifying in the courtroom as well. Since this method falls under social science, the *Daubert* ruling (see page 47) applies. In other words, whether or not a profiler can testify is subject to the judge's discretion. In court, a profiler may

- testify about how a profile was devised from the crime scene and victim analysis
- assist attorneys to understand the methods of profiling
- elucidate the offender's mental state at the time of the offense, based on databanks of similar crimes
- discuss the types of offenders and how the defendant fits a certain class
- assist attorneys with cross-examination
- assist with risk assessment analysis at sentencing and parole hearings

Assisting the Forensic Artist

On a cold November day in Westfield, New Jersey, in 1971, John List systematically shot and killed his elderly mother, his wife, and each of his three children as they came home from school. He placed them on sleeping bags in the ballroom of his Victorian mansion, turned down the heat, turned on all of the lights, and left. He had written extensive notes to his minister detailing what he'd done and why, but there was no clue as to where he had gone.

Over the years the trail went cold, although detectives made several attempts to update the file. By the mid-eighties, they were using computer-enhanced photos to indicate what they believed List would look like that many years later. Somewhere, someone would recognize this man.

Then in 1988, the television show *America's Most Wanted* decided to take on the unsolved case. They hired forensic sculptor Frank Bender to make a three-dimensional clay bust of the fugitive to display on the show.

Bender knew he'd have to work up an entire psychological profile to be able to accurately depict the way the aging process would show on List's face. For that he teamed up with criminal psychologist Richard Walter. They looked over what was known of List's past, what he had written in the murder notes, and what others had to say about the man. Then they decided which of his traits would remain intact, despite his attempt to take on a new identity. They figured he'd still wear the same type of glasses, work as an accountant, overspend, and would likely be remarried. He'd be paunchier, with drooping skin around the jowls, deep worry lines, and a receding hairline. He'd not have opted for plastic surgery. Most notably, List had a pronounced scar behind his right ear.

They also had to think about what would drive a man who was reportedly so religious and conservative to kill his entire family. They spent several days thinking about the buildup of anger and despair, as well as what List would have planned for his escape. Even with all of that, they felt sure List would still be involved in church activities.

Bender went to work on the bust, and it had its intended effect. After the show aired in 1989, a tip came in that led to the arrest of accountant "Bob Clark," who looked so much like the bust it was uncanny. Fingerprints affirmed his identity as John List, and he was convicted of five counts of first-degree murder.

There are many types of forensic art, from drawings to photography to three-dimensional replicas like the List bust. Whether it's used to find a missing person, work from a corpse for purposes of identification, or snare a fugitive, the artist can always benefit from the psychological information that a mental health professional can provide.

Psychological Autopsy for Equivocal Death

In Patricia Cornwell's novel *The Body Farm*, one of the investigating officers in a murder case is found dead in his home. He was wearing woman's underwear and from all appearances had died from accidental autoerotic asphyxiation. That is, he had put a rope around his neck to increase pressure to the carotid artery in order to have a heightened sexual experience. Apparently, he had underestimated his ability to escape, and the investigators were about to chalk his death up to accidental suicide. However, medical examiner Kay Scarpetta looked more closely at the evidence. A condom wrapper in the bathroom wastebasket—an odd thing for a man with a noose around his neck to do—alerted her to the possibility of murder. Then a woman's fingerprint on the panties added to her impression that she was dealing with an equivocal death—one in which the circumstances are ambiguous. That meant she had to do a more thorough analysis of the victim, which gets into the area of psychological autopsy.

> **Psychological Autopsy**
> When the circumstances surrounding a death can be interpreted in more than one way, psychologists can help compile information about behavior and motive to distinguish between accident and homicide or suicide.

One of the most famous psychological autopsies was done by Dr. Raymond Fowler following the death of Howard Hughes. He practically wrote a biography; in fact, the methods of biography are not dissimilar. Some mental health professionals estimate around twenty to thirty hours worth of work, while others believe it could take much longer. Fowler's autopsy took several years. The amount of time put into the psychological autopsy depends on the goal.

Often where a death seems likely to be an accident or suicide, the police wrap up the case quickly, but there may be more to it than they realize. Pathologists on the scene may misunderstand the importance of body position and then only provide a cursory pronouncement of death with an estimate of time of death. However, in questionable cases the position of the corpse is profoundly important, such as in the following instance.

The female victim of a hit-and-run appeared to have been sitting "Indian style" on or near the road at the time of death, apparently hit from behind by a car and dragged face down by the undercarriage. The body was found with legs crossed, and the right thigh was fractured. Her skirt was pulled up, and her stockings were torn at the knees, which were severely abraded. One pathologist questioned that she could have been sitting thus while accidentally hit. The tire tracks at the scene indicated a small automobile, which would have no room underneath for such a position. The pathologist felt that the body would have been pushed forward and the legs would have straightened—unless significant rigor mortis had already set in, which was not the case. He believed the body had been pulled and pushed toward the lower extremities—as if the vehicle had dragged the body back and forth. Blood marks on the pavement indicated that the victim had been dragged several times in an attempt to dislodge her from beneath the car. This was probably no accident but a homicide. This information changed the nature of the investigation altogether. In that case, a psychologist could help determine possible scenarios for a person to be treated like this.

A medical autopsy determines cause and means of death by examining the body. In cases where the manner of death is unexplained, such as someone hit by a car, and it's not clear whether it was a suicide, a homicide, natural, or accidental, a psychological autopsy may assist the coroner or medical examiner in clearing up the mystery. The idea is to discover the state of mind of the victim preceding death. The results may be used to settle criminal cases, estate issues, malpractice suits, or insurance claims. First used in the 1950s in Los Angeles, psychological autopsies are now a more standard resource, although still questioned in some courts as a rigorous scientific technique.

The investigator examines numerous factors to make the proper determination. In a suspected suicide, for example, it's important to rule out accident and such unfortunate incidents as autoerotic asphyxiation. The database generally consists of the following:

Examining Cloth Fragments for Clues

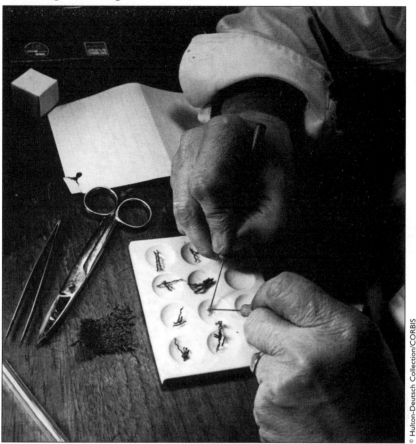

In this photograph, a forensic scientist at Scotland Yard is shown examining fragments of a cloth from a car and clothing found at the scene of a "hit and run" incident.

- an examination of the death scene (similar to the examination of a crime scene)
- a study of all documentation pertaining to the death, such as witness statements and police reports
- interviews with family members and associates
- medical autopsy reports
- history of taking medication
- reports about conflicted relationships or other stressors
- unusual recent behavior

- all relevant documents pertaining to the individual's life history, like school or employment records, letters, and diaries
- changes in wills or life insurance policies

A close examination of the death scene may indicate degree of intent and lethality—a secluded place and the use of a gun indicating a higher degree than using slow-acting pills in a place where the victim is likely to be discovered.

The investigator needs to be proficient in deception detection as well; it may be that people who knew the deceased have motives for concealing what may have happened. At times, the results will be clear, while at other times, the deceased's state of mind prior to death cannot be stated with certainty. If the psychological autopsy evidence is allowed in court, the methods must be clarified.

In his first novel, *Certifiably Insane*, Arthur Bahr made his protagonist— a forensic psychiatrist—a specialist in psychological autopsies. A good description of the procedures can also be found in Roy Hazelwood's *The Evil That Men Do* in the FBI's controversial behavioral analysis of the deceased man thought responsible for the 1989 explosion aboard the *USS Iowa*.

Psychological Investigator/Consultant

This is a hybrid between a psychologist and a detective, although not quite fully either one. Investigative psychologists generally take courses in applied psychology programs, such as the one offered in Liverpool, England, and then learn police investigation techniques. They act as assistants who have some background in human behavior, but they don't necessarily have graduate degrees in psychology nor are they licensed. What they do is get involved in applied projects in police work. Specifically, they help gather information that then gets interpreted within a scientific framework that involves background in sociology, geology, and psychology. They might also interview inmates, conduct studies, write reports or work products, do documentation searches, and offer presentations on motivational aspects of crime.

They cannot testify in court. However, a psychological investigator might make for an interesting fictional character because she would go to a crime scene, follow the investigation closely to provide specific consultation, and coach the police in specific behaviors. She might be involved in the various stages of solving a crime, while also bringing it to a new level informed by behavioral and sociological research. Thus, clues could come from some obscure study or from connections made by knowing about a number of vaguely similar cases. However, the writer would need to understand the limits of this type of profession.

Stalker Evaluations

In 1990 California was the first state to pass an antistalking law, which went into effect the following year. This happened in response to the murder of actress Rebecca Schaeffer, with whom Robert John Bardo had such an obsession that he felt he had to eliminate her. Another actress was stabbed ten times by a man who flew in from another country with the intention of killing her because that was the only way they could be together—in the afterlife.

Within another year thirty more states had passed similar laws, and by 1993 the entire country had followed suit. And they were needed. The U.S. Department of Justice estimates that every year over a million and a half people are stalked—more than two-thirds of them women. While many stalkers only threaten harm, a small percentage carry out their threats—including damage against property or harm to pets. With the rise in popularity of the Internet, cyberstalking has become yet another avenue of danger.

The unrelenting harassment of stalking causes great emotional stress in the targeted victims. Some people lose their jobs or have to change their identities and move. They may suffer from post-traumatic stress disorder—anxiety, sleep disorders, depression, and reliance on medication. Some consider suicide. Even if these incidents get reported, restraining laws can do little against the verbal harassment. In fact some laws require that there be a genuine risk of danger or a pattern of incidents before formal protection will be offered.

There is no clear way to tell who might become a stalker: It could be a former boyfriend, girlfriend, or spouse; a fellow employee who has spotted his target in some casual encounter; a hostile neighbor; even a stranger who happens to see the victim on the street. Celebrities are often the targets of stalkers who become obsessed with them through photographs, songs, or movies. Even people who were not abusive prior to their obsession can become so in the throes of it.

The stalker often views the relationship in ways that have no basis in reality. A stalker feels certain that the target person "loves" him or was meant to be with him, or he may feel the person needs to be punished in some manner. Any gesture on the part of the victim—even a restraining order—is perceived as a way to be connected. (The singer/actress Madonna pointed this out when she had to go to court against her stalker: He had achieved his dream of having her pay attention to him.) Stalkers may never go away. One woman was stalked by her former husband for thirty-one years. Another woman discovered her stalker camped out beneath her house at night, tapping her phone.

While most stalkers are males obsessed with females, it can also be the other way around: It can be men obsessed with men or children, women stalking women (someone they love or the girlfriend of someone who broke up with them), anyone stalking a couple, and someone of either sex simultaneously stalking more than one victim. Stalkers exhibit a broad range of traits and motivations. Generally, there is some extreme dependency need and overriding character instability. They have exaggerated reactions to rejection. Some may even be mentally ill or have personality disorders, such as narcissistic personality disorder or borderline personality disorder. Some may abuse drugs or alcohol.

Psychologists have provided several theories, most of them centered on attachment issues. The idea of attachment theory is that children develop certain ways of attaching to others, and those patterns will persist into adulthood. Children will either have a positive or negative type of attachment, but the one that results in the most abusive behavior is when the person feels negatively about both himself and the person to whom he attaches. It is a fear-based relationship, mixed with self-hate and abandonment issues. The stalker desires but also distrusts relationships. She may have been traumatized in a past relationship and overreacts with rage when rejected.

Another scenario develops with a person who may have overvalued a significant other (caretaker, parent, teacher) early in life, so she needs constant approval and affirmation from someone else. That means she will experience severe anxiety over needing a person in her life who validates her, and this need can precipitate anger and abuse.

There are several stalker typologies used by mental health professionals, but according to psychiatrist Michael Zona and his colleagues in threat management, stalkers appear to come in three basic varieties.

1. **Simple obsession:** The most common form of simple obsession is a male with a female with whom he was once sexually intimate. He cannot deal well with the end of the relationship, so he instigates a campaign of harassment.

2. **Love obsession:** A love-obsessed stalker tends to idealize a celebrity or someone he has seen from afar. He develops an unrealistic belief that the target person will feel strongly about him once they meet.

3. **Erotomania:** Someone suffering from this obsession believes he or she is loved by the victim. No one can convince her otherwise. This type tends to be female and can be quite aggressive in her pursuit of a supposed relationship.

According to stalking expert J. Reid Meloy, a central component in motivating and maintaining stalking is fantasy—in other words, a delusional behavior. A narcissistic link is developed by the stalker such that he believes the other person is essential to the fantasy and will fulfill it. Stalkers tend to be unemployed or underemployed but are smarter than other criminals. They often have histories of failed intimate relationships. They tend to devalue and sexualize their victims. They also idealize certain people, minimize what they are doing, project onto people motives and actions that have no basis in truth, and rationalize that the victims deserve to be harassed and violated.

Mental health professionals with expertise in this behavior may present expert testimony, consult with attorneys, or assist the police in helping predict what stalkers might do. They also participate in threat management programs. These consist of risk assessment based on analyzing actuarial data, monitoring information, and proving an array of intervention strategies that take into account the individualized nature of such cases.

One odd phenomenon that mental health professionals might encounter involves what is known as "false victimization syndrome." There are people who claim they are victims of stalking when they are not. They report harassment, threats of violence, and even actual attacks that never took place. They tend to consume more medical services and to thrive on the attention. What sets them apart is that they usually seek help before true stalking victims would, and they are less likely to claim that their harassment came via letters (hence they don't have to produce evidence). Real stalking victims are generally embarrassed to acknowledge this is happening to them, so when someone seems to relish the attention, false victimization syndrome should be suspected.

A Fictional Case

In *Romeo*, a crime suspense novel by Elise Title, female psychiatrist Melanie Rosen profiles a San Francisco serial killer nicknamed "Romeo." She discusses why he likes power over his victims, who all seem to be competent professional women who'd each gone on a date with him. Evidence of bondage from the crime scenes indicates that these women might have been linked by a need to submit to a powerful man. He also cuts out each one's heart and leaves behind the shriveled heart of his previous victim. Rosen assists the police in their investigation and crime scene analysis, and she also discusses her understanding of this brutal offender on a television show. She offers a clear explanation of a sexual psychopath, but some of her psychoanalytic insights are highly speculative. When she faces the killer, she finds out that he doesn't quite agree. He finds her formulas amusing and is eager to show her—by killing her—that she didn't quite guess right about him. Whether she did or not is moot, because in her case, he changes the scenario.

Whenever mental health professionals are used for profiling, consultation, or investigation, writers need to remember that the professionals are not detectives or law enforcement personnel (unless like James Patterson's Alex Cross, they have credentials in both fields). During legal proceedings, mental health professionals will generally serve as consultants, helping with court strategies and providing insight about information that police and detectives dig up. Of course, that does not prevent them from being stalked.

One of crime fiction's standard formulas is to have the expert become a target, as in *Romeo*. In that case, a good knowledge of the types of stalkers—particularly when the mental health professional has expertise in it—is a bonus. *Copycat* is an excellent example of a movie that achieves this.

12

Other Applications

A Quick Overview

Besides criminal transactions, psychologists are used in some civil proceedings and for consultation on psychological issues, such as stress effects on mental fitness. Outside the courtroom, mental health professionals have some presence in emergency service fields, including fire control, corrections, and law enforcement. They may be asked to consult with police departments on hostage negotiations, provide assessments on preemployment exams for police officers, give fitness for duty evaluations, and help with special unit (SWAT, Tactical Response Team) evaluations. Additionally, they might serve as jury consultants and offer behavioral expertise on other types of forensic projects.

Civil Proceedings

The difference between criminal and civil trials is that in criminal proceedings, government prosecutors enforce the law through fines and incarceration. In civil arenas, disputes are enforced by private individuals, and financial awards are given for violations and damages. Sometimes mental health professionals get involved to assess competency or degree of pain and suffering. Civil proceedings include the following general areas:

- personal injury and property damage
- intentional misconduct, such as assault, slander, trespass, and invasion of privacy
- negligence, such as malpractice, wrongful death, or emotional distress
- liability, such as product liability, animal control, insurance, and class-action lawsuits

- contracts
- intellectual property
- family law
- estate planning

Mental health professionals tend to get involved in civil commitment, civil competencies, emotional suffering, mental injury, sexual harassment, child abuse, and child custody issues.

1. Civil Commitment

Civil commitment is the state-sanctioned hospitalization of someone who is deemed a danger to self or others and who is judged to need treatment. It involves the state's authority to protect the community, as the guardian of infants and lunatics, although the risk of error to the individual must be minimized.

Commitment involves the standard of "clear and convincing evidence." No limits are imposed by law on the length of time a person can be committed, although it usually is decided in increments of six months. Commitment decisions once were made solely at the discretion of psychiatrists, but it was found that this discretion was frequently abused. Civil liberties lawyers stepped in and got some needed changes (although some have argued that they have taken things too far and in the name of freedom have an unwittingly endangered people). There were challenges even from within the mental health community to using labels to legitimize the segregation of bothersome individuals; many said there was no justification for this curtailment of liberties and believed there were serious consequences to the individual. People in institutions were stigmatized. Even worse, they were also thrown into horrendous living conditions. The situation finally evolved in which the mere existence of a mental illness was insufficient for involuntary commitment. To subject a person to this it had to be an exercise of police power, not parental care. The state cannot confine an individual who can survive safely in freedom—and lawyers are now stepping in to enforce this.

Some of these issues are explored in the 1987 film *Nuts* when a call girl who murders her client in self-defense is subjected to a competency hearing.

Her parents want to get her declared mentally incompetent, so she can be involuntarily committed. She resists.

The mental health professional's role in civil commitment proceedings is often to provide an evaluation of dangerousness—which is highly controversial. At best, he should provide descriptions of current behavior, assess treatment needs, judge the patient's ability to survive outside an institution, and provide options for meeting those needs. The mental health professional can mention factors that might be likely to enhance or reduce violence, but the court should decide the ultimate issue. Mental health professionals can also serve as consultants to attorneys who are seeking alternatives to commitment.

2. Civil Competencies

The civil competencies area involves making assessments about whether there exists a functional inability to make important decisions or perform certain tasks. Some of the issues involve property control, treatment specifications, self-determination, and the agreement to participate in experiments.

In an episode of *Law and Order*, a judge who wanted to disconnect life support after she was shot was evaluated for whether she was competent to make such a decision. Keeping her alive was in the court's interest in a pending criminal case, so they had her daughter sign an affidavit to the effect that the judge was too depressed, and thus incompetent, to make a rational decision about her life.

One issue involving civil competency is guardianship, or the state of authority over another person or an estate. For example, children are presumed incompetent to make certain decisions, so they are subject to the decisions made on their behalf by their natural guardians. Civilly committed adults are likewise assumed to be incompetent, especially with respect to refusal of treatment or decisions about their estates. The issues in guardianship proceedings are as follows:

- deciding if a guardian is necessary
- deciding who shall be appointed
- deciding what things that person shall be required to do

When courts view guardianship as involving issues of due process, function-specific mental health evaluations may be done. In other words, a mental health professional assesses whatever mental capacity is in question, from presence of mind to ability to manage someone else's affairs.

Another civil competency issue is competency to make treatment decisions. Informed consent is a primary aspect of this, which involves full disclosure, voluntary choice, and competency to understand. The person involved must be given sufficient information to make a decision, except in emergencies or where such disclosure poses the potential for psychological damage. Competency is generally assumed for most people, excepting children, the elderly, and the mentally incapacitated. The competency tests involve getting information about the following:

- expression of preferences
- understanding the issues
- appreciation of what's at stake
- reasonableness in decision-making
- ensuring a reasonable outcome

The methods that most respect personal autonomy are observed.

An evaluation involves talking to the person in question. She is asked what she has been told about the treatment, and if she displays ignorance on several points, the mental health professional must see if the person can comprehend those points once informed—specifically the risks and benefits. She must also be asked her reasons for refusing treatment and whether she is aware of alternatives. There may also need to be an evaluation on the likelihood that she may deteriorate or become dangerous without medication.

Testamentary capacity is another area of civil competency, and it has to do with state of mind while executing a will. Being of "sound mind" involves

- knowing that one is making one's will
- knowing the extent of one's property
- knowing those to whom one is passing one's goods
- knowing how the will specifically distributes one's property

Only a low threshold of functioning is required for legal standards. The trick for a mental health professional in these evaluations is that, in most cases, the testator is dead. Some of the information needed to determine competence and knowledge will be found in the will or in statements made to other people, similar to the way a psychological autopsy assesses state of mind prior to death. A mental health professional may be needed to figure out the person's values and preferences with regard to family relationships.

3. Emotional Suffering/Distress

Monetary damages in cases of tortious misconduct (private wrongs) are decided by juries, including pain and suffering or any form of mental anguish. The harm is compensable if the law defines it as important enough to hold the person who causes it liable for it. If mental suffering is a clear consequence of an independent tort, such as slander, the harm can be compensated. This is generally presented in terms of what a "reasonable person" would consider offensive or distressful.

Clinical evaluations in mental injury cases require documentation and plenty of information-gathering to determine whether injury has actually occurred and whether it is clearly related to the defendant. There is also an investigation into whether there were any pre-existing conditions or disorders. A determination is then made as to the extent of the damage to the plaintiff's ability to function, especially with regard to the future and to his or her ability to earn money.

One of the more popular approaches to mental injury is to diagnose post-traumatic stress disorder. This is also used in workers' compensation cases. Mental health professionals should be familiar with the checklists and diagnostic instruments devised specifically for post-traumatic stress disorder.

One such list asks for the clinician to determine whether the following symptoms are present:

- repeated recall of the incident
- sleep disturbances
- fatigue and agitation
- sadness, anxiety, depression
- quick startle response
- detachment, irritability, anger
- memory difficulties
- pervasive feelings of guilt
- loss of appetite and interest in life

In addition, mental health professionals must be alert to malingering. Certain conditions are easily faked, such as post-traumatic stress disorder, so third-party corroboration and a documented history of symptoms is important. A prognosis should also be made, including statistical information about chances of rehabilitation.

4. Workers' Compensation for Mental Injuries

Tort law is the law of civil wrongs. The same act can come into both criminal and civil court, as happened in the case of O.J. Simpson when he was prosecuted for both the murder and "wrongful death" of his former wife. Tortious conduct may be intentional, negligent, or involving liability. Because of the way the tort system emphasizes fault, other compensation systems have arisen. The workers' compensation proceeding ignores the potential fault of the injured party and provides coverage for anyone who is employed. Part of what is covered is mental injury. In such cases, a mental health professional may be asked to assess the impact of certain work-related events on a worker's mental functioning. This could come from physical trauma or from a mental stimulus (discrimination, harassment) that causes a physical or mental injury. Some condition of the employment, such as long periods in isolation, might also aggravate a pre-existing disorder.

5. Sexual Harassment

Business law covers a variety of situations, from wrongful termination to employment discrimination. One of the areas in which mental health professionals get involved in court and in research is sexual harassment or gender discrimination. This involves any unwelcome advances or conduct that makes the working environment difficult in a sexually charged way. This may include jokes, inappropriate gestures or noises, magazine pinups, suggestive touching, and sexual coercion. A mental health professional may be asked to evaluate the mental injury in a particular case or to provide general information about the concept of what a "reasonable person" might believe about a given situation—the typical standard when opinions may vary widely. Often one of the parties may lie, deny, or exaggerate, so the mental health professional involved must make judgments about whether or not abuse or harassment has occurred—especially when there are no clear lines drawn. Sometimes a test battery that uses projective assessments yields clarity about the sexual ideation of both the alleged harasser and the alleged victim. Note that some people will claim harassment where none actually exists, so mental health professionals need to be careful.

6. Child Abuse

The state has an interest in and a duty to protect children and can invoke its authority where children are neglected and abused. Since this can interfere with family privacy, which the state also protects, the issues can get confusing. For example, it can be unclear in a given situation whether children are better off with difficult parents or with the child care services of the state. It can also be unclear whether a temporary removal from the home is sufficient or whether it needs to be made permanent. The most difficult issue involves the lack of consensus among mental health professionals (and the courts) on what constitutes abuse and also on how this abuse is discovered.

A mental health professional may be involved in evaluating the child and/or treating the parents or family. Her initial involvement in the legal process is through investigation, and she may also enter a case on an emergency basis. The mental health professional must find out what happened and what can be done, which means taking statements from all parties involved. That gets into issues of deception detection, using the evaluation to make exaggerated statements as payback on some grudge, and whether young children can make accurate statements. It becomes quite difficult when the abused and the abuser are related, especially in positions of dominance and dependence.

If things proceed to court, then there are issues about whether the child is competent to testify. A mental health professional must determine whether the child remembers and can communicate the events that occurred, whether he knows the difference between fantasy and reality, and whether he understands the importance of telling the truth. There are different criteria for statements about different types of abuse (sexual, emotional, negligent). Mental health professionals must be familiar with the legal differences.

Any mental health professional involved in such proceedings needs to consult the latest research on children as witnesses and to learn to evaluate a child's ability to communicate in different contexts. Web sites like www.find law.com may have the most recent issues, and using a search engine like www.google.com can get writers to plenty of professional sites. Use search words like children, competency to testify, and court witness. It's unlikely that a book or even a professional journal will have the latest developments. Writers may join child abuse foundations like the National Clearinghouse on Child Abuse and Neglect (www.calib.com/nccanch) to get newsletters. Web sites include http://child-abuse.com for the Child Abuse Prevention Network and www.childabuse.org.

A mental health professional may also be involved in expert testimony about such things as the characteristics of abused children and the traits of a child abuser. She may make assessments about alleviating the current psychological harm and about preventing further mistreatment. This may involve medicating a parent with a mental illness or devising a program for anger management or substance abuse. One further duty for a mental health professional, in the event the child is removed from the home, might be placement evaluations.

7. Child Custody

In Virginia a man requested custody of his unborn child. He claimed the woman carrying the fetus would be unfit and would raise the child in a dangerous inner-city environment. The woman countered with the statement that the father of her child wanted nothing to do with her once she was pregnant. Each believed that he or she would be a better parent for the child than the other. The issue became not just one of parental fitness but also of whether the court had jurisdiction over an unborn child. A mental health professional in this situation would evaluate whether one of the parties was clearly unfit.

It is estimated that mental health professionals are involved in only about 10 percent of custody cases. Their best function is to gather facts for the court and report research on the psychological effects of various custody arrangements (such as a daughter's chances of adapting well to a father custody situation). If a mental health professional was a therapist for one of the parties, he is advised by the American Psychological Association to refrain from offering testimony except to report evidential facts.

Perhaps the custody situation most likely to involve mental health professionals are those that deal with special populations, such as same-sex couples.

The courts often make assumptions based on false stereotypes, such as homosexuality being an illness, so mental health professionals can set the record straight with research data.

In the event that there are serious parental competence issues, the mental health professional may submit the parties to a battery of assessments. This might involve self-report statements, questionnaires, attitude surveys, IQ testing, substance abuse evaluations, the child's conceptualization of the parents, the child's emotional functioning, and emotional evaluations. There are also parental competency screening devices such as the Michigan Screening Profile of Parenting and the Ackerman-Schoendorf Scales for Parent Evaluation of Custody (ASPECT).

8. Insurance Liability

While insurance liability appears to offer nothing dramatic for writers, it might be a topic that's worth pursuing. Former FBI profiler Roy Hazelwood is a member of the Academy Group, Inc., which consists of other profilers who are available for research, consultation, and expert testimony on a variety of cases that involve violence. One liability case Hazelwood worked on involved a brutal murder. He was there to assess whether the presence of a security guard would have deterred the attacker.

The victim was a twenty-one-year-old girl who was learning disabled. She had just gotten her driver's license and decided to go to the store one evening to buy some yogurt. Her mother was on her way out to attend a Bible study class, so the girl went alone. The store was not far away, but she just happened to arrive at the wrong place at the wrong time.

A man who had killed several young women was on the lookout for a victim. What he often enjoyed was pulling up to a woman and pointing what looked like a real 9mm gun out the window to frighten her. He spotted the girl and decided to scare her. However, she got into her car before he could get her attention, so he followed her. He figured he could pull along beside her at the first stop sign, but there were none, so he ended up following her to where she lived.

Just when she pulled up to the gate, the security guard disappeared to go to the restroom. She used her key card to get in, but the gate stayed up long enough for two cars to get through. With no guard to observe this happening, the killer slipped in easily behind his victim and went right to where she parked.

He pointed the toy gun at her and said nothing. Since she did not understand such things, she put down her purse and yogurt cup, saying, "Please don't hurt me." At that moment, he changed tactics. She would be easier than he thought. He told her to get into the van, and she meekly complied. Then he joined her in the back, tied her up, and used a screwdriver to kill her. Once that was done, he drove away and dumped the body. He was later arrested and brought to trial.

"My job on this case," Hazelwood said, "was to talk about the type of killer he was and to say what would or would not have stopped him. I knew from police reports that on previous occasions when this guy was confronted, he would leave, so that was his pattern. If you as a woman were walking down the street and he started following you, and you turned around and said, 'What are you doing? Get the hell out of here!' he would just go. That convinced me that had a gate guard been present and challenged him for not having a sticker on his car, he would have backed off and left." In other words, the community that allowed the gate to go unprotected for any length of time by having only one guard on duty was liable for whatever might happen. The victim's mother won the case.

Screenings for Police Officers

Psychology makes a contribution to understanding the police and their function in society. A mental health professional looks at biases such as personality factors, stress, and police-community relations that may affect an officer's performance and competence. Mental health professionals can help police to more effectively talk with victims and question offenders. More often they assist with personnel issues, such as helping partners work with each other or deal with stress on the job.

In the 1960s, police psychology became an established specialization, and increasingly more police departments used standard scoring assessments given by mental health professionals. In many states the assessments became a requirement. Forms were developed to help determine who was best fitted for police work and who should be screened out.

As liability issues become more expensive for municipalities, some sort of psychological screening may become mandatory to prove that the city has taken all necessary precautions to hire stable employees.

Psychologists who test police officers rely on

- interviews
- observations in structured situations
- psychological assessment devices

The interview helps build rapport and gather initial information but is insufficient as an evaluation tool in itself. Situational tests might involve memory, perception, problem-solving skills, and emotional maturity. Psychological tests include IQ and personality inventories that have some predictive capacity for certain behaviors, such as being anger-prone or resistant to authority. While criteria vary for the "ideal" police officer, departments tend to seek well-adjusted, nonreactive, honest, logical, and people-oriented types for further training.

There are also fitness-for-duty evaluations. If an individual officer appears to be psychologically impaired, a series of tests can make a determination about that person's ability to perform the job. Confidentiality is balanced against public safety, but the psychologist must also be able to detect when an officer is distorting answers to project his or her job. Some departments employ a police psychologist to do all such evaluations and provide treatment. Others separate the evaluation from the treatment process to avoid conflict-of-interest situations.

Psychologists might also train police officers in such things as crisis intervention. When officers are called into situations involving mentally ill people, they can be educated as to what to expect from different types of psychosis and medication reactions. If there is no obvious danger to self or others, the officers can provide temporary on-the-spot counseling. If an arrest must be made, psychologists can educate police on how best to handle a potentially violent person. At the very least, education can help officers minimize their own fear factor.

Domestic disturbances generally require education in abuse and battered woman syndrome. Training programs by police psychologists generally focus on strategies that avoid arrest. Role-playing gives officers a chance to see how certain situations feel and to better prepare them to handle those situations in the field. They learn techniques for calming people, reducing tension, getting people to talk, and decreasing the potential for violence. Officers also learn the facts about domestic violence so they don't fall prey to myths that a battered wife provokes violence or that family violence occurs mostly in areas of high poverty.

Police interrogation techniques also can result in false confessions. Police need to be educated in the effective use of this approach so that they do not cross the line into the sort of intimidation and coercion that gets controversial results.

Hostage negotiation often involves people suffering from mental disorders or going through serious personal crises. At the heart of it may be depression, delusions, or schizophrenia. The hostage takers may also feel powerlessness and may be suicidal. Some are attempting to commit victim-precipitated death or "suicide by police," which means they want the police to shoot them. An excellent film on the psychology of hostage negotiations is *The Negotiator*, in which a professional hostage negotiator himself ends up taking hostages. He demands the services of another top-rated professional, and their conversations reveal the subtle psychological nuances and stress of this job.

Such situations involve a high degree of fear, both with the hostages and the perpetrator, and can be extremely dangerous. Even when planned, such as in a terrorist situation, emotional conflicts can escalate the danger. The successful negotiator must understand the various dynamics so he or she can manipulate the situation toward decreased volatility. If captivity of hostages is prolonged, the dynamics change, particularly in terms of the hostages feeling dependent. They can begin to experience positive feelings toward their kidnapper—the Stockholm Syndrome—and the negotiator needs to understand both how this works and how to take advantage of it for peaceful resolution. There may also be a debriefing session for the victims once released, so a psychologist can help suggest what the hostages may be feeling.

Lastly, psychologists are often needed in police departments for stress management. Officers are constantly evaluated for how effective they are, and public criticism can take a toll. There may also be times when an officer is separated from his or her family for a period of time. Officers are constantly exposed to the potential for physical and psychological threats, temptations to compromise their standards, and frustration with unresolved cases. They may also fall into dehumanizing people just to be able to cope. In addition, they may suffer from nightmares, emotional numbing, anxiety, substance abuse, family conflicts, and any number of other psychological difficulties that increase their stress factors. Psychologists can assist with such strategies as the following:

- standardized stress survey
- counseling
- peer counseling groups
- specific interventions, such as overuse of certain tactics
- post-incident debriefing

Despite popular notions in the culture at large, police psychologists are not used as profilers—that's not their expertise—or as investigators. They have specific functions in police departments and may encounter resentment if they try to become detectives.

Innocence Projects

David Milgaard was arrested in 1969 in Canada for the rape and murder of a young woman. He served twenty-eight years in prison before it became apparent that someone else had committed the crime. Eventually DNA evidence exonerated him, but his mind had been seriously damaged by his ordeal. It turned out that controversial police interrogation tactics had been used to pressure two of his friends to falsely place him at the crime scene with a knife. Then, a prosecutor manipulated a jury of older men to believe in the stereotype of dangerous young men with long hair. A better understanding of the psychological effects of the investigation methods and of social biases in a jury might have convinced the U.S. Justice Department to look into his case long before they actually did. The evidence of the real perpetrator's previous crimes were offered, and witness statements were recanted, but the justices initially ignored all of that. An education in the effects of police manipulation could have set the scales of justice straight.

Social science research has been valuable for pointing out numerous problem areas in the legal process, such as false confessions, eyewitness testimony, and manipulative interrogation procedures. As such, mental health professionals can consult on aspects of the various programs being set up around the country to prove the innocence of people who were wrongly incarcerated. Although many of these programs focus on DNA evidence, which has nothing to do with social science research, some investigators are looking at other things, such as profiling, character, and actuarial statistics on behavior.

Gary Graham, for example, is on death row in Texas for killing a man during a robbery when he was seventeen. He was convicted based on the testimony of a single eyewitness who saw him in the dark from some distance away. A store clerk who saw the shooter flee did not testify—although he was ready to claim that Graham was not the man. There was no DNA or fingerprint evidence to test, so this is clearly a case where character analysis and risk assessment techniques could assist. To convict someone and sentence that person to die based solely on an eyewitness with poor visibility is a poor procedure. To add the fact that eyewitnesses who are confident are often wrong means that certain court traditions must be reevaluated.

Defense attorneys—particularly if they are assigned to cases by the court—have limited resources and sometimes offer inadequate counsel. There are also clear cases of prosecutorial misconduct, tampering with evidence, and poor fact-finding procedures.

In fact, a journalistic investigation of 285 death penalty cases in Illinois found that half involved incompetent defense attorneys, questionable jailhouse snitches, questionable hair analysis results, or obvious racial biases. DNA analysis exonerated thirteen of these men, prompting the governor to place a moratorium on executions in the state. This event started with the cases of four black men, two of whom were slated to die, in the 1978 murder of a white couple near Chicago. A couple of journalists turned up evidence that the men were innocent. Then, DNA tests exonerated them altogether. Finally, three other men confessed.

It was chilling to think four innocent men had been incarcerated and two had nearly been put to death. Then, other cases followed—thanks to the legwork of journalism students at Northwestern University. Another man was only two days from execution when his conviction was overturned. He had an IQ of 51 and should never have been that close to the death chamber.

According to a report in the Associated Press, two-thirds of death penalty appeals from 1973 to 1995 were successful. This is a shameful testament to

Using DNA in Criminal Investigations

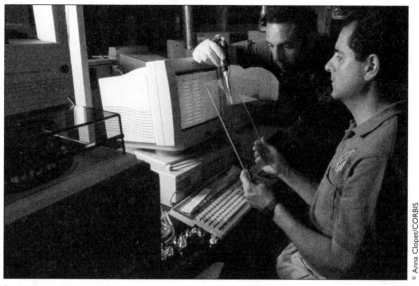

Forensic specialists use the facilities at the FBI Academy in Quantico, Virginia, to investigate the use of DNA taken from dandruff samples at a crime scene. Through DNA testing, many suspects have been proven to be innocent of crimes where it seemed they were undoubtedly guilty.

the enormous number of mistakes made in some very serious cases.

A mental health professional may not have the power to exonerate someone, but she can bear research that indicates perception problems in eyewitnesses, the psychological pressures of a jury system, the problems with confession evidence, and even the effects of expert witnesses who might be influential but nevertheless wrong. One experiment, for example, pitted two tire tread experts against each other in a murder case. The older and more experienced man had a greater air of authority. He said quite definitely that the tire tread pattern from a hypothetical crime scene matched the tire of the car driven by the suspect. The other expert saw problems with that and refused to make such a strong statement. He was right, the older man was wrong, and yet the jury sided with the one in error. Why? According to the poll, he just seemed more convincing.

Unfortunately, what social science experts have to reveal about the judicial system is often disallowed. However, they can still act as consultants for attorneys.

Mental Health Court

A mental health court in Florida is set up to provide care to individuals with mental disorders or substance addictions who are waiting for their misdemeanor cases to be heard. Doctoral students in psychology are responsible for screening the cases and making referrals. They look for the reasons why a person is arrested, because a pattern for certain offenses like substance abuse or disorderly conduct signals a potential mental health issue. They then ask about prior mental health treatment, head injuries, and previous drug treatment. If they find someone who qualifies, they alert the public defender's office and make a referral to the mental health court. They may also have to make a case for treatment in front of a judge.

A few other jurisdictions in Washington, Illinois, and California have followed this model. It is hoped that more states will see the benefit and allocate funding.

Clinics like this help to mitigate the fact that so many people with mental disorders end up in prisons rather than in places where they can receive medication and counseling. To this point, about 75 percent of the mentally ill have been sentenced to prison, and 16 percent of the prison population suffers from a mental illness. This may be the result of the reduction of mental health services in many states and the shutdown of numerous psychiatric facilities.

It is likely that in the future there will be more such mental health courts. Writers should be able to find plenty of material from potential cases.

Litigation Consulting/Jury Analysis

Psychology experts are often part of a legal team in the courtroom. Sometimes they work as freelance consultants and sometimes as part of consulting firms. They have several functions, most specifically that of evaluating the various people going through *voir dire* to become jury members.

First, however, a psychology expert needs to know the nature of the case before he can decide which traits he wants to seek in potential jury members. The goal is to help attorneys assemble a group of people who will listen with an open mind to the client's story. Thus, the expert prepares a "juror profile," a list of the attributes of the kind of person who will view the specific case favorably. In other words, the expert has to look at such things as racial bias, gender issues, and conservative values. He examines what people wear, what their body language expresses, and aspects of behavior that reveal "predictive traits"—those characteristics most likely to affect a person's beliefs that are relevant to the case.

As part of the process, the psychology expert might conduct a mock jury trial in the community, a telephone survey, or a focus group to try to determine the types of responses he can expect in a given area. He asks each person who participates a list of questions that will yield clues about what the person might think of a case. The consultant then records age, sex, race, employment history, hobbies, experiences growing up, marital status, and other habits. This provides a database from which to develop a profile.

In a mock trial, the consultant can ask questions specific to the case and get reactions to the key issues, such as capital punishment, attitudes toward the police, or settlement awards. The replies help build correlations between attitudes and personality traits. This helps the consultants know what to look for and how to prepare specific questions for the real jurors. In short, the jury consultant is looking for patterns.

Basically, the consultant examines traits that provide information about socioeconomic background, compassion, and life attitudes. A focus group composed of people likely to represent the typical juror can help the consultant offer advice on developing arguments and opening and closing speeches, determining the effectiveness of visual aids, developing questions for *voir dire*, making notes for jury instruction, and for revealing less obvious aspects of the case. (Many consulting firms use at least three focus groups for better objectivity.)

Then during jury selection, the expert assesses candidates for their degree of empathy, attention to detail, analytical abilities, life experiences, prejudices, and personality traits. Research indicates that juries make decisions based more firmly on their values, beliefs, and experiences than on the facts of cases. Some cases, such as those involving the death penalty, require particular care in certain areas, such as authoritarian attitudes or the urge to punish. In civil cases, personal experience may be more important.

A litigation consultant believes it's essential to know what she is looking for in a case before the selection starts and to be completely objective in evaluating each person. She also wants to warn lawyers to avoid the most common errors: attempts to indoctrinate the jury, poor strategies for bonding with the jury, and overselling—especially selling the case too soon. Lawyers need to listen to individual jury members when they ask questions, and they need to take the process seriously. Otherwise they will pay dearly for their inattention when jury members feel alienated and unimportant.

A jury consultant might also get involved in the following areas:

- witness preparation
- identifying jury leaders
- judging jury sympathy
- reading the opponents
- file reviews for civil litigation
- trial testimony evaluation
- argument strategy
- demographic research
- exhibit preparation for easy comprehension
- attorney seminars
- evaluation of monetary damages for psychological suffering

A scenario that involves litigation consulting by a mental health professional would be the following.

A case involving a highly technical engineering firm required several dozen witnesses whose testimony was difficult for the average person to follow. The defense counted on the case being over the heads of the jury, but the consulting psychologist managed to rehearse witnesses for the plaintiff to speak clearly and simply. This aided jury deliberations and made the jury more appreciative of the side that took the trouble to help them understand the case. They expressed that appreciation in their award to the plaintiff.

To prepare for your writing, read a range of criminal cases and pay attention to civil proceedings to determine how best to use a mental health professional in an original situation. There are many possibilities for drama and plot twists, even in something as seemingly innocuous as product liability.

13
Ethics

Ethical Errors

Hannibal Lecter probably demonstrated the worst breach of professional ethics possible: He killed and ate some of his patients, and (no pun intended) he did it with relish. Fortunately, most mental health professionals have lesser concerns, but there are many ways psychologists and psychiatrists can get themselves into trouble in the forensic arena.

A good example is the following case: A psychologist named Paul Dell was called into question regarding an ethical issue when he came forward after the arrest of Tom Donney for killing his nineteen-year-old daughter in North Carolina in 1987. Dell had read newspaper reports about Donney's apparent lapses of memory, and he introduced himself to the defense counsel as an expert on multiple personality disorder. He suspected that Donney might be suffering from this and wanted to evaluate the man. After a clinical interview, Dell put Donney under hypnosis, which he videotaped. Dell seemed to get nine other personalities coming through, which he said were manifested by odd finger tapping. He also appeared to be coaching Donney to the effect that if those personalities did not come through, Donney would be facing a probable guilty verdict. In other words, he gave Donney every good reason to pretend—and did this while Donney was in a highly suggestible state.

Dell then testified on the stand that this was a clear case of a man who was not responsible for his actions because a personality named "Satan" had made him murder his daughter. First of all, it was hardly a clear case, and second, Dell's method of eliciting the "personalities" was highly questionable.

Hannibal Lecter Behind Bars

Reprinted with permission of PhotoFest, Inc., New York

Anthony Hopkins's gives a chilling portrayal of cannibal Hannibal Lecter in *The Silence of the Lambs*, which was based on a novel by Thomas Harris. Through the character played by Jodie Foster, this movie provides a fictional example of a profiler who tracks down a killer.

The jury didn't buy it and found Donney guilty. Dell was criticized by colleagues as a man who had used the case to boost his own career, noting that both the use of hypnosis and a diagnosis of multiple personality disorder were controversial in the field.

However, in 1992, a state-appointed psychiatrist evaluated Donney and presented evidence that he was not competent to have been on trial. A mistrial was declared, and the case remains unresolved. Donney himself, now in a psychiatric facility, claims he never stated to anyone that he had more than one personality. This appeared to be a case of a mental health professional reaching for evidence that fit his theory—to the point of seeming to invent it himself—rather than looking at what was actually there. In the case of theories as controversial as multiple personality disorder, mental health professionals have to be even more alert to how they interpret ambiguous behaviors. The temptation is always there to make more of some symptom than is warranted—especially for a mental health professional who develops a reputation on a certain psychological syndrome.

This kind of problem was clearly illustrated in the movie *Primal Fear*. When a neuropsychologist who testifies in a case of multiple personality disorder is asked about her credentials, she admits that she does not specialize in the disorder and has little clinical experience. In fact, she is an academic who bases her testimony strictly on research. She not only did not conduct any of the appropriate clinical tests for personality factors and possible malingering but declared her diagnosis after only a superficial clinical interview. It soon became clear that she was reaching well beyond her expertise, which ought not to be allowed under any circumstances, let alone in a capital case. Because she was inexperienced, she was easily deceived by a clever offender. Although such things do happen in real cases, it is unlikely that she would have qualified in a real *voir dire* as an expert in such a case. As it turned out, her limitations and apparent ignorance of what goes into a full-scale forensic examination contributed to a verdict that freed a guilty man. In real life, this would be an egregious breach of professional ethics.

Ethical Principles for Mental Health Professionals

In the courtroom, no matter which roles they provide, mental health professionals should uphold the general standards of their profession. In 1992 the American Psychological Association addressed forensic psychology in their Ethical Code. There was also a guide published in the *Law and Human Behavior* journal called the Specialty Guidelines for Forensic Psychologists.

Accordingly, mental health professionals should conduct themselves as representatives of the profession, both morally and legally. If they consult on topics, they should know their limits of expertise and not allow themselves to be pressured to offer testimony or opinions on subjects about which they have little experience. Likewise, they should not oversell themselves as experts on subjects if they have limited experience with them. They should provide services and techniques only when they are qualified to do so, and they should observe the integrity of the legal system at all times—even when the layers who hired them do not. They need to learn courtroom protocol and conform their behaviors to it.

During the Menendez trial, for example, an obvious and embarrassing breach of ethics occurred that could have resulted in a lesser sentence. Eighteen experts were called in to testify during the three-week penalty phase. During the second week, Dr. William Vicary, the psychiatrist who had treated Erik Menendez, admitted that Erik's defense lawyer, Leslie Abramson, had asked him to doctor his notes. He had done so, leaving out whole sections in which Erik had made incriminating statements. This was discovered when Abramson inadvertently gave the entire set of notes to the prosecutor's expert witness, Dr. Park Dietz. If it were not for this mistake, no one would have known. It turned out that Vicary had rewritten ten pages and removed twenty-four pages to avoid any suggestion that the murders had been planned. He clearly had violated professional ethics.

No mental health professional should purposely distort his report to support a legal strategy. Attorneys know this, but some may resort to this anyway. While it is permissible to ask a mental health professional to discard irrelevant information or rephrase jargon, it is not okay to use psychological information in a way that clearly misrepresents the actual report.

Mental health professionals are ethically charged to guide lawyers in the use of their work so it is not inappropriately applied. A forensic psychologist working with an attorney for a young man who was arrested for dealing drugs did an involved workup. The results of her test battery indicated that the man needed structure but would not do well too far from his family connections. The lawyer wanted to get him a stint on a special ranch for young men, because he could then avoid a sentence. However, the ranch was too far away for his family to visit him, so the lawyer asked the psychologist to restructure her findings to support what he wanted to do. This meant downplaying the severity of his dependent personality by removing any statements about his need for family support. She resisted, claiming her test results failed to support this alternative to incarceration and might even damage the boy. She also pointed out that the offender did not want to go to the ranch. Then, the lawyer pressured her with economic blackmail—either she change the report to his liking or she would get no more cases from him. Against her better judgment, she rewrote the report. What she did is unethical, because it was in her best interests, not those of the client. It was her duty to guide the lawyer on the defendant's mental well-being, not allow the lawyer—who had no mental health expertise—to guide her.

However, it can also be the case that a mental health professional might try to pressure a lawyer to discard another mental health professional's testimony, which is also unethical. People who move in and out of the same courthouse often get to know each other, and using an acquaintance to pressure for a different tactic violates professional boundaries.

An episode of *Law and Order* provided a context for this, although it was never made clear that the mental health professional had been unethical. In the case where a ten-year-old girl had murdered a seven-year-old boy in cold blood, the district attorney had a forensic evaluation performed by the court psychiatrist, Emil Skoda. After a cursory evaluation, Skoda pronounced the child an incurable sociopath. To counter him, the defense hired Dr. Elizabeth Olivet, a specialist in child psychology who had often worked for the district attorney's office on other cases. She felt Skoda had dismissed the child's possible rehabilitation too easily, and in court she criticized his tendency to rely on drug therapy. During a court recess, she went to the district attorney to use their past association to pressure him to listen to her rather than to his own expert. This kind of behavior should not have been allowed. Olivet crossed the line in terms of professional ethics.

Ethical standards apply no matter what capacity the mental health professional serves in. In some positions, such as investigator or profiler or consultant, the standards can be less clear. However, in each position, mental health professionals have an obligation to represent the profession and to avoid abusing their positions to provide special services to someone that could violate ethical codes. For example, the film *Basic Instinct* involves a plot that turns on the unethical behavior of a police psychologist. Dr. Beth Garner is supposed to be evaluating Nick, a detective, for his ability to be on the job. Nick was involved in a shooting incident that resulted in the death of two tourists. He abused alcohol and cocaine and was suffering from depression after his wife's suicide. Clearly stress is getting to him, but he uses his previous affair with Garner to pressure her to turn in a clean bill of health so he can stay on the job. Garner agrees to cover for him. However, when Nick becomes intimate with her college rival, also a murder suspect, Garner's affections take a decidedly dangerous turn. She clearly has trouble observing the boundaries of her job, although when asked to do a profile of a murder scene, she acknowledges the limits of her expertise and calls in another expert. How ethical!

The Relationship With Attorneys

There are many ambiguities in the area of expert mental health opinions, and it can be difficult to judge the difference between an attorney's attempt to get a hired gun and her honest pursuit of sound clinical judgment. A contingent

Ethics in *Basic Instinct*

The affair Nick Curran (played by Michael Douglas) has with murder suspect Catherine Tramell (played by Sharon Stone) places not only his career, but potentially his life, in jeopardy. Their relationship and the murder investigation ultimately revealed the unethical behavior of police psychologist Beth Garner (played by Jeanne Tripplehorn).

Reprinted with permission of PhotoFest, Inc., New York

fee arrangement should never be accepted. Any mental health professional approached to do an evaluation needs to have a clearly written agreement, signed by the attorney, that he will be paid for his services, regardless of the assessment outcome or the verdict. That is one way to ensure objectivity.

This practice differs from state to state. In some states, if an expert is retained by the defense attorney but reaches a conclusion about the defendant that fails to support what the attorney hoped for, the results are privileged. However, some states have decided that if a psychiatric issue is raised for a defendant, the attorney-client privilege is no longer in effect, and the results are made available to the prosecutor.

In all states, if the court or the prosecutor orders a mental health evaluation, all materials deemed to assist the defense must be turned over. A court-ordered evaluation also goes to all parties.

The mental health professional needs to be aware of the laws in order to observe the appropriate protocol. If an evaluation for the defense is not going to be confidential, for example, the mental health professional must inform the defendant of the parties to whom the information is to be sent and have a confidentiality waiver signed. (The defendant, of course, must be deemed competent to sign such a waiver and to understand what the lack of confidentiality means.) Without this consent, the mental health professional should not proceed.

One error mental health professionals are prone to involves making assessments of legal competence from diagnostic criteria for mental illness. All mental health professionals who make evaluations for the court must learn the difference between clinical opinion and legal assessments of competence, diminished capacity, and insanity.

Each competency issue must be evaluated separately because incompetence demonstrated in one function (e.g., to testify) may not be related to competence in some other function (e.g., to waive the right to an attorney).

If the mental health professional suspects the attorney may be withholding relevant information about the client, then it is her duty to address this issue. Otherwise the missing information could lead to inadequate preparation and even a faulty diagnosis. All such suspicions should be documented for her own records in case the defendant charges his attorney with insufficient defense. In a case where a prosecutor fails to turn over information that might support insanity or incompetency, there are clear grounds for an appeal.

Another issue that might cause friction occurs when the mental health professional senses that the client has been coached on what to say (or not say) and do for the evaluation. Trying to get someone to feign symptoms is manufacturing evidence, and no mental health professional should go along with this. Likewise, when helping prepare a defendant for trial, the mental health professional should not feel pressured to coach the client regarding how to answer questions in a way that feigns symptoms and perpetuates fraud.

Whenever the mental health professional feels the attorney is misusing her data, she must speak out. She is bound by the attorney-client relationship from informing the other side, but she should take steps to make her objections known and to document every conversation. If the attorney senses hostility, he probably won't call her as a witness anyway.

Mental health professionals must also avoid the conflicts of multiple relationships that can impair objectivity. In other words, mental health professionals should avoid being therapists if they are hired to do forensic evaluations. Social workers should also avoid getting involved in family issues. If a mental health professional is already treating the defendant and gets called as a witness, he should maintain the role of lay witness only, not expert witness. He should also honor as much as possible the confidentiality of his relationship with the defendant.

Another ethical obligation involved in forensic work is to be as thorough as possible. To do only a clinical evaluation and fail to obtain information from third-party sources or other records is negligent and incomplete. Such a witness will falter under cross-examination. In one case, a psychiatrist testifying in a capital offense case had not even met with the defendant. There is no doubt that he violated his professional code.

However, any attempt to contact third parties or obtain records must be done with prior approval of the attorney and client. Mental health professionals are not to play detectives and go off on their own leads. All information is to be gathered for the work product and guided by the standards of the profession. (Writers, beware of the temptation to have your mental health professional proceed on her own—she could be sued or severely sanctioned.)

Mental health professionals also need to be sure that court protocol is followed. If a defense expert is asked to turn over records to the prosecutor, but the prosecutor refuses to provide the name of the expert who will examine the records, the defense expert should resist. He must also file a motion to quash the subpoena. The judge then makes the decision about the disposition of the records.

Also, if the defendant makes incriminating statements during an evaluation, the statements can only be admitted into evidence if relevant to the mental health issue for which the defendant is being evaluated. For example, if the defendant talks about other crimes or other mental problems, they are not to be included in the written evaluation.

One of the most troubling ethical dilemmas for a mental health professional in court is the controversial ultimate issue—whether or not to state one's opinion on the legal issue consideration by the triers of fact, specifically insanity and competency. Some mental health professionals believe an evaluator ought only to describe the behavior relevant to the issue and leave the judge or jury to decide on the legal issue; others say even that goes too far. They believe that mentioning behavior that will decide the issue, rather than just offering assessment results, is tantamount to deciding the issue.

However, many legal and mental health scholars have pointed out that if a mental health professional refuses to testify on the ultimate issue when asked, it could be referred to someone less competent and less ethical for a declaration. In other words, if the court is determined to get this opinion from a mental health professional, it will get the opinion from someone. As long as there is a good basis for the opinion, the mental health professional may feel it is in the client's best interests that the professional address it if pressured to do so by the court. This will have to be judged on a case-by-case basis.

Controversial Topics

In the case of Tom Donney mentioned earlier, Paul Dell offered expert testimony through hypnosis about multiple personality disorder. Since both the diagnosis and technique are contestable, it's up to the judge to decide whether to allow such testimony; however, many defense attorneys are not aware of how controversial some areas of social science research can be. They might proceed in good faith when in fact they've put their clients on tentative grounds.

For example, during the late eighties, many cases were brought to court—and people were convicted—based on "repressed memory" testimony. Helped along by mental health professionals, plaintiffs claimed that childhood sexual abuse was suppressed from consciousness through a memory-filtering mechanism that worked via dissociation. The abuse was so traumatic that victims could store the memories for many years and not recall them until they were adults. They had personal injury claims, they said, even though the injuries had happened many years in the past. Therapists who saw the signs could bring the memories forth with hypnosis.

It wasn't long before other mental health professionals demonstrated that "repressed memories" could be planted and manipulated, and some of the most high profile cases were soon discredited. The professional community became polarized, with those who had invested their careers on repressed memories defending their turf against those who distrusted the phenomenon entirely. To date there is no clear consensus, so "expert witnesses" are not offering scientifically verified information. The *Daubert* rules for scientific research and methodology apply, but allowing such testimony becomes a matter of how well informed the various court personnel are about the research.

Four basic legal postures have emerged from rulings at the appellate level.

1. Legal rulings about a plaintiff's injury may not apply to repressed memory cases.
2. A recovered memory claim does not extend the statute of limitations as a disability.
3. Independent corroboration (evidence or witnesses) about any accusation based on recovered memories is required.
4. The reliability of the theory must be determined by scientific verification before there is any consideration of extending the statute of limitations.

In a 1986 case of recovered memories, the Washington Supreme Court ruled that there was no verifiable empirical evidence to support the claim of a wrongful act and resulting injury. To rule otherwise, the justices rightly stated, would open the door to numerous spurious claims. In 1995 the Michigan Supreme Court noted that the issue was sorely lacking in objective verification. Numerous other courts have likewise recognized the weakness of scientific support for recovered memory claims.

Other similarly controversial areas are post-traumatic stress disorder and battered woman syndrome (a form of learned helplessness via emotional erosion), both of which involve the effects of trauma on a person's ability to judge a situation. Battered woman syndrome has often been invoked in murder trials where a woman had killed her spouse or her children.

Some research has indicated that traumatic memories are retrieved in the form of dissociated mental imprints of sensory elements of the traumatic experience. A memory's accuracy is affected by the emotional context, with highly emotional events imprinting in greater intensity and detail. Introducing trauma, however, can lead to extremes of forgetting because the mind resists their integration. However they are treated, such memories appear qualitatively different from normal memory processes. Some researchers believe the memories are encoded differently, but no one has proven this theory.

In any event, mental health professionals who rely on research studies about trauma to support diagnoses of post-traumatic stress disorder or battered woman syndrome will need to be fully informed about the controversies. There are numerous Web sites devoted to these issues, which change all the time, so the best thing to do is use www.google.com as a search engine and locate a Web site that includes updated articles. Ethically, mental health professionals must be objectively convinced by the data and not just be defending their own research or attempting to make a name for themselves in some high profile case. The mental health professional must also be prepared, if the judge allows the testimony, to be thoroughly cross-examined by the opposing counsel, who may have very good researchers on her team.

Further research may strengthen these defenses, but until that time, mental health professionals who claim to be experts may have difficulty in courts with the demand for scientific support.

Dangerousness Assessment Ethics

Given the evolving state of risk assessment, some professionals feel that mental health professionals should not address this in court at commitment, sentencing, or parole hearings. Others believe that when good empirical support is offered for a prediction of violent recidivism, there is no reason not to do so. This involves identifying studies that have shown that certain traits (e.g., impulsivity) or social support groups (e.g., gangs) are significantly linked to violent behavior. The assessment's intent is to provide guidelines for certain liberty restrictions, such as convicted child molesters being actively monitored by law enforcement officials.

Ethical guidelines for such predictions include the following.
- demonstrate that the subject being evaluated appropriately fits the research subjects used in the actuarial studies
- make estimates of risk that are appropriately based on data comparable to that used in the studies

- recognize that actuarial data has not been gathered on the most dangerous offenders, who remain locked up, or on offenders who have not been caught
- make every effort to collect clinical data where none exists, and be able to show logical steps in making a risk assessment prediction from the information

Where research is being actively developed on issues that infringe on human liberty, as in the field of risk assessment, mental health professionals who testify must stay updated with the very latest information. Risk assessment covers subjects from juvenile to adult or disgruntled employee to stalker. Writers who want to use mental health professional characters in this area should use the Internet to check on the specific subject. There's no single site devoted to the entire range of risk assessment, but there are many for each area. The Web site www.findlaw.com may also have cases and the latest legal news on the subject.

Duty to Warn/Protect

Prosenjit Poddar, a native of India, attended the University of California at Berkeley in the late 1960s and met Tatiana Tarasoff at a dance. They became friends, and he developed a strong romantic interest in her. When they shared a quick New Year's Eve kiss, he interpreted this as a sign that they were engaged. Tatiana was uninterested in such a relationship, which confused Poddar. He developed a delusion that she in fact had feelings for him, and this obsession became increasingly more intrusive. He soon suffered an emotional breakdown and attempted to end all contact, but she called him to say how much she missed their discussions. His obsessions returned and became paranoid to the point that he believed he would have to kill Tatiana.

During the summer of 1969, Poddar sought outpatient psychiatric services at a hospital in Berkeley. The treating psychiatrist diagnosed paranoid schizophrenia and prescribed antipsychotic medication. He then referred Poddar to a psychologist, Dr. Lawrence Moore, for counseling. Despite their sessions, Poddar persisted in his delusion that Tatiana would one day love him. To prove himself, he purchased a handgun to orchestrate a life-threatening situation from which he could rescue his beloved. Moore said he might have to take steps to restrain Poddar, which sent Poddar angrily from his office. Poddar had talked about his need to get even with Tatiana for violating his honor.

Moore talked with colleagues about these threats and mentioned to the campus police that Poddar was unstable and was threatening to kill a girl. Officers questioned Poddar and thought he appeared rational. He promised to stay away from the girl. Moore's department chief believed Moore had overreacted to the situation and ordered him to falsify records to the effect that he had not contacted the police on this matter.

In October 1969, Poddar's delusions had reached a breaking point. He went to Tatiana's house armed with a knife and a pellet gun. She ran from him and he shot her, then stabbed her fourteen times, killing her. Poddar turned himself in and at his trial pleaded not guilty by reason of insanity. He was convicted of second-degree murder and released after serving five years.

Tatiana's family instigated a civil case of negligence against the Regents of the University of California. In 1974 the California Supreme Court found that, despite patient-psychotherapist confidentiality, a duty to warn exists when the therapist determines a warning is essential to avert a danger rising from the patient's condition.

The mental health profession quickly responded that mental health professionals have no inherent abilities to predict violence and that such a ruling violated their confidential relationships and would prevent patients from trusting them. It could also generate false positive predictions as a means of diverting liability just in case something happened. Overall, this would be a detriment to those needing treatment, as well as a deterrent to clients who might otherwise expose their violent fantasies.

The court agreed to rehear the case and issue a second opinion. They still found that therapists have a duty to potential victims, but they need only use "reasonable care" to protect the person. That is, the therapist may only have to civilly commit or voluntarily hospitalize the patient to avoid the potential for harm.

Most jurisdictions now recognize the *Tarasoff* decision, but some limit it to situations in which the patient communicates a serious threat of physical violence against an identifiable victim. Standards vary from state to state.

Therapists are legally obligated because they are in special relationships—assuming care and custody of patients, which encompasses the potential victims of each patient. The therapist's involvement with and control over the potential assailant presumably is "significant," and the therapist should possess some expertise in predicting who may be violent.

However, this does not constitute an automatic duty to warn a potential victim. In fact, issuing a warning has proven ineffective because more violence occurs after a warning than if no warning is issued. In any event, there are alternatives, such as notifying law enforcement or involuntarily committing the patient.

Disclosure

Disclosure (and violation of confidentiality) need only occur where there are sufficient indicators of dangerousness to lead a competent physician reasonably to conclude that an individual will act out violently toward a specific person.

The critical factor is that there be a comprehensive assessment and a treatment plan that logically flows from the assessment, such as increasing sessions, referring for medication, or doing a neurological workup. Proof, aided by hindsight that the therapist erred, is insufficient to establish negligence.

In fact, in some cases where a victim's family has sued, such as in *Shaw v. Glickman*, it was found that the victim contributed to the violence. Thus, the therapist was not liable. In that case, too, there was no threat made toward an identifiable third party.

If a threat is made and it's vague, as in *Thompson v. Alameda County* (CA), where a juvenile in detention threatened to kill a child (without naming any child in particular), a therapist can do little in terms of warning or protecting someone. In that case, mental health professionals can't be held accountable. However, having no specific target person to protect does not free the therapist from the duty to *manage*. If a patient is assaultive when psychotic and goes off medication, an alternative would be to commit that person. Otherwise, the therapist may be held liable for damages.

That does not mean that any obsession constitutes a threat. There must be clear intent against a third party. To hold a therapist negligent for any possible act of his patient would be to hold him accountable to a standard of care that does not exist in the field.

Hedlund v. Superior Court of Orange County extended the therapist's civil liability not only to an intended victim, but to anyone within a "zone of danger." The American Psychological Association protested this concept as unworkable. One justice dissented, saying the majority opinion in this case perpetuated the myth that mental health professionals have clairvoyant abilities to predict dangerousness. This same idea played out in *Jablonski v. United States*, in which a man killed his wife, and although he did not threaten her specifically, the court concluded that she fit the general profile of previous victims whom he had assaulted. To have to extrapolate from a specified third party to anyone who fits a similar profile forces the special relationship into an unmanageable association.

Yet the idea of the special relationship is evolving, particularly with court cases citing standard of care in the profession. If psychologists are saddled with the duty to warn third parties, potential third parties, people in a zone of danger, or even to foresee damage to property, it limits what they can do therapeutically. Mental health professionals should be granted legally recognized options, such as establishing documented treatment plans that reduce the likelihood of acting out, so they can function as therapists. In *Littleton v. Good Samaritan Hospital and Care Center,* the court determined that as long as therapists exercise judgment consistent with the standard of care in the profession (level of practice of average professional), they are not liable for what their patients do.

Nasser v. Parker more specifically challenged the idea of the special relationship assumption. After an abusive patient from an institution killed his girlfriend, the court found that the psychiatrist in charge of the case did not have much control because the patient had voluntarily committed himself and was free to leave. However, there is still some question as to whether any therapist controls or should control patients. That mental health professionals influence behavioral change is not the same as control. There is a trend that suggests psychotherapy is not a special relationship in terms of prediction or control, although the danger is that with reduced liability there may be a diminished standard of care.

245

A mental health professional faced with a situation where a threat is made needs to keep clear records, especially if a specific target is identified. If the threat is vague, then the therapist must develop a treatment plan that shows specific management of the anger and also indicates awareness in the latest developments of risk assessment.

The mental health professional would have to examine the nature of the violent behavior implied by the threat (use of a weapon, poison, ambush, etc.) and indicate precisely how she engaged the patient in discussing it (particularly in terms of family history of violence). Any interchange on the subject should be meticulously recorded, along with notations on any type of red flag behavior, such as dissociation or evidence of neurological damage. A mental health professional cannot be expected to be clairvoyant, but she can make an informed guess about whether a patient is likely to act out, and she can come up with a behavior management plan that would decrease the likelihood of actual violence against a specific target.

A Fictional Scenario Involving Ethics—How to Turn the Plot

On the television show *The Practice*, a psychologist was asked to testify in the case of a woman who had gunned down the suspected rapist and murderer of her seven-year-old daughter. The shooting had been recorded live on camera because a news crew was present for the suspect's arrest, directly after which the defendant shot him. She had walked up to him with steady deliberation, taken a position, shot him twice, and then dropped the gun and allowed herself to be taken into custody.

For a ten-thousand-dollar fee, the defense team hired a psychologist to provide an assessment with which they hoped to prove temporary insanity. The psychologist saw the news clip and told the defense team he could not testify that the defendant had been suffering from temporary insanity. She certainly looked as if she knew what she was doing, and her state of mind was calm. They protested that they had paid him, and he reminded them his fee was for his expert assessment, not his role as their spokesperson. He was more concerned about his reputation and the ethics of the situation than about any repeat business from them.

When he left, they dropped back on their second plan—to hire a psychologist who made a living testifying in court, i.e., a hired gun. They knew the psychologist would say whatever they wanted him to. There's always someone.

Such dilemmas make for good fiction.

Glossary of Legal and Psychological Terms

A priori investigative bias—Crime scene personnel come up with theories not based on facts, and their bias influences the kind of evidence collected and the strategy used.

Accused—The person charged with a crime.

Acquittal—A court finding of not guilty in a criminal trial; made by a judge or a jury.

Action—A dispute brought before the court for resolution.

Actus reus—The physical act or omission required for conviction of a crime; the person must have conscious physical control.

Admissible—Evidence that can be admitted for consideration by the trier(s) of fact.

Affidavit—A written statement given under oath.

Affirmative defense—A legal reason presented at a trial to justify why the accused did what he did.

AFIS—Automated Fingerprint Identification System.

Aggravating circumstances—Conditions that make a crime more serious, such as knowing the risk involved that may lead to injury or death.

Allegation—A statement about what the alleging party will address in court.

American Board of Forensic Psychiatry/Psychology—Professionals who certify other professionals in this field via examination and review of experience.

American Law Institute rule—A ruling stating that a defendant is not responsible for criminal conduct when, as a result of mental disease or defect, that person lacks substantial capacity to appreciate the criminality of the conduct or the ability to conform his or her conduct to the requirements of the law.

Anger-excitation behavior—A classification of sexual violence motivated by arousal at the suffering of the victim.

Anger-retaliatory behavior—A classification of excessive sexual violence motivated by revenge over imagined wrongs.

Answer—Statement made by a defendant to allegations in a complaint.

Ante-mortem—Wounds made prior to death.

Antipsychotic drugs—Drugs used to control psychosis.

Antisocial personality disorder—As defined in the *DSM-IV*, it emphasizes antisocial behavior over psychopathic personality traits.

Appeal—The process that gets a case before a higher court for review.

Appellate court—A court that reviews the decisions made in a lower court, generally on proper legal procedure and interpretation.

Arbitration—Alternative dispute resolution, usually through a neutral third party.

Arraignment—A defendant is informed in court of the charges pending and enters a plea of guilty or not guilty; sometimes this occurs at the preliminary hearing, sometimes afterward.

Arranged crime scene—A disposal site where an offender has arranged the body and other items to serve a ritual fantasy.

Attention deficit disorder/attention deficit hyperactivity disorder—A person whose impulsivity and inability to focus for very long causes problems with distractions and disruptions.

Automatism—A legal defense that involves a lack of conscious control over one's actions. It has been used successfully in some cases of apparent sleepwalking.

Beck Depression Inventory—An assessment device used to discover thinking or behavior that indicates a serious, perhaps suicidal, problem with depression.

Behavioral evidence—Forensic evidence suggestive of certain behaviors, generally used for criminal profiling.

Bench trial—A nonjury trial, decided by a judge.

Bender-Gestalt Test—A psychological assessment technique that measures perceptual development and organic conditions.

Beyond a reasonable doubt—The degree of proof that will convince the trier of facts to a near certainty that the allegations have been established. This is the highest of the three standards of proof in a courtroom, used in all criminal trial proceedings.

Bifurcated trial—A trial that is separated into two phases for different issues, such as criminal intent and punishment, or guilt and sanity.

Bind over—Court order to place someone into custody to be brought in to face charges.

Bipolar disorders—A group of mood disorders that consist of recurrent cycles of manic behavior and depression.

Blitz attack—The delivery of overpowering force.

Borderline personality disorder—Instability in relationships, job, mood, and self-image, including uncontrolled flashes of anger, impulsive behavior, and self-mutilation.

Brandeis brief—A brief using social science research to support its points.

Brief—The written argument filed by a lawyer on behalf of a client.

Burden of proof—The necessity of proving a fact in dispute, according to the standard of proof required in a specific proceeding (beyond reasonable doubt, preponderance of evidence, clear and convincing).

California Psychological Inventory—A self-administered test comprised of 462 true/false statements that help to organize information about feelings and typical behavior patterns.

Capital offense—A crime for which the death penalty may be used.

Capital punishment—A death sentence imposed for a given crime. The method used varies by state.

Case linkage—Finding links among cases that had seemed unrelated.

Catathymic offense—A crime committed from the buildup of pressure that issues in a sudden overwhelming release.

Cause of action—A legal claim, or the basis for a lawsuit.

Character disorder—A personality disorder that manifests in habitual maladaptive patterns of behavior.

Civil procedure—Noncriminal legal action where one party brings a claim against another to assess damages.

Clear and convincing proof—The second-highest standard of proof, stronger than preponderance of evidence but less stringent than beyond a reasonable doubt. Generally thought to be about 75 percent certainty, it is applied in matters in which civil liberty interests are at stake.

Closing argument or statement—An attorney's summary of the evidence that is made at the end of a trial.

CODIS—Combined DNA Index System.

Cold case—Unsolved case no longer under active investigation.

Comorbid—The simultaneous occurrence of two or more disorders or illnesses.

Competency—Sufficient ability to participate in proceedings, such as to stand trial, to waive rights, to testify, and to die. One must understand the legal proceedings involved and have the ability to consult with an attorney.

Complaint—Statement of the cause of legal action in civil cases; formal charge in criminal cases.

Conduct disorder—A disruptive behavior in childhood that involves violating the rights of others, conflict with authorities, truancy, and petty crimes. There are several categories of conduct disorder, depending on the specific behavior of the child.

Confabulation—Fabrication of stories in response to questions about situations that are not recalled.

Confession—Incriminating evidence offered by the defendant in the form of a written or verbal statement. Some confessions are false or pressured, which was a motivating factor in creating the Miranda rights.

Confidentiality—Certain communications are protected by a trust relationship and are not legally permitted to be disclosed or used as evidence in court.

Consultant—The role a mental health professional might take in offering expertise or research results on a legal issue, policy, or proceeding.

Corpus delicti—Essential facts that indicate a crime has occurred.

Crime reconstruction—Using evidence to determine the actions involved in a crime.

Crime scene staging—Attempting to misdirect an investigation by making it look as if one type of crime has taken place to cover up a different one.

Criminal procedure—Legal action in which a city, county, state, or federal district prosecutes an individual for breaking a law.

Criminal profiling—The use of observation of the crime scene and pattern of crimes to determine investigatively relevant characteristics of the perpetrator; it guides police in narrowing the field of suspects and devising a strategy for questioning.

Damages—Monetary compensation from a lawsuit.

Dangerousness—The degree of risk of danger posed by someone, typically a person who has already committed a crime.

***Daubert* ruling**—The 1993 court decision about the admissibility of scientific evidence. The court decides whether the methodology is scientific and can be applied to the facts at issue.

de facto—Something that is actually in effect.

de jure—Something considered lawful, rightful, or just.

Decision—The judgment in a hearing or trial.

Defendant—The individual charged in a wrongdoing.

Delusion—A false belief based on an incoherent inference about reality.

Deposition—The pretrial statements, given under oath, by any witnesses in a proceeding.

Designer defense—An excuse offered for a defendant that falls outside the psychiatric code books; generally uses psychological language to add credibility.

Determinate sentence—A sentence whose length is established at the time the sentence is handed down.

***Diagnostic and Statistical Manual of Mental Disorders (DSM)*—**The official classification manual of the American Psychiatric Association for mental disorders, revised several times and now in its fourth edition.

Diminished capacity—A psychological defense indicative of an inability to appreciate the nature of the crime or to control one's actions. Not used in all states.

Discovery—The process through which parties in dispute find out facts about the case.

Disorganized offender—Person who commits a crime haphazardly or opportunistically, using weapons at the scene and often leaving clues.

Disposition—The closing of a case with a sentence.

Dissociation—Detachment from an idea or location such that it can alter normal organization of thinking; consciousness or identity can be lost.

Dissociative identity disorder/multiple personality disorder—A disorder characterized by more than one personality sharing the same body; often malingered by defendants seeking a way to escape responsibility for a crime.

Diversion—Routing a juvenile or adult out of the criminal system and into alternative rehab programs.

Due process—Guaranteed steps in a legal proceeding.

Durham rule—One of the tests for insanity, reformulated from the M'Naghten Rule.

Evidence—Documents, statements, and all items included in the legal proceedings for the jury's sole consideration in the question of guilt or innocence.

Expert witness—A person with specialized knowledge about an area or with a special skill that is germane to the proceedings, such as hair analysis, DNA, or a mental illness. This person assists the fact finders in understanding complicated information.

Explosive personality—A disorder of impulse control in which episodes of unprovoked aggression lead to assault or destruction of property.

Fact finder—The person (judge) or persons (jury) who weigh the evidence in a trial to determine a verdict.

Felony—A serious crime for which the punishment in federal law is generally severe, including capital punishment.

Forensic—Associated with the court.

Forensic art—An artistic method that is used for legal purposes, such as sketches, enhanced photography, or three-dimensional sculpture.

Frye test or standard—A test that governs the admissibility of scientific evidence, such that evidence entered into a case must be generally accepted by the relevant scientific community.

***Gault* decision**—A landmark Supreme Court decision that granted juveniles the same right to due process as was accorded adults, except for the right to trial by jury.

Geographic profiling—Using aspects of a geographical relationship among crime scenes to infer offender characteristics.

Grand jury—A closed proceeding in which a group of citizens reviews evidence in a crime and decides whether to issue an indictment; these proceedings differ from state to state, but generally the defendant has no right to present his or her side.

Guilty but mentally ill—A court finding that the person on trial has a mental illness but is still legally guilty.

Habeas corpus—An order to bring a party before a judge for evaluation of appropriateness of hospital retention.

Hired gun—A phrase used for professionals who sell their testimony and say what they're hired to say rather than offering an objective opinion.

Histrionic personality disorder—An enduring personality pattern characterized by excessive emotion, instability, and attention-seeking behavior.

Hung jury—A panel of people who confer on the evidence presented at trial who cannot come to an agreement on the defendant's guilt or innocence.

Hypnotically induced or refreshed testimony—Use of hypnosis to aid in the recall of material relevant to the legal proceeding; has an uneven history in the courts and is only admitted in qualified circumstances.

Immunity—The prosecutor promises not to prosecute a defendant in exchange for his or her cooperation in another trial.

Impeach—To try to make a witness lose credibility through cross-examination.

Indeterminate sentence—A sentence whose length remains open as to the maximum time to be served. The minimum is set at the sentencing, but the maximum is left to officials who come into contact with the person sentenced.

Indictment—Accusation issued by a grand jury that charges an individual with criminal misconduct.

Infanticide/Neonaticide—Murdering one's child.

Informed consent—A person gives his or her consent to a treatment only after informed about the method and possible ramifications.

Insanity—A legal term for a mental disease or defect that if present at the time of a crime absolves the person of responsibility.

Intelligence tests—Psychological assessment techniques to determine cognitive functioning and problem-solving abilities. The most common are the Wechsler Adult Intelligence Scale and the Stanford-Binet.

Intent—Mental state ranging from purpose to awareness of consequences.

Involuntary commitment—Detaining someone against his or her will in a mental hospital when the person is considered a danger to self or others.

Irresistible impulse test—A way to determine whether the defendant knows that what he did was right or wrong; if that person would have done it even in the presence of a police officer, then he was either acting on an irresistible impulse or he failed to appreciate the nature of the act.

Jesness Inventory—An assessment used with adolescents to classify juvenile delinquents according to problem behaviors.

Judgment—The final decision in a lawsuit.

Jurisdiction—A court's authority to exert power over individuals or legal matters within a defined geographic area.

Jury consulting—Use of principles of social science to select members of the jury that predictably will favor a certain side. The consultation derives from surveys, demographic studies, and focus groups.

Jury nullification—Option for a jury that allows it to disregard the law and the evidence in order to acquit the defendant if they believe such an act is justified.

Jury view—When a jury leaves the courtroom to view the scene of the crime, accompanied by the judge, bailiff, attorneys, and court reporter.

Locard's Exchange Principle—The theory that anyone entering a crime scene both leaves and takes something.

Malingering—Deliberate simulation of a mental illness to obtain personal gain.

Memory hardening—When hypnotically aided recall results in transforming a belief into a memory that appears to be true.

Mens rea—The mental state that accompanies a forbidden act, required for conviction.

Mental status exam—An initial observation of a client, along with a list of questions, to obtain psychological and behavioral information.

Millon Clinical Multiaxial Inventory (MCMI)—A standardized self-report assessment questionnaire that focuses on personality traits and emotional adjustment.

Minnesota Multiphasic Personality Inventory (MMPI-2)—A personality assessment test composed of items that the test taker scores as applied to him or herself. The test contains ten scales for clinical assessment, as well as for exaggeration, defensiveness, and lying.

Minnesota Multiphasic Personality Inventory for Adolescents (MMPI-A)—The same test, scaled specifically for the juvenile population.

Miranda rights—The required statement that a police officer gives to a suspect upon arrest, informing that person of the right to remain silent (not to self-incriminate) and to have legal representation before questioning.

Misdemeanor—A lesser crime than a felony, generally punished by a fine or a short sentence in jail.

Mitigating factors/circumstances—Factors such as age, motivation, duress, or unstable home life that can diminish the degree of guilt in a criminal offense.

M'Naghten Rule—A legal rule first proposed in Britain's common law that states the grounds for a defense of insanity: At the time of committing the act, the accused was laboring under such a defect of reason, from a disease of the mind, as not to know the nature and quality of the act, or if he did know, that he did not know what he was doing was wrong.

Modus operandi **(MO)**—An offender's method of carrying out the offense.

Motion in limine—A legal request for a judge to make a pretrial ruling on some matter of law that might become an issue at trial.

MSO—Acronym for "mental state at the time of the offense."

Narcissistic personality disorder—An enduring pattern of behavior characterized by excessive attention to oneself, grandiose thinking, and need for admiration.

No bill—The grand jury's finding that no indictment should be issued.

Non compos mentis—Not of sound mind.

Opening statements—An overview of the evidence given by each side before the evidence is presented.

Organized offender—Person committing a crime in a planned, premeditated manner, leaving few or no clues.

Parole—When a defendant is freed from prison before his sentence allows. This is conditioned on adherence to certain rules, such as seeing a parole officer on a regular basis.

PCL-R—The revised Psychopathy Checklist, which is currently in use to assess psychopathic traits and behaviors and to aid in risk assessment.

Per se—A Latin term meaning by itself, or inherently.

Peremptory challenge—The opportunity given to each side to exclude certain citizens from serving on a jury; how many each side gets varies among jurisdictions.

Peri-mortem—Injuries inflicted in the time interval just before death.

Perjury—Telling lies under oath.

Personality disorders—Enduring patterns of thought and behavior that are maladaptive, causing impairment and distress. For criminal proceedings, the most common are antisocial, borderline, narcissistic, paranoid, and schizoid.

Plea—The defendant's statement at a trial of "guilty" or "not guilty."

Plea bargain—The government charges a defendant with a lesser crime in exchange for foregoing a trial and pleading guilty to the lesser charge.

Polygraph—A machine used to determine through changes in physiological functions whether a person is lying.

Postmortem—Injuries that occurred after death.

Power-assertive behavior—Using aggression to restore an offender's self-confidence, authority, and control.

Power-reassurance behavior—Behaviors used to restore self-confidence through low aggression means, suggestive of a sense of inadequacy.

Preliminary hearing—A hearing held before a judge to decide whether there is sufficient evidence to go to trial.

Preponderance of evidence—The standard used in civil suits; the evidence on one side outweighs the evidence on the other. This is the lowest of the three standards of evidence (beyond a reasonable doubt and clear and convincing proof), generally estimated at 51 percent certainty.

Pretrial conference—A meeting of the judge with the attorneys to determine the primary issues and to outline procedures.

Privilege—A legal doctrine that permits the patient, under limited circumstances, to prevent the disclosure of information shared between patient and a treating clinician; also covers information shared exclusively between client and attorney.

Probative—Serving to prove.

Profiler (criminal)—A mental health professional or law enforcement officer with behavioral science training who helps determine the traits of an unknown offender from aspects of the victim and crime scene.

Prosecutor—The attorney who represents the government in a criminal proceeding.

Psychological autopsy—Methods used to determine the state of mind of a person where the scene of a suicide is ambiguous and therefore questionable.

Psychopath—Personality disorder defined by long-term unsocialized criminal behavior by a person who feels no guilt or remorse and is not inclined to stop.

Psychopharmacology—The study of the effects of psychoactive drugs on behavior.

Psychosis—A major mental disorder in which a person's ability to think, respond, communicate, recall, and interpret reality is impaired. The person shows inappropriate moods, poor impulse control, and delusions. Often confused with insanity, which is a legal term, and psychopathy, which is a character disorder.

Psychotropic—Drugs that act on the psyche, such as antidepressants.

Rape trauma syndrome—A collection of behaviors common to the after-effects of rape.

"Reasonable person" standard—A reference to what a reasonable person might do or think in a certain situation, used in cases like sexual harassment to try to determine if a plaintiff is overreacting.

Rebuttal—Evidence used to counter or disprove facts introduced at a trial, including witness statements.

Recidivism—Repeat criminal behavior.

Remand—To send a case back to a lower court, generally with instructions to carry out certain orders.

Rogers Criminal Responsibility Assessment Scale (R-CRAS)—An assessment test for organic impairment or major mental illness specific to the time an offense is committed.

Rorschach test—A projective psychological test that relies on inkblots and free-association to detect patterns of functioning.

Schizoaffective disorder—A psychotic condition in which a manic state or a major depression develops along with the symptoms of schizophrenia.

Schizophrenia—A group of disorders manifested in delusions, disturbances in language and thought, mood shifts, and maladaptive behaviors.

Scripting—When an offender forces a victim to say or do certain things that fulfill a ritual scenario.

Serial crimes—Any type of crime occurring in a pattern that indicates a single offender.

Signature crime—A crime scene that bears a personality stamp of an offender, characteristic of a need for ritual or theme. These acts are not necessary to complete the offense.

Sociopath—According to some theories, a person with behavior identical to a psychopath, but the personality was forged by social forces and environment.

Souvenir—A personal item taken from a victim and kept by the offender as a memory aid to relive the crime. *See also* trophy.

Statute—Law or act passed by a legislature.

Subpoena—A command to appear at a certain time and place to give testimony on a certain matter.

Subpoena duces tecum—A command to produce specific records or documents at a trial.

Suppression hearing—A hearing before a judge to exclude certain evidence from a trial.

Syndrome—A cluster of symptoms that collectively characterize a group of people that shares them.

***Tarasoff* decision**—Court decision deriving from a 1976 murder case in California that stipulates that psychotherapists have a duty to use reasonable care to protect third parties when a patient presents a risk of violence to a foreseeable victim.

Test battery—A standard group of psychological and neurological assessment devices used for specific conditions or circumstances.

Thematic Apperception Test (TAT)—A projective technique consisting of a series of pictures about which the examinee is asked to create stories.

Tort—An injury or wrong committed to a person or property that is subject to lawsuit by private individuals.

Trophy—*See* Souvenir.

259

True bill—The finding of a grand jury that a criminal indictment is warranted.

Ultimate issue—The actual legal issue at stake in a proceeding, e.g., competence or insanity.

Undoing behavior—An attempt to reverse a crime, generally by returning the victim to a natural-looking state.

UNSUB—The term used in criminal profiling to refer to an unknown suspect.

Vacate—To set aside a prior decision.

Venire—A panel of prospective jurors drawn from lists.

Venue—The place where some part of the crime took place and where the trial can be held. The judge may be asked to change this if conditions are adverse for a fair trial.

Verdict—The decision of a judge or jury after hearing and considering the evidence.

ViCap—Violent Criminal Apprehension Program—the FBI's nationwide data information center, designed for collecting, sorting, and analyzing information about crimes.

Victim Impact Statement—A written document collected from a crime victim providing recalled details about the crime, along with the effects on the victim afterward.

Victimology—A study of victim information to find clues about the offender's opportunity and selection process.

Voir dire—Process by which a judge and attorneys interview potential members of the jury; they hope to uncover biases that may undermine a fair trial.

Waiver—Process by which a defendant gives up his or her rights.

Wechsler Adult Intelligence Scales (WAIS-R and WISC-III)—Multi-part assessment devices used to gauge the examinee's intelligence quotient relative to the general population.

Wide Range Achievement Test (WRAT)—An assessment device used with juveniles to ascertain their level of educational achievement.

Writ—An order of the court the requires a specified act, such as to deliver records.

Roles of Mental Health Professionals

Elements of a Legal Proceeding	Potential Role of Mental Health Professional
Criminal Investigation Criminal Complaint/Grand Jury Indictment Arrest and Booking of Suspect	Profiling/Consultation
Interrogation Arraignment/Plea Bail or Detention	Competency Issues
Preliminary Hearing Discovery	Evaluation/Consultation
Pretrial (Plea Bargain or Trial)	Use of Clinical Report/Competency Hearings
Voir Dire Prosecution Opening Statement Defense Opening Statement	Consultation
Prosecution Direct Examination	Expert Testimony
Cross-Examination by Defense	Consultation
Redirect by Prosecution	Consultation

Recross by Defense Prosecution Rests (Defense's case follows same pattern)	Consultation
Rebuttals and subrebuttals Opening Argument by Prosecution Closing Argument by Defense Closing Argument by Prosecution Judge's Instructions to Jury Jury Deliberations Jury Verdict	Consultation
Sentencing	Evaluation/Risk Assessment
Appeals	Use of Reports
Corrections	Treatment
Parole Hearing	Risk Assessment
Capital Sentence	Competency Evaluation
Release	Follow-up/Programs

Forms

Forensic Intake Sheet Information Form

> ### Attorney's Name, Phone Number(s), and Address.
>
> Indication of whether the client is the plaintiff, defendant, or juvenile or whether this is a court-appointed evaluation.
>
> Indication of type of forensic evaluation procedure (e.g., competency, insanity, IQ). List of assessment devices indicated.
>
> ### Basic Facts of the Case.
> List of things that must be achieved, such as types of records needed, questions for intake interview, and which assessments to administer; this may include a schedule of when each task must be finished and when a report written.
>
> ### Fee Structure.
> Pretrial meeting dates/attorney appointments/trial dates.

Example of a Confidentiality Waiver for Records

Please read, sign, and date this Permission Form for the Release of Confidential Information to:

_____ (Person requesting records)

You will be asked questions for information about your background, and you will be given psychological tests. The results may be released to the person named above.

Permission is hereby granted to _____ to release

clinical information to _____

for the purpose of _____ .

Name of examinee:

Date:

Signature of examinee:

Clinical Observations Sheet

Client's name:

Date:

Initial observations:

Mental alertness and orientation:

Speech/voice:

Posture and motor coordination:

Hearing:

Degree of cooperation:

Eye contact:

Overt behaviors prior to testing:

Significant behaviors during testing:

Evidence of specific symptoms:

Competency Evaluation Form

Name:

Date:

1. Understands the charges
   ☐ Yes
   ☐ Unclear   Elaborate:
   ☐ No

2. Knows what the judge and jury do
   ☐ Yes
   ☐ Unclear   Elaborate:
   ☐ No

3. Understands the adversary nature of the proceedings and the need to assist his legal counsel
   ☐ Yes
   ☐ Unclear   Elaborate:
   ☐ No

4. Appreciates the nature of the possible penalties
   ☐ Yes
   ☐ Unclear   Elaborate:
   ☐ No

5. Can be attentive in court
   ☐ Yes
   ☐ Unclear   Elaborate:
   ☐ No

6. Can discuss facts pertinent to case
   ☐ Yes
   ☐ Unclear   Elaborate:
   ☐ No

Psychological Autopsy Evaluation Sheet

Name of subject: _____

Date: _____

Age: _____ Marital status: _____

Children: _____

Living arrangements: _____

Type of employment: _____

History of health problems: _____

History of mental health treatment/commitment: _____

Medications: _____

Date of death: _____

Circumstances: _____

Autopsy report: _____

Evidence of emotional disturbance (grief, anger, frustration): _____

_____

Possible precipitating events: _____

Evidence of hopelessness/depression: _____

Evidence of constricted or confused thinking: _____

Suicidal ideas: _____

Recent physical complaints: _____

Approaching or recent anniversaries: _____

Use of substances like alcohol or drugs: _____

Past suicide attempts: _____

Reported changes in routines: _____

Change in religious activity: _____

Malingering Checklist

Conditions that signal deception, distortion of facts, or malingering symptoms:

1. Dramatic manner

2. Exaggerated symptoms

3. Embellished descriptions of the event

4. Sudden onset of condition

5. Symptoms that are rare or uncharacteristic of syndrome

6. Scale 3 of MMPI-2 exceeds Scale 4, or Scales 4 or 9 are highly elevated

7. Presentation of absurd symptoms

8. Inconsistent abilities (cannot work, but can go sailing)

9. Financial motivations or motivations to avoid a penalty

10. Evidence of character pathology prior to evaluation

11. Discrepancies between what is claimed and what shows up on objective measures

Day in Court Checklist—What to Remember

☐ Pack all charts, test scores, written reports.

☐ Review deposition and written reports.

☐ Discard extraneous materials.

☐ Index possible backup material.

☐ Confirm time and place with attorney.

☐ Ensure attire is conservative and clean.

☐ Map the route to court and parking.

☐ Pack something to read while waiting.

☐ Arrive early.

☐ Let bailiff know of arrival.

☐ Avoid other witnesses, the press, or opposing attorneys.

☐ Avoid taking notes.

Bibliography

Allen, F. "The Psychopathic Delinquent Child." *American Journal of Ortho-psychiatry* 20 (1950): 223–265.

Anolli, Luigi, and Rita Ciceri. "The Voice of Deception: Vocal Strategies of Naïve and Able Liars." *Journal of Nonverbal Behavior* 21 (1997): 259–284.

Arrigo, Bruce A. *Introduction to Forensic Psychology.* San Diego: Academic Press, 2000.

Athens, Lonnie H. *The Creation of Dangerous Violent Criminals.* Urbana, Ill.: University of Illinois Press, 1992.

Bahr, Arthur W. *Certifiably Insane.* New York: Simon & Schuster, 1999.

Barefoot v. Estelle 463 U.S. 83 (1963).

Beer, M.D. "Psychosis: A History of the Concept." *Comprehensive Psychiatry* 37 (1996): 273–291.

Benedek, Elissa P., and Dewey G. Cornell, eds. *Juvenile Homicide.* Washington, D.C.: American Psychiatric Press, 1989.

Beren, Phyllis, ed. *Narcissistic Disorders in Children and Adolescents.* Northvale, N.J.: Jason Aronson, 1998.

Black, Donald W. *Bad Boys, Bad Men: Confronting Antisocial Personality Disorder.* New York: Oxford University Press, 1999.

Butterfield, Fox. *All God's Children: The Bosket Family and the American Tradition of Violence.* New York: Avon, 1995.

Cassal, Paul G. "The Guilty and the 'Innocent': An Examination of Alleged Cases of Wrongful Conviction From False Confessions." *Harvard Journal of Law and Public Policy,* (spring 1999).

Cleckley, Hervey M. *The Mask of Sanity,* rev. ed. St. Louis: C.V. Mosby, (1941), 1982.

Cornwell, Patricia. *The Body Farm.* New York: Scribner's, 1994.

Cunningham, M.D., and T.J. Reidy. "Antisocial Personality Disorder and Psychopathy: Diagnostic Implications in Classifying Patterns of Antisocial Behavior in Sentencing Evaluations." *Behavioral Science and the Law* 16 (1998): 333–351.

Currie, Elliott. "Crime in the Market Society: From Bad to Worse in the Nineties." *Dissent.* (Spring, 1991).

Daubert v. Merrill Dow Pharmaceutical 509 U.S. 579 (1993).

Deyoub, Paul L., and Gretchen V.K. Douthit. *A Practical Guide to Forensic Psychology.* Northvale, N.J.: Jason Aronson, 1996.

Diagnostic Criteria from DSM-IV. Washington, D.C.: American Psychiatric Press, 1994.

Diagnostic and Statistical Manual 3d ed. rev. Washington, D.C.: American Psychiatric Association, 1987.

Diagnostic and Statistical Manual of Mental Disorders: DSM-III, 3d ed. Washington, D.C.: American Psychiatric Association, 1980.

Diagnostic and Statistical Manual of Mental Disorders: DSM-IV, 4th ed. Washington, D.C.: American Psychiatric Association, 1994.

Dinwiddie, S. "Genetics, Antisocial Personality, and Criminal Responsibility." *Bulletin of the American Academy of Psychiatry and the Law* 24 (1996): 95–108.

Donaldson-Pressman, Stephanie, and Ronald Pressman. *The Narcissistic Family: Diagnosis and Treatment.* San Francisco: Jossey-Bass Publishers, 1997.

Dostoevsky, Fyodor. *Crime and Punishment.* New York: Modern Library (reprint), 1996.

Douglas, John E., with Mark Olshaker. *The Anatomy of Motive.* New York: Scribner, 1999.

———. *Broken Wings.* New York: Pocket Books, 1999.

———. *Mindhunter.* New York: Scribner, 1995.

Dusky v. United States 362 U.S. 402 (1960).

Eddy, J. Mark. *Conduct Disorders.* Kansas City: Compact Clinicals, 1996.

Edgerton, Jane, ed. *American Psychiatric Glossary.* 7th ed. Washington, D.C.: American Psychiatric Press, 1994.

Ekman, Paul. *Telling Lies: Clues to Deceit in the Marketplace, Politics, and Marriage.* New York: W.W. Norton, 1992.

Englander, Elizabeth Kandel. *Understanding Violence.* Mahwah, N.J.: Lawrence Erlbaum Associates, 1997.

Engstrom, Elizabeth. *Lizzie Borden.* New York: Tor Books, 1991.

Ewing, Charles Patrick. *Kids Who Kill.* Lexington, Mass.: Lexington Books, 1990.

Exner, John E. *The Rorshach: A Comprehensive System,* vol. 1: *Basic Foundations.* 2d ed. New York: Wiley, 1986.

Frick, P.J., and Robert D. Hare. *The Psychopathy Screening Device.* Toronto: Multi-Health Systems, 1996.

Frick, P.J., B.S. O'Brien, J.M. Wootten, and K. McBurnett. "Psychopathy and Conduct Problems in Children." *Journal of Abnormal Psychology* 103 (1994): 700–707.

Friedlander, K. "Formation of the Antisocial Character." *The Psychoanalytic Study of the Child* 1 (1945): 189–203.

Frye v. United States 293 F. 1013 (D.C. Cir. 1923).

Garbarino, James. *Lost Boys: Why Our Sons Turn Violent and How We Can Save Them.* New York: Free Press, 1999.

Graham, John R. *MMPI-2: Assessing Personality and Psychopathology.* New York: Oxford University Press, 1993.

Gilmore, Mikal. *Shot in the Heart.* New York: Doubleday, 1994.

Greenacre, P. "Conscience in the Psychopath." *American Journal of Orthopsychiatry* 14 (1945): 495–509.

Grisso, Thomas. *Evaluating Competencies: Forensics Assessments and Instruments.* New York: Plenum Publishing Corporation, 1986.

———. *Forensic Evaluation of Juveniles.* Sarasota, Fla.: Professional Resource Exchange, 1998.

Groth-Marnat, Gary. *Handbook of Psychological Assessment,* 3d ed. New York: John Wiley & Sons, 1997.

Haney, Craig and Zimbardo, Philip. "The Past and the Future of U.S. Prison Policy: Twenty-five Years After the Stanford Prison Experiment." *American Psychologist* (July 1998): 708–724.

Harding v. State [*of Maryland*] 5 MD App. 230, 246 A2d 302 (1968).

Hare, Robert D. *The Hare Psychopathy Checklist-Revised.* Toronto: Multi-Health Systems, 1991.

———. *Without Conscience: The Disturbing World of the Psychopaths Among Us.* New York: Pocket Books, 1993.

———. "Psychopaths and Their Nature: Implications for the Mental Health and Criminal Justice Systems." In *Psychopathy: Antisocial, Criminal, and Violent Behavior,* edited by T. Millon, E. Simonsen, M. Birket-Smith, and R.D. Davis. New York: Guilford Press, 1998. 188–212.

Hare, Robert D., and D.N. Cox "Clinical and Empirical Conceptions of Psychopathy, and the Selection of Subjects for Research." In *Psychopathic Behaviour: Approaches to Research,* edited by Robert D. Hare and D. Schalling, 107–144. Chichester, England: John Wiley & Sons, 1978.

Harrington, Alan. *Psychopaths.* New York: Simon & Schuster, 1972.

Harris, Thomas. *The Silence of the Lambs.* New York: St. Martin's Press, 1988.

Hart, S.D., and R.J. Demptster. *"Impulsivity and Psychopathy."* In *Impulsivity: Theory, Assessment, and Treatment,* edited by C.D. Webster and M.A. Jackson. New York: Guilford Press, 1997.

Hart, Josephine. *Damage.* New York: Alfred A. Knopf, 1991.

Hazelwood, Roy, and Stephen G. Michaud. *Dark Dreams: Sexual Violence, Homicide and the Criminal Mind.* New York: St. Martin's Press, 2001.

Heide, Kathleen M. *Young Killers: The Challenge of Juvenile Homicide.* Thousand Oaks, Calif.: Sage Publications, 1999.

Hess, Allen K., and Irving B. Weiner. *The Handbook of Forensic Psychology,* 2d ed. New York: John Wiley & Sons, 1999.

Hodgins, S. "An Overview of Research on the Prediction of Dangerousness." *Nordic Journal of Psychiatry* 51 (1997), 73–95.

Holmes, Ronald M., and Stephen T. Holmes. *Profiling Violent Crimes.* Thousand Oaks, Calif.: Sage Publications, 1996.

In re Gault 387 U.S. 1 (1967).

Jenkins, Susan C., and Mark R. Hansen. *Pocket Reference for Psychiatrists,* 2d ed. Washington, D.C.: American Psychiatric Press, 1995.

Kapardis, Andreas. *Psychology and Law.* Cambridge, England: Cambridge University Press, 1997.

Kassin, Saul, and Christina Fong. " 'I'm Innocent!' Effects of Training on

Judgments of Truth and Deception in the Interrogation Room." *Law and Human Behavior* 23 (1999): 499–516.

Kelleher, Michael D. *When Good Kids Kill.* Westport, Conn.: Praeger, 1998.

Kent v. United States 383 U.S. 541, 556 (1966).

Kernberg, Otto F. *Borderline Conditions and Pathological Narcissism.* New York: Jason Aronson, 1975.

———. *Severe Personality Disorders.* New Haven, Conn.: Yale University Press, 1984.

Kirwin, Barbara. *The Mad, the Bad, and the Innocent: The Criminal Mind on Trial—Tales of a Forensic Psychologist.* Boston: Little, Brown & Co., 1997.

Lanyon, Richard. "Detecting Deception." *Clinical Psychology* 4 (1997) 377–387.

Lasseter, Don. *Killer Kids.* New York: Pinnacle Books, 1998.

Leo, Richard, and Richard Ofshe. "The Consequences of False Confessions: Deprivations of Liberty and Miscarriages of Justice in the Age of Psychological Interrogation." *Journal of Crime and Criminology* 88 (1998).

Lewis, A. "Psychopathic Personality: A Most Elusive Category." *Psychological Medicine* 4 (1974): 133–140.

Lilienfield, S.O. "Methodological Advances and Developments in the Assessment of Psychopathy." *Behaviour Research and Therapy* 36 (1998): 99–125.

Lindecker, Clifford. *Killer Kids: Shocking True Stories of Children Who Murdered Their Parents.* New York: St. Martin's Press, 1993.

———. *The Vampire Killers.* New York: St. Martin's Press, 1998.

Little v. Armontrout 835 F2d 1240 (8th Cir 1987).

Lowen, Alexander. *Narcissism: Denial of the True Self.* New York: Collier Books, 1985.

Lykken, David T. *The Antisocial Personalities.* Hillsdale, N.J.: Lawrence Erlbaum Associates, 1995.

Lynam, D.R. "Pursuing the Psychopath: Capturing the Fledgling Psychopath in a Nomological Net." *Journal of Abnormal Psychology* 106 (1997): 425–438.

———. "Early Identification of the Fledgling Psychopath: Locating the Psychopathic Child in the Current Nomenclature." *Journal of Abnormal Psychology* 107 (1998): 566–575.

Magid, Ken, and Carole A. McKelvey. *High Risk: Children Without a Conscience.* New York: Bantam, 1987.

Magnet, Myron. *The Dream and the Nightmare: The Sixties' Legacy to the Underclass.* New York: William Morrow, 1993.

McConkey, Kevin M., and Peter W. Sheehan. *Hypnosis, Memory, and Behavior in Criminal Investigation.* New York: Guilford Press, 1995.

Meloy, J. Reid. *The Psychopathic Mind: Origins, Dynamics, and Treatment.* Northvale, N.J.: Jason Aronson, 1988.

———, ed. *The Psychology of Stalking: Clinical and Forensic Perspectives.* San Diego: Academic Press, 1998.

Meloy, J. Reid, and C.B. Gacano. "The Internal World of the Psychopath." In *Psychopathy: Antisocial, Criminal, and Violent Behavior,* edited by T. Millon, E. Simonsen, M. Birket-Smith, and R.D. Davis 95–109. New York: Guilford Press, 1998.

Melton, Gary B., John Petrila, Norman Poythress, and Christopher Slobogin. *Psychological Evaluations for the Courts: A Handbook for Mental Health Professionals and Lawyers,* 2d ed. New York: Guilford Press, 1997.

Millar, Murray, and Karen Millar. "Effects of Situational Variables on Judgments About Deception and Detection Accuracy." *Basic and Applied Social Psychology* 19 (1997): 401–410.

Miller, D., and J. Looney. "The Prediction of Adolescent Homicide: Episodic Dyscontrol and Dehumanization." *American Journal of Psychoanalysis* 34 (1974): 187–198.

Millon, T., E. Simonsen, and M. Birket-Smith. "Historical Conceptions of Psychopathy in the United States and Europe." In *Psychopathy: Antisocial, Criminal, and Violent Behavior,* edited by T. Millon, E. Simonsen, M. Birket-Smith, and R.D. Davis, 3–32. New York: Guilford Press, 1998.

———. *The Million Inventories.* New York: Guilford Press, 1997.

Monahan, John, and Henry J. Steadman, eds. *Violence and Mental Disorder.* Chicago: University of Chicago Press, 1994.

Mullally, David S. *Order in the Court: A Writer's Guide to the Legal System.* Cincinnati: Writer's Digest Books, 2000.

Myers, W.C., and R. Blashfield. "Psychopathology and Personality in Juvenile Sexual Homicide Offenders." *Journal of the American Academy of Psychiatry and the Law* 25 (1997): 497–508.

Nesca, M., J.T. Dalby, and S. Baskerville. "Psychosocial Profile of a Female Psychopath." *American Journal of Forensic Psychology* 17 (1999): 63–77.

Noll, Richard. *The Encyclopedia of Schizophrenia and the Psychotic Disorders.* New York: Facts on File, 1992.

Ofshe, Richard. *Making Monsters: False Memories, Psychotherapy, and Sexual Hysteria.* New York: Charles Scribner's Sons, 1994.

Orne, M.T., D.A. Soskis, D.F. Dinges, and E.C. Orne. "Hypnotically Induced Testimony." In *Eyewitness Testimony: Psychological Perspectives*, edited by G.L. Wells and E.F. Loftus, 171–213. New York: Cambridge University Press, 1984.

Patterson, James. *Along Came a Spider.* New York: Warner, 1993.

Perry v. Louisiana 610 So. 2d 746 (La. 1992).

Pope, Kenneth S., James N. Butcher, and Joyce Seelen. *The MMPI, MMPI-2, and MMPI-A in Court.* Washington, D.C.: American Psychological Association, 1993.

Quinsey, V.L., M.E. Rice, C. Cormier, T. Harris, and C.A. Cormier. *Violent Offenders: Appraising and Managing Risk.* Washington, D.C.: American Psychological Association, 1998.

Rabasca, Lisa. "A Court That Sentences Psychological Care Rather Than Jail Time." *Monitor on Psychology* (July/August 2000): 58–60.

Reed, J. "Psychopathy: A Clinical and Legal Dilemma," *British Journal of Psychiatry* 168 (1996): 4–9.

Reiser, Martin. *Handbook of Investigative Hypnosis.* Los Angeles: LEHI Publishing, 1980.

Revitch, Eugene and Louis B. Schlesinger. *Sex Murder and Sex Aggression: Phenomenology, Psychopathy, Psychodynamics, and Prognosis.* Springfield, Ill.: Charles C. Thomas, 1989.

Reznek, Lawrie. *Evil or Ill: Justifying the Insanity Defence.* New York: Routledge, 1997.

Robins, L.N. "Conduct Disorder." *Journal of Child Psychology and Psychiatry* 20 (1991): 566–680.

Rock v. Arkansas 107 S.Ct. 2704, 97 LEd2d 37 (1987).

Rogers, Richard, and Daniel W. Schuman. *Conducting Insanity Evaluations*, 2d ed. New York: Guilford Press, 2000.

Rogers, R., J. Johansen, J.J. Chang, and R.T. Salekin. "Predictors of Adolescent Psychopathy: Oppositional and Conduct-Disordered Symptoms." *Journal of the American Academy of Psychiatry and the Law* 25 (1997): 261–271.

Rutter, Michael, Henri Giller, and Ann Hagell. *Antisocial Behavior by Young People*. Cambridge, England: Cambridge University Press, 1998.

Ryzuk, Mary S. *Thou Shalt Not Kill: The True Story of John List*. New York: Popular Library, 1990.

Samenow, Stanton E. *Inside the Criminal Mind*. New York: Times Books, 1984.

Schreiber, Thomas, and Susan Sergent. "The Role of Commitment in Producing Misinformation Effects in Eyewitness Memory." *Psychonomic Bulletin and Review* 5 (1998): 443–448.

Sells, Scott P. *Treating the Tough Adolescent*. New York: Guilford Press, 1998.

Shapiro, David L. *Criminal Responsibility Evaluations*. Sarasota, Fla.: Professional Resource Press, 1999.

Sheflin, Alan W., and Jerrold Shapiro. *Trance on Trial*. New York: Guilford Press, 1989.

Slovenko, R. "Responsibility of the Psychopath." *Philosophy, Psychiatry, and Psychology* 6 (1999): 53–55.

Smith, M.C. "Hypnotic Memory Enhancement of Witnesses: Does it Work?" *Psychological Bulletin* 94 (1983): 387–407.

State [of New Jersey] v. Hurd 432 NJ A2d 86 (1981).

State [of Minnesota] v. Mack 292 MN NW2d 764 (1980).

Taylor, Karen T. *Forensic Art and Illustration*. Boca Raton, Fla.: CRC Press, 2001.

Tithecott, Richard. *Of Men and Monsters*. Madison, Wisc.: University of Wisconsin Press, 1997.

Tsushima, William, and Robert Anderson, Jr. *Mastering Expert Testimony*. Mahwah, N.J.: Lawrence Erlbaum Associates, 1996.

Turvey, Brent E. *Criminal Profiling*. San Diego: Academic Press, 1999.

Vitelli, R. "Childhood Disruptive Behavior Disorders and Adult Psychopathy," *American Journal of Forensic Psychology* 16 (1998): 29–37.

Wertham, Frederic. "The Catathymic Crisis," In *Violence: Perspectives on Murder and Aggression*, ed., I.L. Kutash, S.B. Kutash, and L.B. Schlesinger. San Francisco: Jossey-Bass, 1978.

Wrightsman, Lawrence S., Michael T. Nietzel, and William H. Fortune. *Psychology and the Legal System*. Pacific Grove, Calif.: Brooks/Cole, 1994.

Zona, Michael, Russell Palerea, and John C. Lane. "Psychiatric Diagnosis and Offender-Victim Typology of Stalking." In *The Psychology of Stalking: Clinical and Forensic Perspectives*, ed., J. Reid Meloy. New York: Academic Press (1998): 70–84.

Index

Index